Organization
Woman

Organization Woman

The Story of the National
Union of Townswomen's Guilds

MARY STOTT

HEINEMANN:
LONDON

William Heinemann Ltd
15 Queen Street, Mayfair, London W1X 8BE

LONDON MELBOURNE TORONTO
JOHANNESBURG AUCKLAND

434 74800 5

Printed and bound in Great Britain by Cox and Wyman Ltd,
London, Fakenham and Reading

Contents

This book was written in affection and admiration for Organization Women everywhere — for my mother, Amalie Waddington, the Organization Woman who set the pattern of my life; for the Townswomen and many others with whom I have worked, and for Women In Media, to whom I owe more than I can say.

List of Plates

Between pages 164 and 165

The Gift at the Scala Theatre:

The Nightmare scene and 'Life's a Proper How D'you Do'

NUTG's first annual dinner

An old couple at the Ried camp

Acknowledgments

The author would like to thank the following for permission to reproduce photographs:

The Press Association for the photograph of Dame Margery Corbett Ashby facing page 37; *The Birmingham Post and Mail* for the Birmingham Townswomen group between pages 68 and 69; G. Macdomnic for the portrait of Imogen Holst facing page 132; J. R. J. Parrish for the photograph of Leslie Crowther and Glenda Jackson, the London *Daily Mail* for the photograph of the lace-maker, and Topix for the photograph of landscape painters between pages 132 and 133; Angus McBean for the photograph from the *Brides of Begerin* facing page 133 and for the photographs from *The Gift* facing page 164; Rawood Ltd for the NUTG's 1938 London dinner between pages 164 and 165.

The drawings are reproduced from *The Townswoman* from contributions by Guild members.

1

In the Beginning

One of the oddest notions that people have about people is that women cannot work together. However did it come to be accepted? They must always have worked together in the fields, in convents, in the 'extended families' of many cultures beside our own. In the UK they have been working together in organized groups for at least 150 years. During the agitation for the Reform Bill there were a number of women's associations, and some of their members were killed at Peterloo. There were women's associations, too, among the Chartists, in the 1830s. There were early groups of women trade unionists in all industrialized countries.

Women, in fact, have banded together for all sorts of reasons, as they still do. They have banded together for political purposes; to fight oppressive laws and economic conditions; to raise the status of women from that of criminals, bankrupts and minors; to succour the deprived; to achieve improvements in the education, health and welfare of women and children; to give one another support in their trades and professions; to widen their own horizons; to have an escape from the confining four walls of home. And they have banded together for company and friendship, because, contrary to a powerful old myth, they *like* being together. Nearly a quarter of a million women have banded together in the National Union of Townswomen's Guilds, and the overriding reason for joining was company and fellowship. But having joined, they like what they get in their Guilds—the activities, the stimuli, the making it all work, the enlargement of horizons. The existence of all these Guilds, of all the Women's Institutes, of the Women's

Clubs, the branches of this and branches of that religious, social or political organization throughout the length and breadth of the UK shows up that notion about women being unable to work together as so remote from the truth as to make one suspect that it is a self-protective male invention. There must be literally millions of women meeting together, doing things together, to vouch for the reality of that admirable, indispensable human being, Organization Woman.

Before Organization Woman could flourish there had, of course, to be a drive to set the female sex free from the repressive social customs of middle-class Victorian England. Working women, despite their shockingly hard lives, had the freedom to link together with their menfolk in a trade union or a political grouping. But Ladies never, never, spoke in public, for to do so was to disgrace their husbands as well as themselves. When the World Anti-Slavery Convention met in London in 1840 there were four women among the American delegation. The leading British delegates were shocked. 'The claim that the women should attend the conference was,' they said, 'subversive of the principles and traditions of the country and contrary to the word of God.' All day, while the men wrangled over whether to allow the women to participate in the conference, the women sat behind a curtain. The decision went against them. The conference continued with no women delegates—but the American women went home to start a women's rights movement. And who can wonder?

A women's rights movement was inevitable in Britain too. There were good middle-class fathers who believed that their daughters had a right to a proper education. There were good husbands who believed that their wives had a right to use their brains and their mental energies. Such wives and daughters could not be content to be shut up in a cage. Inevitably they began to get together. A few, in 1855, linked up to collect signatures for a Married Woman's Property Bill—just as today women might link up to collect signatures for Child Benefit to be paid to the mother. These women were from the same sort of social and cultural background. They got used to working together. They liked and trusted one another. They had a deep and true longing to improve the lot of women. And they were getting a taste for organizing. A few of them started, in 1865, The Kensington

Society, a Ladies Discussion Society for women aspiring after higher education. At their first meeting they discussed 'the limits of parental authority'. They then went on to debate 'Should women take part in public affairs?' To their own surprise and certainly everyone else's, all present were in favour of women's political activity, even to the extent of women's franchise. From that meeting began more than sixty years of suffrage agitation. From that ladylike little society stemmed the National Union of Women's Suffrage Societies, and from *that* grew many an influential women's society, including the National Union of Societies for Equal Citizenship, the Fawcett Society and, in 1928, the National Union of Townswomen's Guilds.

The Kensington ladies were what might be called a benevolent conspiracy. Among them were Emily Davies, who was the true founder of Girton College, Elizabeth Garrett Anderson, the first woman doctor to qualify and practise in England, Sophia Jex-Blake who led the fierce battle for medical education for women in Edinburgh, and those famous headmistresses Miss Buss and Miss Beale. These clever, independent-minded women could not confine their energies to a struggle for that far-off goal, the vote. They set about organizing for more immediate benefits and satisfactions. Frances Mary Buss, for instance, the headmistress of the North London Collegiate School for girls founded in 1874 the Association of Headmistresses. Ten years after the headmistresses, the assistant mistresses formed an association. The Royal College of Midwives was formed in 1881 and the Queen's Institute for District Nurses in 1887. In the 1890s more women banded together, the Health Visitors, the Teachers of Domestic Science, the Women Writers and Journalists, and the Farmers and Gardeners. Who would guess, now, that there were enough women pharmacists to form an association as long ago as 1905? The medical women did not formally unite until 1917 (but probably met together within the confines of the BMA). Women engineers followed; the British Federation of University Women united many professional women from 1907 and women musicians formed an association in 1911.

These self-help, mutually supportive organizations gave their members confidence and assurance in a largely man-dominated world but in those days most of their membership was of dedicated

spinsters. The married woman turned to philanthropic organizations as an extension of her interests. In our times 'Lady Bountiful'
has come to be a much sneered-at figure, but kindness to the
disadvantaged is an aspect of our national character that should
never seriously be mocked. The oldest philanthropic society for
women is the Young Women's Christian Association (1855); the
Girls Friendly Society followed in 1875 and in 1891 there was a
development almost as remarkable in its results as the Kensington
Ladies Discussion Society: the Ladies Association for the Care of
Friendless Girls, formed by a Miss Ellice Hopkins, and the Ladies'
Unions of Workers Among Women and Children which had been
set up in Birmingham, met together in Liverpool. Under the
chairmanship of Mrs Albert Booth these thoroughly worthy
ladies set up a Central Conference Council of Women Workers,
which came to be known as the CCC, to sit throughout the year
to collect and disseminate material about women's work in general
and 'especially with reference to all that is being carried on for
the social, moral and religious elevation of their own sex'. The
Duchess of Bedford became president and by 1893 there were 99
members of the CCC who could afford to pay a subscription of
five shillings or more—or sixpence a session.

The sessions always opened with prayer and the subjects they
talked about included district nursing, how to get women on
hospital committees, the training of philanthropic workers, old
age pensions—all topics that might well be discussed in a
women's organization today except perhaps 'The Responsibility of
Women of Wealth and Leisure'. It was at a conference in Nottingham in 1895 that the CCC disbanded and reformed as the
National Union of Women Workers. Three years later it affiliated
to the International Council of Women, and in 1918 the 'women
workers' became that highly respected and influential 'umbrella'
organization, the National Council of Women.

Another important strand in the web of women's organizations
was what one might call 'the supporters clubs'—the ancillary
organizations of the churches and political parties. Of these the
first was the Mothers' Union, in 1876, with the primary object of
'promoting Christian family life'. The National Free Church
Women's Council (1908), the Catholic Women's League (1906),
and the Church of Scotland's Women's Guild (1882) all aimed to

serve the wider community as well as upholding spiritual values. The Women's Liberal Federation was the first of the political organizations, in 1886. Perhaps the forerunner of the National Union of Townswomen's Guilds with most in common with it was the Women's Co-operative Guild, formed in 1883 by Mrs Arthur Acland (later Lady Acland) who was then editing a small section for women in the *Co-operative News*, and Mrs Mary Lawrenson, daughter of a Woolwich printer (Mrs Lawrenson herself trained as a printer). The Women's Co-operative Guild was, of course, an ancillary organization to the great consumer co-operative movement but, like the NUTG later, its primary aim was to educate home-making women to take an active part in public life. Its members were drawn almost entirely from the working class and it never lost its working-class basis or attitudes, yet its great and most influential general secretary was exactly of the type who had founded the Kensington Ladies Society. Indeed, Margaret Llewelyn Davies was a niece of Emily Davies, of Girton fame.

The 'philanthropic women' were influential, too. While the suffragists were battling in their constitutional and in their militant societies for the vote, an increasing number of women were working usefully in baby welfare clinics, or schools for mothers as they were sometimes called, for these were voluntary until they became absorbed in the state health system and local authorities took over their running. There were a good many women, too, on the Boards of Guardians which preceded welfare committees, and on school boards. There were women campaigners for temperance and total abstinence, and the MacMillan sisters, Rachel and Margaret, launched the nursery school movement. These experienced, knowledgeable, and devoted women were not numerous compared with the stay-at-home wives and mothers, but they were a yeast working in the population at large.

When the Great War came, in 1914, women were quite able to organize canteens for servicemen and the provision of a steady flow of knitted 'comforts'. No doubt they astonished themselves by what they could learn to do in the man's world—drive heavy lorries and buses and VIPs' cars, work long hours in dangerous conditions in munition factories and on the land. They replaced men, in fact, in scores of jobs that had always been closed to them.

So the vote, for which women had marched and gone to prison
and gone on hunger strike and been forcibly fed; for which others,
like Millicent Garrett Fawcett, had campaigned through constitutional channels for fifty years, was given to women with a minimum
of fuss in 1918—or at least, to as many women as were aged at
least thirty, householders, or the wives of householders. The
following year the Sex Disqualification Removal Act opened the
legal profession to women, enabled them to sit on juries, if they
were over 21 and householders, and admitted them to a few other
'closed' professions such as accountancy. Women were now able
to sit on town and borough councils, and, of course, in Parliament
—though only in the Commons. Though there was a handful of
peeresses in their own right, they were not allowed to take their
seats in the House of Lords until Parliament accepted the idea of
life peers.

The formation of new women's organizations, of all kinds,
naturally slowed down during the war years, but it was in 1915 that
the most successful and enduring of them all was launched in this
country—the Rural Women's Institute movement, which started
in Canada, and within two years of the formation of the first
women's institute in Anglesey had become the National Federation
of Women's Institutes with 137 WIs. There are now more than
9,000, with a total membership of nearly half a million. The rapid
growth and remarkable success of this movement made a great
impression on the thinking of 'Organization Women'. An invaluable blueprint had been provided, and some of the steady
stream of well-educated women from the spate of girls' grammar
schools founded in the 1870s and '80s and from the Oxford and
Cambridge Colleges were there to note it and take advantage of it
when the time came. Many of them, too, had learned the technique
of democratic organization in the suffrage societies. The women
of all classes who rallied behind Emmeline Pankhurst and her
daughters Christabel and Sylvia in the militant fight for the vote
will never be forgotten in British history. They performed feats
of organization almost beyond belief even in these days of the
'demo', but they were self-acknowledged dictators. If you joined
the Women's Social and Political Union you accepted the rule of
the Pankhursts or you were replaced, as even leaders of the quality

and generosity of Frederick and Emmeline Pethick Lawrence discovered.

But the constitutionalists, who were the 'mothers' of the National Union of Townswomen's Guilds, had a tremendous respect for order as well as for law. They thrashed out policy and tactics at delegate conferences. They were 'organization women' of the most dedicated kind, who really understood the democratic process, including the essential process of communicating with the rank and file and securing their support and agreement to policy, strategy and tactics.

Mary Stocks (Baroness Stocks of the Royal Borough of Kensington and Chelsea, as she later became) gave an example of the way the suffragists worked in her autobiography *My Commonplace Book*: 'In 1913 the National Union of Women's Suffrage Societies adopted the policy of selecting constituencies where Labour Party candidates were fighting anti-suffrage candidates and concentrating its resources on the support of such Labour candidates. The Union always had been, and remained, a non-party organization. But the Labour Party had not merely declared its support of women's suffrage as a party, it had pledged itself to oppose any Government Reform Bill which did not include women. The Union's decision to adopt such a policy was not taken lightly and its passage through conference precipitated resignations from the executive committee.' But the women met their policy crises steadfastly and responsibly.

It was ludicrous to say, as Herbert Asquith said when contesting Paisley at the General Election of 1924: 'There are about 15,000 women on the register—a dim impenetrable, for the most part un-get-at-able element, of whom all one knows is that they are for the most part ignorant of politics, credulous to the last degree and flickering with gusts of sentiment like a candle in the wind.' It was ludicrous to say, too, as so many did, that giving the vote to women in 1918 'had made no difference'. On that historic day, in March 1928, which heralded the end of sixty years of struggle to secure the vote for women on the same terms as men, Lady Astor, first woman to take her seat in Parliament, declared in the Commons debate: 'When I first stood up and asked questions affecting women and children, social and moral questions, I used to be shouted at for five or ten minutes at a time. That was when they thought I was rather a freak. But as the women became more and more interested in these questions the more I stood here knowing full well that there was an army outside behind me. I can testify to the change that has taken place in the House of Commons since women had a vote. In the twelve years before they had a vote there were only five measures passed dealing with women and the things that affected women and children. From 1918 onwards we have had twenty measures affecting women and children. I am not blaming men; I am simply showing that already we see the effect women's influence is having on legislation.'

Of course in 1928 there were still men, and perhaps some women, though they were not in the Chamber to say so, who thought that the effect women might have on legislation was dangerous. Brigadier Cockerill told the Commons he thought that MPs with small majorities might be subject to 'unfair pressure' by women. He wanted 'electoral colleges' to ensure an equal weight of men's and women's votes. Colonel Appian declared roundly that 'the wealth of the country from which its revenues are derived is produced by men in relation to women on the scale 10–1. If we are to have majority rule by women we are handing over to them the taxable wealth of the country to which they have only contributed one-tenth.' It is nice to know that MPs laughed at this . . . but Colonel Appian was indignant. 'It is all very well to treat this as a jest,' he said, 'but if we pass a law to permit women to take over the finances of the country, where are we going?'

There must have been many women throughout the country who, reading the reports of the speech of Ellen Wilkinson, shared her emotion. At that time, though entitled to be elected to Parliament, she was not entitled to vote for herself or any other candidate, because she was too young, and she was not a ratepayer or married to a ratepayer. 'I feel this is a very solemn occasion,' she said, 'and I am glad that I have been allowed to take part in it.' When the vote was taken, only twelve Members went into the 'No' lobby. After it had been duly debated in the House of Lords where Lord Birkenhead (F. E. Smith) gloomily advised his fellow peers to vote for it 'with resolute resignation', it became law, in June 1928.

The women organized a great thanksgiving meeting in the Queen's Hall, London. Dame Millicent Garrett Fawcett who had

given her whole long life to the constitutional suffrage movement
showed herself to be, at eighty years of age, still mentally and
physically alert. She was joined by Emmeline Pankhurst, the
militant heroine, survivor of numerous hunger strikes, who looked
pale and ill. Josephine Kamm in her *Rapiers and Battleaxes* says,
however, that when she started to speak—without the aid of a
microphone, of course—she came to life once more and the voice
which had thrilled multitudes in the Albert Hall was as clear and
persuasive as ever.

Mrs Pankhurst had recently agreed to stand as a Conservative
candidate for Whitechapel and St George's, a strong Labour seat,
but she died a fortnight before the Representation of the People
(Equal Franchise) Act became law. Dame Millicent was more
fortunate. She lived another year and actually saw 'the flappers'
(as the newspapers called the new younger women electors) vote
in the General Election of May 1929.

The long-awaited triumph of the suffrage campaigners must have
been very sweet to them. But where did they go from there? There
was plenty of work still to do, and a speech in the House of Commons debate on the Franchise Bill gave a crucial lead. 'The letters
I have received on the Bill,' said Sir Charles Oman, 'are only an
eighth of those I have received on the Totalisator Bill and not a
fiftieth of the number received on the Prayer Book. The country
was really interested in the Prayer Book. It was moderately
interested in the totalisator. But of this Bill not the slightest
notice was, till last week, being taken in the country.'

Despite Lady Astor, Ellen Wilkinson, and the other women
MPs, despite Dame Millicent Garrett Fawcett and her faithful
workers, and the Pankhursts and their vehement cohorts, there was
a sense in which Sir Charles Oman was right. There were five and a
quarter million new women voters coming on to the register and
a vast majority of them had never been politically minded and
were not organization women in any sense of the term. What was
to be done about that? The experienced campaigners had no
doubt—they had to be educated in citizenship.

In 1976 Dame Margery Corbett Ashby remembered it like this:
'By the time we had won the vote for women over thirty we had
300 individual women's suffrage societies up and down the country,
in the countryside as well as in the towns. When the younger

women also acquired the vote it was a real problem as to how they were to be trained for this new responsibility.' It was she who set this training opportunity in motion by moving Resolution 82 at the annual council meeting of the National Union of Societies for Equal Citizenship (the old NUWSS) in March 1927, at which the promise of the Government to give women the full franchise was welcomed. It read: 'This Council resolves itself into a committee to consider by what means those about-to-be enfranchised women who do not yet belong to the women's movement may be drawn into active co-operation with it.' At this time the energetic parliamentary secretary of the National Union of Women's Suffrage Societies, Mrs Eva Hubback, was resting in a nursing-home after an operation, her mind busily engaged on the problem of women voters. Mrs Corbett Ashby went to visit her and naturally they talked chiefly of what they would get up to next and how to find something all their well-trained suffrage workers could usefully do. According to Dame Margery it was Mrs Hubback who first suggested that it might be wise to take the Women's Institutes as a model on which to build a town organization for the ordinary married woman, with quite a simple programme. The WI included agriculture and food production, for that was of great importance during the 1914–18 war when the Institutes began here, but these things were irrelevant to women living in towns.

'We felt that it would be much more in keeping with our philosophy and policy,' said Dame Margery, reminiscing in her ninety-fifth year, 'if we gave the women in the towns not only training in and enjoyment of arts and crafts but also training in the responsibility of citizenship. Our programme was comradeship, arts and crafts and citizenship. We found that there was no organization for the ordinary housewife apart from the organizations attached to the churches and to the political parties. So the Townswomen's Guilds were brought in to give this triple programme to the ordinary women at home.' A founder member of the first Townswomen's Guild, Mrs S. J. Moojen, of Haywards Heath, recalled a meeting in St George's Hall, London, in 1928 'to discuss the disposal of suffrage funds'. 'Mrs Tyrell Godman', she said, 'put forth the proposition that Institutes should be formed in towns on the lines of the village institutes which she and Mrs

Clowes had started in England. I seconded the motion, and it was passed.'

The 'benevolent conspirators', the NUSEC organizing committee, met together in the old suffrage headquarters in Dean's Yard, in the shadow of Westminster Abbey, and Eleanor Rathbone MP gave them £100 anonymously to launch the new movement. Four experimental Guilds were formed, Haywards Heath first, then Burnt Oak, Moulsecomb, and Romsey, and within a year there were twenty-six Guilds affiliated. It all sounds easy, now, but of course it was no such thing. The little organizing group decided where and when to go and, as Dame Margery said, 'it was grinding organization work'. All the 'conspirators' were very busy women, up to their eyes in good works of all kinds, but they found time to go knocking on the doors of women whose names had been given them by the old regional suffrage organizers to invite people to introductory meetings. Often only five or six turned up and it might take two or three meetings before sufficient women showed interest to make forming a Guild worth while. There was some opposition, too. Haywards Heath opened as a 'Women's Town Institute', and the Women's Institutes didn't like that at all, so the next month it became a Townswomen's Guild. But some people didn't like that name either and according to Dame Margery there were 'terrific jeers' from people who thought 'Townswomen' implied women of the street. But the pioneers stuck to their guns, confident that they would live down that sort of nonsense very quickly. As indeed they did.

The pioneers said they planned carefully, developing solidly, not fast, and that they spent a lot of time working out programmes which would be most suitable for different types of Guild, but twenty-six Guilds in a year was an astonishing achievement, and that they had the confidence to rent an office and staff seems even more astonishing to us in this day of high rents and high salaries. The new movement was extremely lucky in taking over the keen young parliamentary secretary of the National Union for Equal Citizenship. In a way Gertrude Horton was a greenhorn—she scarcely knew the difference between the militant and the constitutional movements—but her family had always been enthusiastic about women's rights and her mother had campaigned for Christabel Pankhurst when she stood for Parliament. She had

succeeded Eva Hubback at the NUSEC when Mrs Hubback
became principal of Morley College. She had graduated in science
at London University and married her schoolmaster husband while
there. She herself wanted to be a teacher but could not get a job—
because of the marriage bar—and was lucky, she felt, to be appointed
to the NUSEC job—especially as, like Ellen Wilkinson, at twenty-
eight she was too young to have a vote herself. It was at her first
annual meeting of NUSEC that she heard Dame Millicent Garrett
Fawcett tell the audience 'Now your task is to educate'. The new
committee was lucky too, in having someone who could develop the
educational programme for the Guilds, Mrs H. L. Morgan, who in
1924 had been the chairman of the Advisory Committee of
Women's Evening Institutes. Her aim, like Eva Hubback's, was
to bring adult education to women on a quite informal basis, with
nothing like examinations or certificates of merit. Another taunt
the Guilds had to put up with in their early years was that they
provided 'Woolworth's education'. They stuck out that gibe too,
though it lasted quite a while, because they felt sure that their job
was to awaken women's interest and provide such educational
opportunities as would attract them. Mrs Morgan was involved in
preparing the ground at Burnt Oak, and later recalled how they
recruited by putting chits through people's letter boxes, and held
their first meeting in a builder's hut.

Few people realize now how the suffrage movement spread its
influence throughout the women's organizations. The Women's
Institutes took a lot from the NUSEC including the red, white
and green colours which they share with the National Union of
Townswomen's Guilds. (The red, white and green originally were
taken from the freedom badge of Italy, the symbolism being red
for courage to tackle problems, white for faith in their endeavours
and green for hope that the endeavours would be successful. It
was the militants who chose the colours green, white and purple
which are more often associated with the suffrage agitation.)

The WI national secretary who preceded the much revered
Dame Frances Farrer had been a secretary of NUSEC. Eva
Hubback was very friendly with Lady Denman, chairman of the
National Federation of Women's Institutes, who was friendly
with one of Queen Mary's ladies-in-waiting, Lady Cynthia
Colville. So with this kind of backing it was not too difficult to

raise funds. Lady Cynthia acted as the president of an appeal launched in September 1929 at Lady Denman's Sussex home, Balcombe Place, and what is more, she brought together fifty of her friends to help in the collection of £15,000 to start up Townswomen's Guilds all over the country. Eva Hubback had another inspiration which was to prove of immense value. She brought in as 'voluntary administrator' a most remarkable woman, her cousin, Alice Franklin. She and Gertrude Horton soon became fast friends and it is hard to avoid the conclusion that these two were the real architects of the NUTG, for together they devised its structure and fashioned its rules.

Alice Franklin was the sister of Helen Bentwich (wife of the distinguished Zionist lawyer, Norman Bentwich), a convinced fighter for women's emancipation. Their brother Hugh Franklin was also a suffrage supporter, one of the few men who went to prison for the cause. He was drawn into the movement while at Cambridge and was active in the Men's Social and Political Union which supported the militant suffragettes. He left Cambridge in 1910 and soon afterwards attacked Winston Churchill— always a target for suffragette hostility—with a dog whip in the corridor of a train. He was arrested and imprisoned and soon after his release he set fire to a railway train. As it was the Franklins' local line he was recognized and again sought by the police. For many weeks he escaped arrest, but eventually he was caught and sentenced to nine months' imprisonment. He was one of the first suffrage prisoners to go on hunger strike and be forcibly fed, which seriously undermined his health. When he was released under the Cat and Mouse Act, because he had become physically frail, he escaped to the Continent, dressed as a woman. 'Once again, after his escape we were closely watched by detectives,' wrote Helen Bentwich, 'and they would sometimes follow Alice and me as we set out in the morning. But this stopped after Alice one day turned round and said to the detective "If you insist on following me you might at least carry my despatch case." This the abashed young man did, and we were followed no more.'

The Franklins were a strongly Liberal family—Herbert Samuel was their uncle by marriage. But Alice was a Socialist and honorary secretary of a group of young intellectuals who called themselves 'The Utopians'. Helen also decided at fourteen that she was a Socialist and so was Hugh, six years younger than Alice. They were a very orthodox Jewish family and when two brothers, Hugh and Jack, married non-Jews, their father cut them out of his will. Alice became a Care Committee worker in London and later was the secretary of the Society for the Overseas Settlement of British Women. Her job was to try to amalgamate the societies interested in helping women who wanted to emigrate—it was the period when the youngish women whose potential husbands had been killed in the ghastly slaughter of the trenches in World War I were known as 'surplus women'. So Alice was used to dealing with the wives of High Commissioners and similar top-level people.

But when her father fell ill she made no bones about giving up her job to help her mother and so was available when Eva Hubback was inspired to draw her into the Townswomen's Guild movement. She never had a salary but for nearly twenty years worked untiringly as honorary secretary and treasurer. Whenever Miss Franklin's name is mentioned today to the older Townswomen who can remember her, their faces light up. She must have been middle aged when she took the job on, but she cannot have lacked remarkable energy. 'She was a marvellous old creature,' said Miss Bilbie, once assistant secretary of the NUTG and later warden of Crosby Hall, the residential centre of the British Federation of University Women. 'She was a good old war horse, a great personality. She was well into her seventies when I knew her and lived to be about eighty. People like her jollied the NUTG along. They were full of enterprise and without them it would have been very "worthy".'

Perhaps Alice Franklin's sense of fun did not always go down very well with her committees. Some members were antagonistic to her, and objected when she teased them by saying 'What a nuisance your husbands are'. Mrs Eileen Coram, national chairman of the NUTG since 1975, said, 'I shall never forget my first meeting with her. She was really marvellous. She came down to the Southwell Community Centre to tell us about a Federation grouping scheme. She stood up and said sternly "Are there any Press here? If there are they will leave immediately. This is a private meeting."'

Miss Elias, longest serving member of the head office staff, who joined in 1941 as a newly released German refugee, found Alice Franklin very fearsome at first. Before the rise of the Nazis she had worked as a secretary in a very big company. Overnight the company had to dismiss all its non-Aryan employees and she came to England as a domestic worker in 1937—the only employment refugees were then allowed to take. Her mother was too old to get a work permit, even as a domestic, and she and her other daughter perished.

Miss Elias was interned on the outbreak of war, like all the other refugees, but when British girls were called up for National Service they were allowed to work in offices and public institutions. So she had to brush up her German shorthand and produce an English version of it. Taking letters from Miss Franklin was a trial, she says, for she was very bad at dictating, partly because her sharp brain worked so fast that she didn't always get the sentences out properly, and partly because she usually had a cigarette in her mouth. Miss Elias was a Jill-of-all-trades in the small NUTG office, by that time in Cromwell Place, South Kensington. As there was only a skeleton staff she manned the switchboard when necessary and worked very long hours, often through her lunch hour and always on Saturday morning. 'When I first met Miss Franklin I had to look twice—she looked so like a man with her short-cropped hair. She was rather abrupt and short in her manner—a real character. She and Mrs Horton used surnames without prefixes and would call upstairs for "Elias" or whoever.' One can imagine how the shy refugee was intimidated by her hard task-mistresses. But they, of course, flogged themselves at least as hard as they flogged the staff.

In 1930 when there were already quite a number of Towns-women's Guilds to send delegates to the National Union of Societies for Equal Citizenship council meeting, and for their doings to have a regular page in the historic suffrage magazine *The Woman's Leader*, the limelight was not yet on Miss Franklin, nor indeed on Mrs Horton; and Miss Franklin's name does not appear; but probably Mrs Horton took part in a committee which was set up to formulate rules for the new groups, publish literature, and prepare membership cards and badges. Within two more years it became clear that the mother organization, NUSEC, and the daughter, the Townswomen's Guilds, had to sever the umbilical cord. The daughter was not rebelliously champing at the bit; the mother was in no sense wanting to kick the daughter out into

the cold hard world; but it had become rather obvious that each
was likely to hamper and restrict the growth of the other. So the
executive committee brought forward a motion to divide the work
into two totally separate organizations, and this was carried by a
large majority. One organization, the National Council for Equal
Citizenship, would continue to have a political programme. Its
aims would be 'To enable women as citizens to make their best
contribution towards the common good, and to obtain all such
reforms as are necessary to secure a real equality of liberties, status
and opportunities between men and women.' The other body,
the National Union of Guilds for Citizenship, would concentrate
entirely on *educating* women for citizenship. This organization's
aims were 'To encourage the education of women to enable them
as citizens to make their best contribution to the common good.'

'The pressure groupers' as we might call them today, probably
felt held back by the new groups of women who had not committed
themselves to any political concepts, and the Guild women were
undoubtedly nervous of unauthorized pressure being applied in
their name. The trend must already have become clear, for at the
decisive March 1932 meeting, there were delegates from fifty-one
women's citizens' associations and societies for equal citizenship,
compared with 183 Townswomen's Guilds. Henceforth the older
campaigning societies would shrink and the new social-cum-
educational Guilds would burgeon. It was inevitable, for the major
task of the suffrage societies had been completed and the supporters
inevitably hived off into more specialized societies. They could
not be expected to agree on the whole spectrum of political attitudes.
The suffragists had always been of different political views but
had stood bravely on a common platform so long as the overriding need was, as they believed, to compel some Government,
any Government, to concede the vote to women. When that
overriding need no longer existed, the differences became start-
lingly clear. When Eleanor Rathbone, as successor to Dame
Millicent Garrett Fawcett in the presidency, persuaded the
National Union of Societies for Equal Citizenship to support her
Family Endowment Campaign, Dame Millicent resigned—
regretfully, but quite irrevocably, for she was a Liberal of the old
school who believed that state support of children would endanger
family responsibility.

There were, of course, plenty of causes for the women still to fight, and some lively campaigning organizations to fight them—there were the strongly feminist 6-Point Group and Open Door Council; the Married Women's Association, the Status of Women Committee and a handful of more 'sociable' organizations like the National Association of Women's Clubs (1933), the British Legion Women's Clubs and the Inner Wheel Clubs for the wives of Rotarians. It is hard to remember now that this was what Claude Cockburn named 'The Devil's Decade'—the years of the slump, the Depression, or whatever one prefers to call those unhappy years—when Ellen Wilkinson was less concerned with feminist issues than with walking with the Hunger Marchers from Jarrow to Westminster. It was in these years when the Townswomen's Guilds began to flourish right across Great Britain that the Nazis rose to power and the refugees began to trickle across the North Sea; when the shadow of war began to loom blackly and many of our finest citizens, men and women alike, were deeply involved in the Peace Movement and in recruiting support for the League of Nations and for disarmament. Marjorie Corbett Ashby was herself substitute British delegate to the Disarmament conference at Geneva in 1932, and her commitment to the cause of peace was so strong a thread in her political make-up that it is extraordinary that she found time to be more than a figurehead for the new Guilds. Yet she was a working president if ever there was one, and was still attending National Council meetings in her nineties.

When she stood for the presidency of NUSEC in 1929 before the Townswomen's Guilds 'went independent', Mrs Corbett Ashby said of herself 'After nearly twenty-five years' connection with NUSEC, beginning with my appointment as secretary [that was in *1904!*] it seems unusually difficult to write my views, since I feel so much part and parcel of the Union. When my personal work in connection with the General Election is over [this was the first General Election at which all adult women were able to vote, including those "flappers" whom Fleet Street found as comical—or distasteful—as it later found "Women's Libbers"] and also my work in connection with the Berlin Congress of the International Alliance of Women, I shall throw myself with great zest into the expansion scheme of the National Union.

'I have been connected since the beginning with the Rural

Women's Institutes and know how marvellously they have developed citizenship, initiative and self-reliance among the countrywomen. Our aim should be to combine the feminism of the National Union with the social activities of the Rural Women's Institutes. We should add political and parliamentary work to a programme similar to theirs but adapted to town needs.'

The 'platform' on which Eva Hubback stood for office emphasized general citizenship before equality 'both because the greater includes the less and because the time is past when "equality" can be the rallying cry for a powerful organization. Let us keep,' she urged, 'broad-minded, vital, enterprising, encouraging ever new types of organizations in our affiliated societies. Let us also keep a watching brief on both central and local government and elsewhere and be at the right moment prepared to take action. In this way alone will we attract enough new members of all ages to remain sufficiently well equipped to carry out the equality reforms, with practically all of which I agree though the more important are economic rather than legal.'

Mrs J. L. Stocks (Mary Stocks) was one of the few candidates for office at this time who wanted to stick to a strongly feminist line—she spoke of the antagonism to women doctors and married women teachers, the persistence of unequal pay and the barrier to promotion in the Civil Service. But it was Mrs Hubback's view that prevailed in the new wing of NUSEC which became the NUTG. Mary Stocks retained her interest in the Townswomen and was for many years a vice-president, but the NUTG had not the sort of cutting edge to satisfy her. She was very much an academic, despite that tart sense of fun which years later was to make her perhaps the most popular 'Any Questions' panellist there has ever been. Margery Corbett Ashby could rate as an academic, too, for she was an early Newnham girl. (Her father was such a good feminist that when he heard his son had a suite of two rooms at Oxford and his daughter only a bed-sit at Cambridge he insisted she also have two rooms.) The Corbetts were also 'political'. Mr Corbett was a Liberal MP and his wife a keen member of the Women's Liberal Federation. She herself had been involved in politics, especially international affairs, from her very early years. But the Corbetts lived in a village. They were very close to 'ordinary' life, to the experience and feelings of women whose life-work was raising a family and caring for husband and home. Mrs Corbett Ashby had a very good understanding that what the majority of women were likely to want, first and foremost, was to share the interests they had in common, not battle across party or sectarian lines.

Perhaps this was especially true in the tormented Thirties when the Townswomen's movement began. The NUTG threw open the doors of home, but they opened them into a safe, un-threatened world. Possibly the real key to the rapid success of the organization was 'the common meeting ground'. Coming from the brilliant 'politicos', this showed extraordinary sensitivity and imagination. The NUTG's second object 'To serve as a common meeting ground for women irrespective of creed and party, for their wider education, including social activities' was exactly the re-assurance 'ordinary' women wanted and they soon came flocking in.

No one conducted market research for the founders of the Townswomen's Guilds. No one took test samples of the various socio-economic classes. They acted on their experience and best judgment—as businessmen and industrialists always did before the days of market research 'sampling' to see what kind of products were likely to sell—and they were proved triumphantly right. The day would come when nearly a quarter of a million women from the north of Scotland to the Channel Islands and Northern Ireland would be 'buying their product'. Dame Margery used to say that the NUTG considered any town big enough to support a branch of Woolworth's suitable for a Townswomen's Guild. At its peak the NUTG had 2,700 Guilds. Woolworth's have 1,000 branches. The analogy between the organization of the vast chain of retail stores and the coverage of the UK by a chain of women's groups is not so far-fetched as it may sound. In both cases there has to be a reconnaissance to see if the area is suitable, premises have to be found, staff (committee) recruited and, however independent the Guild (store) may be, it has to be serviced and guided by a central directorate. Presumably directors and staff of F. W. Woolworth Ltd are paid very substantial salaries. For controlling a small head office staff and maintaining fruitful contact with 2,700 'branches' and $2\frac{1}{4}$ million 'customers', the leaders of the National Union of Townswomen's Guilds do not get a penny—except for quite modest travel and subsistence expenses. What satisfactions other than money make this great expenditure of energy, time, and commitment worth while will be considered later in this book.

Four years after the experimental launch of Guilds in 1928, 146 had been set up. A grant of £1,000 from the Carnegie Trust had greatly helped this development, and this was further evidence of the operation of 'the Old Girls Network'. Lady Cynthia Colville, the president of the new organization, was a friend of Colonel Mitchell of the Trust—and indeed Colonel Mitchell had been secretary of one of the men's suffrage societies. He hoped that the new organizations would become 'Townsguilds', but the executive felt that in a man-made world, with the majority of women at home, the new woman voter had a lot of leeway to make up and should be given special and separate consideration. This did not weaken his interest. He was a very faithful friend of the NUTG.

Once again the leadership of the movement was right in its judgment. The potential members wanted company outside the walls of home, but they could only acceptably seek the company of other women. They were not ready for political and cultural independence—and nor were many of their husbands, one suspects, ready for wives who would take an independent political line. Such women needed a supportive organization, with a firm framework. And certainly this is what they got.

Alice Franklin's opposite number in the office, the salaried secretary Gertrude Horton, was probably an academic manqué. She wanted everything just so—and 'just so' at that time meant a written constitution and the most carefully drafted rules for every level of activity throughout the organization. The members felt they needed this detailed guidance: compared with the experienced suffrage leaders who recruited them they were real 'babes in the wood' and astonishingly lacking in confidence. Over and over again one reads of women who trembled like leaves in the wind or turned green at the gills at the thought of proposing a vote of thanks, let alone taking any kind of office in their Guild. Mrs Horton remembers the members who when they were opening a bank account for the Guild asked 'Is the Midland Bank safe?', or 'If I send a cheque do I have to register the letter?'

'We wanted people in regardless of party,' said Mrs Horton, 'and we didn't want the TG to be available for people with an axe to grind. We were trying to recruit people who had not got around to serious thinking.' It was to protect both the organization and the inexperienced individuals who were setting it up that Miss Franklin and Mrs Horton prepared the first NUTG handbook. It sold nearly 2,000 copies in five months.

The first annual report of the National Union of Guilds for Citizenship (set up by the historic conference of 1932) was not quite so euphoric as later accounts of the pioneering days. 'The first five months of 1932,' it reads, 'were of necessity devoted to preparing for the change of constitution and to the reorganization consequent upon its adoption. The organization was seriously handicapped at first through our inability to estimate what income should be available for its extension. The development and direction of our movement were further retarded by the loss of the wide knowledge and experience of former executive committee members who left the National Union to form the National Council for Equal Citizenship. Guild members will always remember with gratitude the help given in the early stages by Miss Eleanor Rathbone, Miss Elizabeth Macadam [an officer of NUSEC] and Miss Picton Turbervill.'

Alice Franklin and Gertrude Horton were dedicated to the idea of referring everything to first principles. When they wrote letters to Guild officials, as they increasingly did as the organization grew, they drafted a 'mini lesson'. Even with the hindsight of forty years, Mrs Horton remained convinced, in 1976, that organization was a matter for trained people—not necessarily professionals or paid staff, but certainly people who had learned how things should be done. She likened opening a new Guild to having a baby—you need to have a trained midwife to usher the baby into the world, and a trained organizer to launch a new Guild. So almost from the start the Townswomen went in for training schools, very much on the same lines as the Women's Co-operative Guilds. It seems very unlikely that the Townswomen got their ideas from the Co-operative guildswomen, and yet, who knows? One gets a strong impression that there was constant coming and going between the circle of women working for the common good. It is by no means unlikely that Margaret Llewelyn Davies and Lilian Harris, the remarkable women who drafted the structure of the Women's Co-operative Guild and inspired its rank-and-file to become real leaders, knew Eva Hubback and Alice Franklin. But undoubtedly both the Women's Institutes and the Townswomen took the idea of regional federations from the National Union of Societies for Equal Citizenship. They had already formed thirteen federations before they were formally independent of the parent body.

The first TG schools were intended for the recruitment and training of voluntary organizers but it quickly became evident that the new committee and officers needed to *learn* how to organize, how to chair a meeting, write and read the minutes, handle the subscriptions and payments, and even how to propose a vote of thanks. So there were schools at which these diffident debutantes in office could learn their Guild duties and how to plan programmes that would hold the interest of members . . . and also how the national movement worked and was financed, how Federations operated and how individual members could help the movement to expand nationally.

Even at this early stage the idea of specialist advisers was germinating. 'Federations at a distance from London are proposing to form advisory committees consisting of keen Guild members who are prepared to specialize in particular branches of the work.' Already a local government sub-committee and a programme sub-committee had been set up at headquarters. The separate interests for which the leaders wanted to provide included handicrafts, housecraft, including cookery demonstrations, household decorating and 'jobbery', upholstery and electrical repairs, drama, choirs, and 'social intercourse'. Informal tea-parties were held once a month in the office by members of the executive committee, so that specialists could meet with members from the provinces— and even at that early date they came from as far away as Aberdeen and Devon.

In these formative years a very close bond was retained with the National Federation of Women's Institutes. A conference was called between the Guilds and the Institutes, and the NFWI agreed to circularize its county federations informing them of the Townswomen's new policy and asking for co-operation. 'In general a WI is not formed in a town where the population exceeds 4,000 or where there is an urban rather than a rural outlook. But in no case where the size or character of the place makes it uncertain whether a Women's Institute could be formed is a Guild started, or any preliminary work undertaken until a WI county federation has been consulted.'

So the annual report for 1933—only five years after the idea of Townswomen's Guilds was born—included quite an extensive rule structure: thirteen rules, with many sub-clauses for the national body, twelve rules with sub-clauses for the local Guilds and eight rules with sub-clauses for the Federations which had already been established to make for quicker and easier communication and support between the local Guilds. Almost everything, from the maximum size of a Guild committee to the minimum number required for a quorum is laid down and one is driven to ask whether it was really necessary. Today's groups of young 'liberated' women would think this tight, hierarchical structure absurd as well as frustrating. They manage very well without written rules and constitution and frequently without any formally elected officers and committee. They have, of course, a great deal more confidence and sense of independence than their mothers and grandmothers, but as Mrs Kathleen Kempton, the thoughtful and experienced general secretary of the Co-operative Women's Guild, said, 'Groups without rules run into difficulties because they have no machinery to resolve differences.' And alas, in the happiest of groups of human beings, male, female, or both together, differences of opinion as to what has to be done *will* arise and a previously agreed method of resolving them can prevent hard feelings, and indeed hurtful and destructive acrimony.

One of the reasons for the swift success of the Townswomen's Guild movement was the very wide range of its activities. An early handout leaflet gave its aims as:

> To encourage the science and practice of homemaking and housecraft.
> To stimulate interest in the preservation of the beauty of the town and countryside and in architecture, local history, folk lore and natural history.
> To promote interest in Handicrafts, Arts and Science.
> To encourage the study by women of their opportunities and responsibilities as voters.
> To take an active interest in matters relating to the town, the

nation and the Empire and questions of international
importance, peace and the League of Nations.
To enable women as citizens to make their best contribution
towards the common good and to obtain all such reforms
as are necessary to secure a real equality of liberties, status
and opportunities between men and women.

One observes that the leaflet put homemaking and housecraft
at the top of the list and citizenship and equal status at the bottom.
The 'founding mothers' were realists, and anyway, they had the
reports from the Guild meetings to show what the favourite
activities were. An analysis of 120 local Guild annual reports,
made, no doubt, by Alice Franklin, and printed in the 1933 annual
report, revealed that handicrafts were right at the top of the
popularity poll with 230 lectures or demonstrations on rugmaking,
dressmaking, toy-making, embroidery, glovemaking, and so forth;
homecraft and gardening came next, then civics, and, curiously,
health was at the bottom of the list. Nowhere was the status of
women, or the education of women to make good use of the vote,
mentioned at all.

The new organization had an asset that few new organizations
have nowadays—a well-established monthly magazine. It sprang
from the suffrage *The Common Cause* and under the name *The
Woman's Leader* it had served the suffrage movement for twenty-five
fruitful years. From 1930 it carried reports of the Townswomen's
Guilds whose doings took up an increasing amount of space. But
its publishers, the Common Cause Publishing Company, were
faced with increasing financial difficulties as the circulation of the
magazine in the 'post-suffrage' period naturally declined. In
1933 the firm went into voluntary liquidation and the new organization, not now the National Union of Guilds for Citizenship but
the National Union of Townswomen's Guilds, acquired the rights
of publication. The annual council meeting agreed to this step,
but when the chairman of the meeting, Mrs Corbett Ashby,
proposed, for the executive, that the Council should decide on the
new title of the paper, the rank and file rebelled. The title of the
paper, they agreed, should be *The Townswoman*. So the April
issue, Volume 1, No 1 of the new monthly, carried the front page
announcement, 'The Woman's Leader is dead. Long Live the

Townswoman' and indeed it has had a longer and probably more influential run than its predecessor, for it is now on its way to its half century, a much larger and more handsome periodical than the sad little *Leader* which perished in 1933.

Sometimes, reading *The Woman's Leader*, the early issues of *The Townswoman*, the annual reports, and especially the pre-war Handbooks, the whole set-up sounds uncomfortably worthy and serious-minded, but for the people involved it was not like that at all. 'It was *fun*,' Gertrude Horton insisted. 'It was very exciting in those early days of the movement. Everything we did was experimental and you never knew whom you would meet or what would happen next.' And interviewed on her ninetieth birthday, Dame Margery Corbett Ashby said to the interviewer, 'Perhaps you'd like to mention one thing—the tremendous fun and loyalty there was working with women for a common object, disproving all the clichés about women being petty, jealous and ineffective.'

2

Grass Roots

So it was fun; it was positively exciting, for the Top Ladies who got the National Union of Townswomen's Guilds off the ground and saw it develop into the second largest federation in the country. But what was it like in the church halls, schoolrooms, and community centres where the first recruits gathered together? Were they having fun too? There are not very many original members still around, after fifty years, but the story of the first Guild to be be formed, Haywards Heath, Sussex, launched on 25 January 1929, is surely typical of many a Guild throughout the country. It seems a quiet and unadventurous tale, but talking to women who have been members since before World War II, one has a strong impression of the way it has enriched the lives of many of its members.

The meeting room now is the Centenary Hall. A window all along one side looks out on to grass, trees, and distant low hills. When the Guild was formed, very near to the home of Mrs Margery Corbett Ashby, Haywards Heath was a small market town. It is now a commuter area but the atmosphere in the Townswomen's Guild seems to have changed very little. Members sit and chat round small tables covered with green and white cloths, some adorned with posies of flowers. There is usually a speaker, always a raffle, often a sales table to which members bring goods, mostly kitchen or garden produce. The Guild takes a small commission on the sales.

The older members agree, 'No, the Guild hasn't changed much.' One regular attender is ninety-two. She is shown a photograph of herself in a play produced in 1939, and is reminded that when

Haywards Heath TG had a choir, it met in her home. Two women who still come regularly actually joined in 1929, the Guild's first year. A former treasurer joined in 1937 and served for nineteen years. 'We have never had any bitchiness in this Guild,' say the older members. 'We have always had a warm, friendly atmosphere. We come for friendship.' And one adds, 'When my husband died the Guild gave me wonderful support'—a sentiment that would be echoed throughout the movement.

On the day the Haywards Heath Townswomen's Guild was formed, 120 women turned up. By the second meeting, a month later, 153 members had joined, and there was 'an orchestral selection by a trio of ladies' while tea was served. There is no music-with-tea at today's meetings, but the 'afternoon tea-ish' atmosphere still prevails. There are only eighty-two members of the afternoon Guild now, but there is a flourishing evening Guild and other Guilds have been formed in the neighbourhood from the original one. The Haywards Heath members are proud that their Guild was a pioneer. At their fortieth birthday the then national chairman, Mrs Mary Sobey, said to them, 'If you hadn't been a success, there would not now be 2,700 Guilds in existence.'

A former Haywards Heath chairman has a delightful collection of early programmes. Each month has a 'motto', some of which are quite witty as well as wise. 'Hard work Makes more Happiness than Easy Chairs'; 'Some people nurse a grouse, others shoot it'; 'Worry is the interest paid on trouble before it is due'; 'After burying the hatchet don't mark the spot'; 'The world's a looking-glass—look pleasant please'; 'We shall never get giddy doing good turns'. Simple competitions and raffles still add a small spice of interest to the monthly meetings. In January 1937 members were asked to bring 'My best piece of china'. In June 1976 the competition was for their 'prettiest piece of china (something small)'.

Early programmes of the Haywards Heath Guild, like so many others, all bear the words 'Let us all work together for the common good', and the members still do just that, outside the Guild as well as within it. Every quarter the Guild provides a team of four to cook, serve, and wash up, lunch for about thirty housebound people. They also cook and wash up for Age Concern. At Christmas they send gifts for about twenty patients at a local geriatric hospital.

They have two sick visitors who keep in touch with members in hospital and take them flowers.

Even during the war years the pattern of programmes did not change very much, despite members' worries about husbands and sons in the Forces and problems with evacuees. They probably regarded the TG as their sheet anchor, as they came together to hear talks on 'some problems of upholstery', 'glimpses of the Emerald Isle' (with cine film), 'Songs from Shakespeare' (in costume), 'African Folklore' and, intriguingly, 'Wits, Bits and Cookery'.

Haywards Heath TG is proud of its financial independence. It gets no grant from the Adult Education department of West Sussex, and pays for its speakers and its room rent out of Guild funds. Money is raised by taking a stall at Haywards Heath Country Market and Cuckfield Hospital Fete. The market stall, selling anything from kitchen mops to jam, raised a useful £117 in 1975. Twice-a-year jumble sales bring in around £70 apiece. In November the Guild has an Arts Exhibition which also adds to Guild funds. Haywards Heath members do not pay any extra fee for the group activities they enjoy so much, such as drama, arts and crafts, and social studies. The Arts and Crafts group had an entertaining and useful season making shopping bags from string, toys, and pewter work. Between March and October an enthusiastic group meets monthly for rambles over the Sussex Downs, and outings by coach are frequently arranged to places of interest.

Was it for this sort of involvement that women all over the United Kingdom queued up throughout the Thirties, Forties, and Fifties (even during the war years)? There can only be one answer . . . 'yes'—for friendship outside the family circle, a widening of interests, and a desire to 'improve themselves'. That largely housebound women were uninterested in social and cultural matters was far from true, but they were inexperienced and lacking in confidence. *Together* they could take the plunge into matters of greater moment than making paper flowers and listening to lecture recitals.

Mrs H. L. Morgan explained very vividly the initial steps towards establishing Townswomen's Guilds, as it happened in Burnt Oak, one of the first five. 'When two or three meetings had

Burnt Oak Townswomen's Guild

Non Party   Non Sectarian

President—Mrs. Corbett Ashby.

Vice-Presidents—

Mrs Monro.   Mrs. Jones

Chairman—Mrs. Calt, 50 Fortescue Road

Vice-Chairman—Mrs. Barker

Hon. Treas.—Mrs. Seddon

Hon. Sec.—Mrs. Alford, 204a High Road.

Committee—

Mrs. Andrews	Mrs. Nall
Mrs. Bond	Mrs. Ristow
Mrs. Daniels	Mrs. Spooner
Mrs. McAlpine	Mrs. Stowers
Mrs. Marsh	Mrs. Wilkins

Programme - 1935
Price 1d.

MEETINGS ALTERNATE THURSDAYS

been held and the organization explained, we held "American teas" to enable us to pay the rent of halls. These involved Bring and Buy sales, and many good craftswomen were discovered. We would arrange to have a birthday party plus entertainment—usually recitations and monologues—and at Christmas carol singing led to the formation of choirs. We found that drama provided an alternative to tear-jerking rhetoric, and performed plays which dealt with women's social problems.' Many an older Guild member will recall those steps to adventure.

A typical member writing to *The Townswoman* thirty years later confirmed the relevance of what Mrs Morgan said: 'How many talents we each have, and how often they are hidden. Through the drama section I find I can act, though I shall never be a star performer. The music section has taught me I can sing a bit. Social studies and handicrafts are two more sections where I am learning to work and play with others. My Guild and Federation have enabled me to make many good and lasting friends. I have become close friends with people whom, had I not been a member of the TG, I should never have spoken to. So my Guild means to me having new interests, something new to talk about each month, being able to take my place as a good citizen for the advancing of good throughout the world, and having good friends who share my joys and sorrows. I shall never cease to be thankful that I became a member of the Townswomen's Guild.'

The present editor of *The Townswoman*. Mrs Gwenllian Parrish, arrived in Blackheath, South-East London, soon after the war with her architect husband. She had worked on various provincial newspapers and found life in the suburbs, even such a 'villagey' suburb as Blackheath, very limiting. She badly wanted company, like-minded company, people she could talk to about subjects of the day, something they could get their teeth into. Her mother had been a committee member of a pre-war Guild in Sussex, a sick visitor, and a firm admirer of Mrs Corbett Ashby. She bubbled with enthusiasm for the Guild. Gwen, being a journalist, was accustomed to using her own initiative. She telephoned the NUTG office; a voice at the other end told her her name would be 'put on a waiting list', and she would be notified if and when a Guild was formed in her area. There was a long queue of people waiting more or less patiently for a staff organizer to come and get things going.

Gwen Parrish was incredulous. Didn't they understand she was
offering to do all the preliminary work? She dialled again. This
time she was put through to Miss Bilbie, the assistant general secretary. Could it possibly be the Miss Bilbie who was the headmistress's secretary at her old school, where she was head girl? It was,
and Miss Bilbie gave this enterprising young woman the go-ahead,
and with Mrs Aldwyth Searles, wife of another architect, she
started Blackheath Evening TG . . . actually the first public meeting was held the day after Mrs Parrish had come home from hospital with her first baby. Also there was Mrs Marjorie Rice, des-
tined to become an outstanding national chairman of the NUTG,
who at the next meeting was appointed Guild secretary.

Naturally, it was a very enterprising Guild, creating its own
identity, its own special activities—like the monthly Mothercraft
Club and Friday morning play group for members' children.
For years this Guild had a big waiting list and 'mothered' half
a dozen or so other Guilds in the area. It was very independent in
spirit, not deeply interested in the TG as a national movement.
But this is, indeed, the pattern of the NUTG as a whole. There
are no 'branches', only Guilds, and all officials have always been
careful to write the word with a capital *G*, perhaps to symbolize
their basic independence of the National Union.

A delightful memory of one of the 1929 vintage of Guilds,
Richings Park, Buckinghamshire, comes from Mrs Joyce Preddle
of the Mid-Hants and Wilts Federation: 'My mother, a former
active WI member, was Richings Park treasurer for many years
and took on the same job when they moved to Horsham, Sussex,
after the war. She used to attend early Council meetings as her
Guild's delegate and in my old diaries, which I have kept since
1927, I have turned up several references, "Mummy going to
London for the Guild", or "Mummy had a Guild meeting this
afternoon". These committee meetings, often held in our home,
were always welcomed by my sister and myself as there were
usually rather special cakes and sandwiches that needed "clearing
up". No committee meetings in those days were complete without
afternoon tea and I'm sure that members were as much regarded
for their excellence as cooks as for their musical or organizing
abilities.'

Probably this still is so in some small towns where afternoon

Guilds still attract a faithful attendance of older members, but 'afternoon tea' with cakes, scones, and tiny sandwiches is a treat that very few young wives find time to prepare now, and the 'refreshment interval' at many Guilds, especially evening ones, is more likely to be a single cup of tea or coffee and a plate of biscuits handed round. Perhaps this is why all 'sales tables', as at 'bring and buys', coffee mornings, and the like, are very quickly cleared of all homemade cakes and jams—they must remind many of the buyers of the lost treats of their young days.

Mrs Preddle has one very special memory of her mother's Guild enthusiasm. 'I was told to hurry home from school and come straight round to the hall, as my mother wanted me to meet "a very interesting lady". I think I must have been about fifteen, and was becoming very interested in international affairs and the old League of Nations. The lady with whom I shook hands was the then Mrs Corbett Ashby.' Mrs Preddle recalled this incident when she talked with Dame Marjorie at the National Council meeting in 1974. Dame Marjorie came over and spoke to her after Mrs Preddle's motion on aid to the developing countries was defeated.

A leading North Manchester member, Miss Goodyear, was recruited actually during the war in very different circumstances from the isolated young suburban mother or the keen Guild member's daughter. She took a job at Birtley, Co. Durham, as a Labour Officer employed by the Ministry of Supply at the Royal Ordnance Factory. She was fixed up in lodgings—for the first time in her life—in a bungalow on the Great North Road and had hardly settled in when her landlady persuaded her to go with her to the Townswomen's Guild. Miss Goodyear wrote regularly to her parents in Failsworth, Manchester, and her carefully preserved letters give an intimate insight into the running of a north country Guild and the lives of the women who formed its membership. On that first night a local postman told his life story. He came of a seafaring family and even his mother and sisters had been in the Senior Service as nursing sisters. He himself had been a diver and served in submarines.

Miss Goodyear returned to a temporary night's lodging, as her 'landlord' was ill at the time, and her temporary hostess kept her up to midnight drinking tea and eating Christmas cake while she told of her husband's meticulous preparations for his death. He wrote his own obituary notice for the local newspapers, bought his wife her mourning outfit, made an inventory for probate and after giving her strict instructions about the arrangement and decoration of his room after his death even told her how to lay him out, and when he was at the point of death assumed the posture he wished to maintain when life was extinct.

Not exactly a cheerful start for a quite young woman working away from home for the first time in a taxing and responsible job, but she became happily involved with the Townswomen's Guild through her landlady and enjoyed not only the meetings but the 'backchat' about the committee's doings. She wrote to her parents: 'At present nominations are going. Voting will take place at the November meeting and December will see the new committee in office. Up the bank, at the back of Braeside, lives a Mrs Evans, a Methodist, full of beans and capable of getting on with something, president of this, that and the other. Also, on and off, for twenty years a bosom friend of my landlady. Well, Mrs Evans has done the awful thing of not making up her mind about standing for the committee and what is being said about her is nobody's business.

'If Mrs Evans still lets her name go forward and eventually sits on the committee and my landlady doesn't, by being adamant and refusing to stand, although she knows where everything is wrong, I can see that skin and hair might be flying around. As it is, the committee of management seems to consist of several women who are married to colliery managers and the treasurer's husband seems to be an area manager or something of the kind, which makes her very exalted. It is as good as a show and I thoroughly appreciate all the cross action.'

Miss Goodyear was young and lighthearted when she wrote those letters home. Later she commented, 'I realize now how I had been tossed about in the affairs of these very energetic ladies who really were very full of good works. My advent into their territory caused a rearrangement of routine for them. I was also an object of interest because my type of work was new to them. I was of the opinion that they were all overworked as a result of the war and were getting tired of one another. Anyway, my arrival provided a kind of safety valve.' Her experience at Birtley laid the foundation of a lifelong interest in the Townswomen's Guild movement and also for a profound interest in social studies. When she returned to North Manchester because of her parents' ill health it was not long before she was involved in forming a new Guild at Failsworth.

An account by another original member, Mrs Smith, is preserved in the Failsworth Guild's records: 'A Failsworth lady had visited a Townswomen's Guild and mentioned that there was not one in Failsworth. Miss Tothill, an organizer, asked me whether I would help her to form a Guild. We had a long talk and I promised to help. I made a list of ladies whom I thought might be interested, and Miss Tothill sent out invitations to these people, to the Churches, etc, to a preliminary meeting to be held at the library. Only four ladies attended and they were all WVS members. I was away on holiday. These four ladies decided a public meeting would be worth calling. We distributed a lot of handbills and had some display bills printed. This meeting was in the Co-operative Hall. Several ladies came from Manchester to assist and when a vote was taken there were more than enough prospective members.'

Mrs Smith skated very lightly over the problems of getting a new Guild going, so it is worth quoting from an excellent account by Mrs Ruth Cockerton, published in *The Townswoman*, of starting a Guild in a London borough. 'It was a notice in a local paper that caught my eye,' she wrote, 'announcing a meeting to be held in the Town Hall to consider the formation of a Townswomen's Guild. As I walked up the steps, two or three young women were just in front of me; "and probably nobody under ninety", a laughing young voice floated back at me. I know; I've said that in my time, too.

'The hall was fairly full with women of all types, shapes and sizes; only a few perhaps in their first youth, but certainly all very much under ninety. The first speaker was a young woman organizer sent by the NUTG. She explained in an admirably lucid manner what a Guild was, what it did or could do and what it cost to belong, and how our Guild, if it was formed, would be linked to others, and so into a National Union. She answered our questions clearly and precisely and it was then proposed formally that a Guild be formed.

'We voted on whether it should be an afternoon or an evening

Guild and decided on the latter. Small envelopes were handed round on which we wrote our names and addresses and into which we were invited to put our subscription—four shillings [in 1952]. While these were being collected and counted the time and place of our first meeting as a Guild were announced—the organizer in anticipation of this happy outcome of our work had already reserved a hall for an evening two or three weeks ahead. The meeting broke up at 9.20 pm and I realized with admiration how much business the organizer had got through without any appearance of haste in less that an hour and a half.

'When we gathered for our first meeting, with the organizer in the chair, somebody had been at work beforehand, for as we came in we were presented with a slip of paper with our name printed on it and a pin and asked to pin it on. So even if we were strangers we knew one another's names. A brief report in a local paper had brought in some new members and there were about fifty of us all told. Our first business was to elect a committee. I wondered how it could be done for we were nearly all unknown to one another. But the organizer had a simple solution for all our difficulties. She invited us to propose our friends, if we had any there and thought them suitable, but she also invited any who were interested in being on the committee to offer themselves for election.

'I turned to the woman next to me and asked if I might propose her. She declined, but she kindly took the hint and in a few minutes I found myself lined up with twelve to sixteen other women, facing the rest of the room. We were each given a large number (I was Number 3) which we displayed to our electors. Voting papers were distributed and voters were asked to choose (by numbers) from those who had boldly come forward. Few of us, perhaps, would be chosen on our looks alone and I rather wished I had worn another hat! A little later I was very pleased to hear that I had been elected, not at the top of the poll but not at the bottom either.

'The next event was our first committee meeting, held at a member's flat. Our organizer was with us still, to guide us with great tact through the still more difficult operation of selecting officers from among ourselves: there were ten women, all unknown to one another—though I was beginning to know one or two of them by sight. It was not an easy thing to do and one could only use one's intuition. It was only because I liked the look of her that when the secretary's post came up I whispered to the woman next to me that I would propose "the lady in grey" if she would second it—and we have never regretted our sponsorship. One took over the Sales Table, another became registrar and so on, and I became treasurer. Our Guild was beginning to take shape. The organizer put us through the hoops of two more meetings and then she bade us farewell, to the echo of our grateful thanks, and as the door closed behind her we looked at her rather solemnly like children left to run the house while mother is away. Now it was up to us.'

Just the same kind of sturdy independent atmosphere which was described by Mrs Parrish at Blackheath is related by Mrs Cockerton: '. . . laid on such good foundations our Guild is beginning to show promise of being a building of which we can be proud. Our membership has nearly doubled; music, arts and crafts, social studies and play-reading groups are soundly, if modestly, established and the treasurer's brow is less furrowed when she broods over the bank balance. We are beginning, too, to make our small impact on the borough and this I regard as very important. We were asked recently to nominate representatives to sit on the local hospital board; to give some help to coloured students in the neighbourhood; and three of us in our best hats and clean gloves attended the Mayor's garden party as Guild representatives.'

Mrs Cockerton speculates, with more insight than any outsider could have, on why women join a Guild. 'We are all busy people,' she wrote, 'with jobs or homes or families or all three. What led us to seek yet more dates in our engagement books? Some, I imagine, wanted something new to think about; some were lonely and hoped to find friends here; some enjoy "running things"; some were attracted by the service that a TG can offer to the community; some wanted to pursue some study or some new craft. And some, having no voice at all, wanted to sing in the Guild choir. The Guild is not a passive entertainment. There are plenty of those elsewhere, and those who sit passively waiting to be amused or to have their boredom relieved may not be satisfied. But, as with so much else in life, the more one puts into the Guild the more one gets out of it.

Alice Franklin and Gertrude Horton who, as honorary secretary and national secretary, were largely responsible for devising the structure of the National Union of Townswomen's Guilds.

Mrs Corbett Ashby (right) at a luncheon given in 1933 to promote the Guilds. It was in the same year that the first issue of *The Townswoman* appeared.

Lady Cynthia Colville, a lady-in-waiting to Queen Mary, was the Guilds' honorary president and a great fund-raiser in its early years.

Mary, Duchess of Roxburghe, president, 1962–72.

Mrs Marjorie Erskine-Wyse, national secretary (1965–76), at the NCM in May 1974.

Dame Margery Corbett Ashby even at 91 could not forego a cause:
here she is campaigning for an anti-discrimination law.

'I have been interested too,' added Mrs Cockerton, 'to consider the effect of the Guild on ourselves, even in this short time. Like most people living in a flat in London, I do not know my neighbours and they do not know me; if I depended on them as friends I should be lonely indeed. But already through the Guild I have made many pleasant acquaintances and more than one good friend. When I was ill for a few weeks I received much kindness from them and I had quite a reception at the Guild meeting when I was well again. The foremost aim of the TG is not the fostering of friends and friendship but it is an important by-product, for these hurrying days hide much loneliness.'

At that time Mrs Cockerton probably little knew how wide the problem of loneliness was—and still is—in the big cities, nor what a notable contribution the Townswomen's Guilds have made, partly just by being there, and partly by organized efforts to bring in people who lack friends. 'We are rather simple people,' concluded Mrs Cockerton. 'Ours is not a sophisticated enterprise or a gathering of high hats or highbrows, but as we gather strength I can see us becoming of real value to the community. I have found a widening of my own interests. I am glad I am a Townswoman.'

A Dawlish member who had been a nurse echoed Mrs Cockerton's view of the importance of the friendship offered. 'From hospital training days I never liked women *en masse*. The Dawlish TG has completely revolutionized that idea for me. Apart from the intellectual activities that I enjoy so much, the thing that impressed me most and still does was the warm friendship of all the members. In all the odd places of the world in which I have found myself I have never met such welcoming kindness. To an essentially lonely person these contacts mean a great deal.' This member had arrived in Dawlish knowing no one at all—this was no new experience for her; she had arrived in many towns and villages knowing no one and left knowing only two or three. But through being recruited to the Townswomen's Guild it was so different in Dawlish that after only a year when she walked down the main street with a little girl they were greeted so often that the child said 'Don't you know a lot of people.'

Some little verses, printed in a 1959 *Townswoman*, sum up this very important aspect of the function of women's organizations:

A spinster, a wife and a widow
All lived in a street in our town.
The spinster was shy
The wife she was young
And the widow was lonely and 'down'.
And none of these three knew the others;
Their days were imperfectly filled—
Till somebody had an idea
And started a Townswomen's Guild.

The spinster, the wife and the widow
All went to the meeting and soon
What a different life they were leading.
To each one the Guild proved a boon.

The first went to classes in drama
And even took part in a play.
The second got help with her cooking—
Ideas galore came her way.
The third found good friends all around her
To help her along in her pain
And all three were busy and useful
And life was worth living again.

There's so much we women can tackle
And so much to learn and to give;
Whether spinster or housewife or widow,
The TG can help us to LIVE.

It would be a great mistake to think that this kind of unsophisti-
cated view of the loneliness of the woman at home, the spinster or
the widow is either old-fashioned or confined to older women.
It was exactly this sort of isolation from like-minded people which
led to the formation of the National Housewives Register in
1961 . . . but when it started, through a letter to the women's
page of the *Guardian* from Mrs Maureen Nicol, the group called
itself 'Liberal-Minded Housebound Housewives'. The likenesses
and differences shown by the older, larger organization and the
newer, younger, smaller group are fascinating. The NUTG was

organized thoroughly from its inception and the younger one grew almost haphazardly, but the need and the response to the need by able and energetic women was just the same. In sixteen years the NUTG set up 640 Guilds, which would mean a membership of at least 60,000. In its first fifteen years the National Housewives Register set up a similar number of groups, but membership was limited to the number that could fit into a member's sitting-room and the nationwide total was around 20,000. The NUTG had from the beginning a headquarters office and a staff. It had that initial £100 given by Eleanor Rathbone and it had public-spirited ladies like Lady Cynthia Colville and Lady Denman to appeal for funds. Its first Ministry of Education grant came in 1945 and this support has been continued ever since.

The National Housewives Register has never had a paid staff, it has never had an office other than a member's home, and it has never had a grant from any public or private body. That it could develop, in conditions like these and entirely by the efforts of enthusiastic housebound young mothers right across the country, is a pretty remarkable tribute to the organizing skill of the very women who used to be satellites of their husbands. Gertrude Horton, Alice Franklin, and the chairman of the Townswomen's Guilds before, during, and after the war years, Joan Loring, would have thought it impossible for such a development to take place without a tight constitutional framework and trained organizers . . . but we move forward on the backs of our predecessors. What was not possible for the newly enfranchised women citizens of the thirties was by no means impossible for the well-educated young Housewives of the sixties and seventies. Most of the early members of Townswomen's Guilds must have left school at fourteen, and some were doubtless anxious to keep up with their children who, from 1948 on, had the chance of a much more extended education. The post-war 'Housewives' were, almost all, able to communicate by telephone and many had the use of a car. Many had husbands much more willing than an earlier generation to share fully in the care of the children and the home.

Because these young women had had business and professional experience before marriage and had trained minds, they did not feel the need of guidance from professional organizers. They found no difficulty in making up their own programmes and they saw

no reason for rigid rules to elect officers and committees. No
doubt someone would volunteer to collect the subs and send the
agreed 75p a head to the national organizer and someone would
volunteer to look after the season's programme and the meeting
places—always in members' homes. There has never been a
written constitution for the NHR and only one 'object' has been
agreed, and two basic rules:

> 'The aim of the National Housewives Register is to encourage
> the formation of and to keep a register of groups which aim to
> encourage participation in stimulating and wide-ranging discus-
> sion, thus creating an opportunity for friendship and other
> activities.
>   'Basic rules: 1. The annual subscription (75p per person)
> should be sent at the same time each year. Local organizers
> should be aware of their responsibility for this. 2. Organ-
> izers should write at least once a year to the National Organizer
> and should keep her informed of changes of local organizers.'

For a number of years one National Organizer, who usually
served for three years or so, coped on her own, keeping the
Register and putting enquirers in touch with local groups, even
producing the newsletter which is the essential link between the
groups. Gradually the work was divided and small honoraria
began to be paid. In 1976 there was a 'National Group' of fifteen,
to co-ordinate activities. The National Organizer lived in Gwent,
the Treasurer and Bookkeeper in Sale, Cheshire, the Archivist
in Angus, the Editor of the quarterly newsletter in Hertfordshire,
the Group Co-ordinator in Worcestershire, the Public Relations
Officer in Buckinghamshire, and other members in Devon,
Hampshire, Harrogate, Renfrewshire, Kent, and Cumbria. All,
of course, were working from their homes and caring for husband
and children, and getting absolutely minimum expenses. Of the
1975–76 group subscription no less than £4,392 was spent on
printing and posting the newsletter to each of the 600 or so groups
and only £1,878 on honoraria, travelling expenses, and clerical
assistance.

But though bigger may be better, growth always means qualita-
tive as well as quantitative change. A group sets itself up and
takes a collection for room rent or stamps at each meeting. As

soon as there is more money in hand than is immediately needed someone has to be found to take care of the surplus and account to the other members of the group for it. Call her what you will, 'collector', 'financial co-ordinator' or 'old money bags', every group very soon has to choose a treasurer, and unless she is to be driven witless by keeping other people's money in her own home, or own bank account, she will have to open a group bank account and the bank will insist on proper 'officials' empowered to sign cheques. And so it goes on—an informal group may decide it is absurd to have anything so official as a chairman, but without someone filling that role, members of the group will talk across one another and no one will hear properly what is being said . . . and the member with the loudest voice or strongest personality will deprive other people of their right to talk. Then if one group wants to communicate with another group, or indeed, with anyone on behalf of the members, there has to be a letter-writer, and she is what is usually called a secretary. And so it goes on.

The Housewives Register groups, unlike the Townswomen's Guilds, developed in just such an informal way, but in the Autumn 1976 Newsletter, Jean Stirk, one of the co-ordinating group was writing: 'Like Topsy, the NHR "just growed"—from the original letter in the *Guardian* to the 20,000 members of today; from one person keeping a register of names and addresses and only now, fifteen years later, to become a constitutioned club run by a team of members.'

The story Jean Stirk tells is in miniature almost exactly the story of the early days of the new Townswomen's Guilds: 'Prospective members asked for help in setting up new groups and needed ideas and publicity material; members asked how to deal with a large group or run a conference. Groups wanted contact with other groups all over the country, so a newsletter was planned and the National Organizers began to visit other parts of the country.' But it was fifteen years before the NHR members faced the necessity of drafting a written constitution, something the TGs had had almost from the word go. 'The sheer size of the National Organizer's job has brought its problems,' wrote Jean Stirk. 'There is no way, by insurance or law, that an unconstitutioned club can limit the liability of its "officers", there are no holidays or sick leave for volunteers without deputies, so at these times the

usual post of 50 or 60 letters a week mounts up unanswered. A
mention in the Press brings the post to between 80 and 100 letters
a week.'

All the organizational problems were discussed at a business
meeting at Crewe in July 1975 and agreement was reached.
The 'constitutioned' NHR was being born. 'To limit the financial
liability of the National Organizer and put the NHR on a more
professional basis we have had to have a constitution and the law
requires certain minimum basics to be included, such as the appointment of trustees, an elected team of officers, an Annual General
Meeting. To ensure that decisions can be made promptly and
effectively, a team of members will help with NHR affairs.'

The Housewives Register illuminates another aspect of the work
of the Townswomen's Guilds—the conflict between the desire
to remain non-aligned or, as the NUTG would say, 'to safeguard
the common meeting ground' and the desire to take action. The
'common meeting ground' which excludes no one and is all
embracing, is still meaningful to today's young 'joiners', but the
desire to influence opinions and events, to act as a pressure group,
in fact, is important to many younger women and is certainly not
alien to the thinking of older women in the NUTG. As an instance
of the conflict of views in the NHR, one may quote a letter in the
Autumn 1976 Newsletter from a Midlands member strongly
deploring what she regarded as a 'biased appraisal of the Dock
Work Regulation Bill' in the previous Newsletter, and a letter
from a Chorleywood member urging support for Chiswick
Women's Aid. The Midlands member wrote, 'One of the delights
of NHR has always been the proliferation of ideas and political
views, and I thought it was understood that if NHR members
felt strongly about an issue they should go elsewhere to put
their point of view.' An Uxbridge reader went further and charac-
terizing the reference to the Dock Work Labour Bill as 'political
propaganda' gave notice that she intended to propose an amendment to the Constitution at the next general meeting which would
'prevent NHR from holding political views or engaging in political
views or propaganda' . . . a stance which reflects exactly the division
of the Guilds from the Equal Citizenship branches when the
Townswomen went off on their own in 1928.

Questions of this kind would almost certainly have brought

some very firm 'guidance' to Townswomen's Guilds from their
first 'Nannies', Alice Franklin and Gertrude Horton . . . and they
not only replied to queries from Guilds painfully anxious to do
what was right and to maintain the 'common meeting ground'
at all costs, but combed the cuttings from local newspapers reporting on local Guild activities and had no hesitation in rushing in
where 1970s 'angels' would have hesitated to tread. Here is the
inter-office memo about the reply to the secretary of the Barnet
Townswomen's Guild who had telephoned to ask whether the
Guild would be in order in being represented at a memorial
service for the rector of Barnet who was very much a public man:
'I explained that this would not really be in order and the secretary
seemed to expect and to agree with that view. As she said, it
could open up the possibilities of attendance at memorial services
for the ministers of all the different kinds of churches.'

The Penrith Guild got an unsolicited rebuke after the secretaries
had read in the *Cumberland and Westmorland Herald* that the
Penrith Guild's choir had sung to a congregation of the Bampton
Methodist Chapel. 'Apparently this was part of a day of celebrations for the new year. I would be glad if you could let me know
whether this Press report is correct, and if so, how it was that the
Guild choir came to give their support to a church body in this way.'

Herne Bay Guild was told that it would not be in order for them
to make a donation to the Friends of Canterbury Cathedral
Appeal, even though this was raised specially, and was not a
donation from Guild funds. 'The point is that as Guilds provide
a common meeting ground for women of all religious denomina-
tions, some members or potential members might be unwilling
to be associated with a Church of England Cathedral.'

Stockton Guild was taken to task for knitting garments for the
local Mission to Seamen, and another Guild for allowing its
choir to sing at a function organized by the British Total Abstinence
Union. 'The position is that a Guild cannot be associated with
any work that is connected with a propagandist organization.
The definition of "propaganda" in the Handbook is "Any form of
endeavour to secure support for one side in a controversial matter".
Total abstinence is definitely something on which Guild members
are very sharply divided.' (Gertrude Horton, the writer of this
letter, quotes being one day at a meeting at a well-known hotel

where a sharp protest was made against meeting on licensed premises, and only the next day being at a Federation meeting where she was invited on arrival to 'come and have a gin and It!')

How narrowly the early NUTG leadership defined 'political aims' can be seen from a fascinating letter from Alice Franklin to Counc. Mrs Farnfield of Hastings, in December 1946. Miss Franklin had read a report in the *Evening Argus* that the Hastings Guild was 'flabbergasted' at the advice the National Union had given them on the subject of affiliation to the National Council of Women. 'I think,' wrote Miss Franklin, 'that we can all agree that the National Council of Women are not in any way party political, but if the Guild studies these extracts from the objects and methods of the NCW I think they must agree that they are political propagandist:

'The NCW objects include: "To work for the removal of all disabilities of women, whether legal, economic or social.

'"Its methods include submitting to the Government and to Parliament recommendations for the amendment of the law and its administration."'

It is easy now to smile at the puritanism which persuaded Alice Franklin that it was compromising the 'common ground' for a Guild to sing at a Methodist Chapel, subscribe to the Canterbury Appeal Fund or knit garments for a Mission to Seamen, but her exposition of the case against affiliating to the National Council of Women is remarkably convincing —even if a little disconcerting, in view of the NUTG's descent, always proudly proclaimed, from the National Union of Women's Suffrage Societies. 'The TG movement has as one of its main objects the keeping of a common meeting ground. That means that care must be taken to keep every Guild and the whole movement such that every woman will want to join a Guild, whatever she believes or does not believe.

'We have a very large number of members in the Guilds who are not feminists and could not subscribe to the objects and methods quoted above. Many a discussion group and debate in the Guild ends with the view that married women should not be employed and that there should not be equal pay for equal work etc. I am making this point, as if the movement were labelled as feminist or propagandist in any direction then a large number of our present members would never have joined the movement.

'I think it is significant that in 1929, when the first Guilds were
formed, there were 80 branches of the NCW. We have now 771
Guilds and the president of NCW recently gave the number of its
branches as 90. This I think proves that by our not being labelled
we are fulfilling a need and attracting women who have not been
attracted by the aims and methods of the NCW.' Perhaps it was
because Miss Franklin was a dyed-in-the-wool feminist herself
and from a strongly feminist family background, that she was so
strongly aware of the hostility which feminist ideals provoked in
many 'homebody' Guildswomen and was especially on her guard
against the temptation to push the Guilds further than they were
ready to go. Even today the NUTG is not affiliated to the National
Council of Women though the NCW umbrella covers at least a
hundred organizations, ranging through all the political parties
and almost every religious denomination—and both the Abortion
Law Reform Association and the Society for the Protection of the
Unborn Child.

Even more surprising than the 'thumbs down' to any taint of
civil rights was the stern face the National Union showed to
Lady Sibley, at Reading University, on 'corporate support for the
United Nations Association', especially in view of the strong
international interests of the founders, such as Dame Margery
Corbett Ashby.

'Corporate members,' said the Head Office letter, 'have to
promise to secure that every member of the group shall become
individual members of the Association. That means that people
joining a TG would be under pressure to join UNA as individuals,
and of course we always make it clear that the Townswomen's
Guild is open to any woman whatever her views may be on politics
or any other subjects.' (However, by 1947 the National Executive
had relaxed sufficiently to notify Federations that Guilds could
now become corporate members of UNA if they wished.)

In emphasizing the simple satisfactions of friendship and
sociability that early Townswomen gained from the membership
of their Guilds, this chapter has underplayed the richness of the
range of subjects offered to members—a lack which will be repaired
in later chapters. One is reminded of an incident which caused a
good deal of feeling in the National Executive in 1962, when the
late Ruth Adam, a well-known, careful and much respected

journalist, writing about women's organizations in the *Sunday Times Colour Supplement* wrote of Townswomen's Guilds in a way that was thought to be very disparaging and unfair. Mrs Adams wrote, 'The typical member is perhaps a small town wife, whose husband is getting ahead and who does not mean to be left behind. Born after the suffrage bitterness was over, it is a mild-mannered organization, given to non-controversial campaigns (better fire precautions and car safety belts) and to culture.'

There does not seem to be anything positively denigratory in that paragraph and the next sentence contains an important truth: 'The NUTG is also typical of the clear-headed kindness thrown up by women's sociable organizations which is less often remembered by the critics than their run of the mill quarrels.'

But it seems as if most women's organizations are touchy about their public image, and the NUTG has proved itself notably so. The then National Secretary, Mrs Lillias Norman, complained on behalf of her executive to the editor of *The Sunday Times* that Mrs Adams had written 'a garbled and misleading account both of our aims and of our activities'.

Mrs Norman's letter for publication in *The Sunday Times* was not published, for lack of space, but it *was* printed in *The Townswoman* and it was such a good exposition of the rationale of the NUTG that it is worth quoting:

'Women are forced by social conditions to spend a large part of their time alone or with young children, at a period of their lives when their minds are most active. The various women's organizations have taken shape to fill this lack in their lives and they are as varied in character as the women who join them. The NUTG has indeed a purpose and all the better for that. It aims to give women a chance to develop their talents, it teaches them procedure, how to handle public money. As a result many go beyond the confines of their Guild to serve the community in local government, to conduct their own business—and even to give some of their leisure to the WVS. The Guilds do demand some discipline but they bring a corresponding satisfaction and however far a woman goes in her chosen work she nearly always holds on with affection and gratitude to membership of her TG.'

Mrs Norman went on to indicate how women who once would have spent all their time more or less contentedly within the four

walls of their home not only had their lives enriched by taking part
in choirs and drama, social studies, and arts and crafts, but learned
how to cope with the logistics of moving hundreds of women across
their counties, even from the far north, south, and west to London,
to take part in schools, festivals, and conferences. Perhaps what
so upset the NUTG executive about Ruth Adams' article was the
introductory sentence (probably not written by her at all, but by
some male sub-editor), 'Men constantly claim that women hate
organizing and being organized. Many women say the same.'
How very odd, if this were true, that something like three million
women in this country are members of all-women organizations.
The pleasure they get from working together, the kindness and
concern they feel for fellow-members shine out from the NUTG
records. So does the fun they share. Here are a few instances of the
heart-warming kindness which women show to one another.

'We had a lady almoner to speak at our Guild. At the end of the
summer our secretary had a letter from her telling us that one of her
patients, a very sick woman, was returning home to our area and
needed help. The patient was not known to any of our members but
the two who lived nearest offered to go and see what was required.
As a result another member [went] regularly to fetch and carry,
prepare lunch if the home help was not there, or just simply to be
with her. This continued until she died.'

'My little daughter recently entered a hospital at Cambridge
for an operation which necessitated her being in a body plaster.
We explained that though visiting was every evening we could
only come on Sundays, and she understood. But my chairman
contacted the chairman of Cambridge TG who at once volunteered to visit and has been several times. Other members of the
Social Studies section have also visited and written to her. It was
a great comfort to me and made a big difference to our daughter.'

In answer to another call for help: 'It was too late to get in
touch with the Guilds near the Royal Northern Hospital before
the weekend so on Sunday morning our secretary just made some
extra cakes, collected some books and flowers and off she went to
find the lonely Townswoman. She had no idea of the ward or the
reason for the stay in hospital but the people at the hospital were
helpful; she was found, and the gifts were handed over. The
secretary arranged for visits for the remainder of her stay.'

Just one more 'sick-visiting' story, from a member confined to bed with a slipped disc whose dependent family were all males: 'Through the goodness of Guild members things have smoothed out amazingly. One has baked, another helped with the washing, another ironed and another done my shopping.'

This chapter opened with the question, 'Was it fun for the rank and file members, as well as for the Top Ladies?' Indeed it was, as this delightful story proves: 'Confronted with five lonely days, an idea came into my mind; I sent out an SOS to my previous TG in Lancashire, a hundred miles away. Almost by return of post came five members for five days. Oh what a time we had! The house shook with laughter and bulged with beds. We toured Nottingham and its most historic interests and the countryside. We had one particularly great day when our Federation chairman invited my guests to coffee and arranged for us to be conducted through the City Hall. Our days were packed full, I had no chance to be lonely, and my visitors now eagerly await my next SOS.'

Mrs Ruth Jewell, later a Public Questions sub-committee chairman, had a similarly happy tale to tell: 'An afternoon in a small motor launch fired five members of the Chiltern and Castle Federation with the idea of hiring a motor cruiser for a week, from Maidenhead, in July. It took us about forty-eight hours to master the art of going through the locks and moorings. We all took turns at the wheel but each kept to her mooring jobs at the locks so that we soon became quite competent at tying up and casting off. We became known as "the five birds in a boat" to lock-keepers etc. Life on board a motor cruiser can be rather a cramped affair but we never had an argument and proved that women can live together amicably if you choose the right women. We all slept extremely well; no one at all under the weather; all had certain jobs to do every day and took it in turns to cook the evening meal.'

Here is a pleasant story about the flexibility of the most northerly Townswomen's Guild, in Orkney, which had arranged to have a talk from a local banker, on Norway. 'Faroes Airways who loaned the speaker a travel film to supplement his own offered to provide a variety of open sandwiches. As the day approached, the wind blew steadily stronger and on the actual day of our meeting a ninety miles per hour gale was whipping round our rooftops. We heard that our sandwiches, flown straight from Stavanger, were hovering above us, unable to land, and were then diverted to the Faroes where they had to remain for forty-eight hours. The sandwiches were put into cold storage and the meeting, delayed for two whole days, turned out to be most enjoyable.'

A Federation official, as good-humoured as she was conscientious, described 'the sorry variety of Guild halls' entertainingly in 1966. 'The corrugated iron, the old army hut, the premises of impoverished churches where mouldering brown and green colour schemes have lasted a whole generation. There are halls so small that we can do nothing but sit in rows; halls so much too large that our members are lost in empty spaces and miserable in winter's cold. How many put up with cracked, discoloured walls, worn paint, draughts from ill-fitting windows, floors of unstained deal worn to a dirty greyness and impossible ever to clean? I know a Guild which meets in a disused chapel. As one member said hopelessly, "What can you do in a pew?"'

'We get, too, many unwanted accompaniments, awkward piles of trestles, shrouded billiard tables, collections of flags and drums and mysterious boxes left by the Scouts, the Cadet Corps or the badminton club. Some halls have limp balloons and paper garlands left from some long-dead party. A delightful room may turn out to be next door to a cinema and we end up shouting against a background of screams, galloping horses and gunshots. Another is on top of a bingo hall whose calls, as well as tobacco smoke, come up through the floor boards.'

Weston-super-Mare had a delightful 'secret friend' scheme: 'At their annual general meeting members write their names and address on a card and the date of their birthday. These are put into a hat and each member draws out one card. The drawer then has the person whose name is on the card as a "secret friend" for a year, sending birthday and Christmas cards and postcards when on holiday, all signed "Your Secret Friend".'

A Townswoman who was recruited because she was a choir singer found when she first arrived that there was 'a roomful of about sixty women, *all smiling*. I vow that is a true statement; wherever one turned one saw faces alight with welcoming smiles and I was given the warmest greetings from I can't tell how many people . . . The wonderfully attractive habit of smiling is, I believe, an infection caught from Madam Chairman, a lady of so pleasantly quiet a personality, until she gathers up a meeting into her hands, when she is still quiet, still pleasant, but very much in command of the situation and always with that lovely smile on her face, which seems instinctively reflected on the faces of Guild members until the whole room appears to shine with a radiance that takes in and welcomes the newcomers. I never saw anything like it. This is Guild life in a small town. Perhaps in large towns members never see one another between meetings, but if there is anything I am not sure about I can pop into the baker's shop in the High Street and ask the smiling Guild secretary about it as she serves me with bread and cakes. The choir conductor does mysterious things in an office two minutes round the corner from my house and is equally available. All very cosy and companionable.'

In case anyone should think this kind of 'cosiness' trivial or superficial, here is a very moving quotation from an account of life in a Northern Ireland Guild in 1972. 'A person peeping into our local meeting place would see quite a large group of women laughing at something which the chairman or speaker has said and would perhaps put us down as being a little inhuman. We know differently. The little woman who makes the best jokes very often goes home and weeps with frustration at the hopelessness of it all. She loses a son every time a bullet cuts down a young soldier.

'There is the member whose husband is blind and who makes us laugh when she describes how she directs him while painting her home—"Left a little, right a little". We laugh because we have no words to applaud their mutual courage.

'At our meetings we hear the dull or loud bang of the bombs and for a fleeting moment we die a little and the chairman is talking to deaf ears. We gather at a handicraft class and truthfully admit that the Arran sweater or the crocheted tea cosy is less important than the need to talk together, but during our chat the sweater is finished and we gain a little courage from shared fears to continue existing amid hatred. We admit that we too can feel the hatred and the fear, but we try to express it only in words ...

'We are not producing sensational miracles of courage and

endurance. We are just using the gifts which women everywhere exhibit during times of trial. We are not brave beyond other women. We may yearn for the normalcy of other Federations, but we appreciate the growth of our understanding, initiative and our own achievements.'

3

The War Years

On that solemn September morning in 1939 when the whole nation listened in to the bleak voice of the Prime Minister, Neville Chamberlain, announcing that we were at war with Germany, our overriding fear was probably of gas attacks—the poison gas that never came. So the natural assumption was that all civilian organizations would be more or less suspended for the duration. No one could have dreamed what a strength to the national morale the voluntary organizations which, like the young National Union of Townswomen's Guilds, were deeply rooted in fellowship, would prove to be. Strange though it may seem, despite some inevitable closures the NUTG was stronger at the end of the war than at the beginning.

But in the first few days of September 1939 it certainly was battle stations at 2 Cromwell Place, South Kensington. In the year of Munich the NU, as the Townswomen's headquarters is still called, had moved from the uncomfortable little bungalow at 4 Smith Street, Westminster. (A large glossy office block stands there now.) The new offices, just across the way from the South Kensington tube station, were in a large and handsome house of five storeys. There was ample room for committee meetings and even 'at-homes' and small 'schools' as well for the staff; one special delight for the staff was that for the first time they had ample room to stock stationery and file documents. There was a basement strong-room, too, and a basement flat for a caretaker.

No one knew then that endurance was the virtue needed above

all others in this war and that the determination to carry on as normally as possible was what would pull us through. In the first issue of *The Townswoman*, compiled as soon as possible after the outbreak of war, the president, Lady Cynthia Colville, wrote, 'The immediate excitement caused by the outbreak of war has subsided.' Nothing about the shock, horror, grief or fear which must be strange to those too young to remember those times. The fact is that there *was* a kind of excitement in the air. The menacing thundercloud that had hung overhead during the year since the Munich crisis had broken and discharged its downpour of hail and sleet. September 1939 was not like August 1914, when the young Wordsworth could have said as with the French Revolution, 'Bliss was it in that dawn to be alive', but there certainly was a sense of being keyed up for great dramatic events. And the first dramatic event was not the expected gas attack over London, but the great exodus of the children and of mothers with their babies and toddlers, from the big cities into the country, their little gas masks dangling from their necks in cardboard boxes.

Within a fortnight the officials—Miss Joan Loring the chairman, Miss Franklin and Mrs Horton—had drafted and despatched a letter to the chairmen, treasurers and secretaries of all the 544 Guilds united in the NUTG, giving guidance on the work which the Guilds could do, and indicating what service the NU hoped to be able to offer. The letter also had to warn that the NUTG's financial situation was grave. The National Union customarily received the bulk of its income in September and October and it was normally at its September meeting that the National Executive authorized the payment of a large number of accounts. 'When the war broke out,' Gertrude Horton recalls, 'we had to find £1,000 to meet our immediate liabilities—and this included the amount owed to Guilds for the fares pool of delegates to the annual national council meeting. On top of this there was £1,735 owed to the friends who lent money to buy the lease of the Cromwell Place house.' No one expected the money to come in just as in times of peace. No one, in fact, expected life to go on in anything like a normal fashion. The National Union could not possibly have guessed that for months people would be talking complainingly about 'the phony war', so the obvious thing seemed to be to cancel the meeting of the TU Joint Council due in October 1939 and the

National Council meeting which was already being planned
for 1940.

The Executive had, of course, previously agreed on emergency
measures to be put into operation in the event of war, and these
included giving all the staff notice. This seems now to have been
an extraordinarily harsh action but it was happening in other
walks of life, too—and some young people, at Cromwell Place
and elsewhere, *wanted* to do national service. The TG staff had
been warned in advance, and no one knew whether there would
be any money coming in to pay their salaries. The organizers in
any event tended to be part-time, working for fees rather than a
proper salary. At the outbreak of war the office staff totalled seventeen and it is typical of the heroic devotion of Alice Franklin that
she immediately offered to keep the organization going single-
handed for the duration. She could not, of course, have carried
the whole organization on her back for long, and in fact, there
was no need for her to try. The Guilds, nationwide, rallied at
once. Some sent money gifts in the first weeks of the war, with the
heartening words 'You must be needing this', and the National
Executive was able not only to pay off all the outstanding accounts
by the beginning of October but to re-engage two members of
the staff and guarantee to keep Mrs Horton employed at least until
the end of the year. (In fact she remained national general secretary
until 1950.) When the December *Townswoman* was compiled,
Mrs Horton was able to report that the Guilds had sent only
£470 less than they had undertaken to contribute during the year.

The NUTG had two built-in assets which helped immensely
to keep the Guilds together and acting in concert during the war.
One was that splendid Handbook published in 1938. From
September 1939 up to the end of the war, 9,000 copies were sold,
and the officials thought that probably its clear advice helped
Guilds most in the early months of the war when some Guilds
were out of touch with the office, and that 'it almost certainly
kept them operating as units of the NUTG instead of degenerating
into just ordinary women's meetings'. The other asset was the
monthly magazine, *The Townswoman*, which not only enabled
the NU to pass on information to every Guild and Federation, but
enabled the Guilds to take heart from what others were doing.
The editors aimed to give news of every Guild's activities once

in three months. The circulation dipped, of course, on the outbreak of war, but had caught up again by the end of it. And indeed it was a bargain: At 9d (4p) for six months it was very good value—a penny per copy and a halfpenny for the stamp!

It may seem surprising that *The Townswoman* does not reflect more of the anxiety over the evacuation of the children with which the civilians' war started. Probably most Townswomen, at the receiving end of this pathetic exodus, were too busy to write much, and we have to remind ourselves that self-censorship was drilled into us day by day. 'Careless talk costs lives' was a very potent slogan. Not until the war was well and truly over did we learn very much of the miseries that afflicted people both in towns and in the countryside. The sort of reaction that *was* reported came from a North Watford member: 'The Guild met on the first Monday in September [the day after the declaration of war], to have their usual monthly meeting—and to learn how to re-cover that dilapidated chair. The speaker turned up, so obviously a little matter of a war breaking out wasn't going to deter her. However, the most important question to decide was "would we be able to continue?" Not knowing exactly what would happen, the Guild decided after a great deal of discussion that the sensible thing would be to carry on. Were we wise? Yes, I think so, because whatever happened, on the first Monday in the month we had a rallying point.'

North Watford was probably fairly typical in being in a 'neutral' area which had no evacuation problems, either of despatching its children or receiving others, so the recollections of this member will strike a chord with women who remember similar problems. 'As time went on more and more of our members were drafted into the Services or to do war work of one kind and another. If we think back, we remember that all women under the age of fifty had to register, and if they had no children of school age or younger they were drafted into work. The older members and those not compelled to work carried on, though at times our membership was down to twenty-four. Turned out of our hall, then the next one and then another taken for military use, we carried on, between running canteens, knitting for the Forces, night-time fire-watching for incendiary bombs, feeding our Home Guard husbands and all the hundred and one jobs that even with a war on required doing, and kept our sanity in what were for so many of us very worrying times.'

For civilians, the war really began in September 1940. London was bombed for fifty-seven consecutive nights and many days, too. Between September 1940 and January 1941, 13,339 people were killed in raids and 17,937 severely injured. There were days when it seemed as if the majority of London's millions spent their nights on the platforms of the Underground railway stations. In fact, a census taken in November 1940 showed that only 4 per cent of London's population was sleeping in the Underground—and probably scarcely any of them were Townswomen for they would mostly be living in the suburbs . . . not safe, but less at risk than the people who lived in the crowded centre. Ninety per cent of those who took shelter settled down in the specially built public shelters and 27 per cent were in domestic shelters, which meant either a cellar or an 'Anderson' in the garden. It was estimated, though, that at one time there were 6,000 people in the Underground at King's Cross. There was nothing illegal in buying a platform ticket for 1½d (½p) and dossing down with your eiderdown, blankets, and pillow wherever you could. It was a pretty horrific experience, for the stench was appalling, though in time the provision of toilets improved. Public shelters were not necessarily better. Sometimes they were worse, for unlike the station platforms they were never swept and people fell asleep on piles of rubbish, in darkness, the head of one against the feet of another.

One of the first reports of a truly alarming air-raid affecting Townswomen came from an East Coast Guild. 'The bowls section has gallantly carried on with just four members until last Friday when we had such a terrible experience that we decided to close until happier times. We were enjoying our usual game in the afternoon when without warning there was a roar of planes and guns started blazing. We had no time to reach shelter and so had to take refuge in the small wooden pavilion, lie flat on the floor and cover ourselves with ground sheets. It was like hell let loose for a few minutes. During a lull we uncovered, to take breath, and I read your letter [from the NUTG office] to the four present. I do not suppose a letter has often been read under such circumstances.'

Life was not exactly easy in Cromwell Place. Arrangements had been made to evacuate the Guild office if necessary, but the small staff centring round Miss Franklin and Mrs Horton stuck it out. Miss Ward-Pearson, who lived in Ross-on-Wye, housed some of the NUTG documents, including an index of Guild secretaries, which was kept up-to-date, and sufficient financial records to enable the work to be reconstructed if necessary. Records of Guilds that had to close were stored in an outhouse in a Dorset village by the chairman's sister. Furniture, typewriters, and supplies were sent there, but work at Cromwell Place was never seriously interrupted. Miss Talbot, the music convenor, was a very welcome visitor when she came to Cromwell Place with cabbages and eggs, and she took some of the records to her home in Hertfordshire. Other documents were put into the care of the Fawcett Society. Mrs Horton, whose schoolmaster husband had been evacuated with his school to the country, moved in with Miss Franklin.

The one member of the staff who experienced war conditions in Cromwell Place and who was still working there in 1977 was Miss Anne Elias, the German refugee who came to the NUTG after release from an internment camp in 1941. 'We had bombs around us,' said Miss Elias, 'and later flying bombs. Mrs Horton kept a look-out and whenever she heard something she whistled, and we all had to go downstairs, four flights of rather steep stairs from the top floor to the ground floor and then down to the strong-room in the basement which was supposed to be the safest place. In the time of the "buzz bombs" we listened for the whistling sound that meant that the bomb was overhead. Then we had to lie flat. The Guild office was lucky. The nearest "incident" was the bombing of the French Institute in Cromwell Road. Some of our windows were shattered, and Miss Franklin went out with a broom and swept up the glass.'

At the time the National Secretary described the Air Raid Precautions slightly differently: 'We are able to minimize the effect of the air-raid warnings by spotting, from the front door step, the spotters on the roof of a Government office at the corner of the road. The two or three of us on the second floor descend to the ground floor, bringing work with us. The general office is on that floor and so continues uninterruptedly. Only if the

spotters disappear do we all go down to the basement corridor
and carry on what we can until the imminence of the raiders is
over. The main effect of the raids is a general slowing up of the
post.' Splendid British understatement of the effect of night after
night, day after day of bombing!

Coventry became synonymous with concentrated bombing and
civilian deaths and maiming. Only one Coventry Townswomen's
Guild, Wyken, reported to *The Townswoman*. This extract is
from its annual report for 1941: 'Two nights after our last annual
meeting our city suffered a most terrible air attack. For some time
after this it seemed as though such things as women's meetings could not continue, so great was the number of mothers
evacuated with their children. However, our Guild has survived.
In spite of our small room with its minimum conveniences and
sometimes no heat at all, we have contrived to come out on top.
Our membership has decreased from 75 to 69. The average attendance at our monthly meeting was 35. Our meetings have been
varied as much as circumstances permit. We had demonstrations
in slipper making, patchwork and cross-stitch, and one of our
members gave a very good dressmaking lesson. A city councillor
spoke on education, the City Architect on "The Future of Coventry";
two members led a debate on Evacuation. The birthday party was
held as usual. Thirty members went by bus to the Federation
meeting at Stratford and took the opportunity to go to the Shakes-
pearian theatre.'

Alas, these brave ladies had to give up other outings because of
'transport difficulties', but they reorganized their choir and it won
second place at festivals in Birmingham and Leamington. A regular
weekly knitting party was held, too, at the chairman's house.

Southampton Central Guild lost both its chairman and the
Federation treasurer by enemy action, and yet was able to report
'The most outstanding thing we have achieved is being able to
carry on all year. The pleasant hours we have spent together have
surely helped us through a very trying year.'

What stayed in the memory of those who lived through the
1914-18 war was the vast, senseless slaughter of a whole generation
of young men. What stays in the memory of those who endured
the 1939-45 war was probably the discomfort and deprivation,
even more than the danger. It was not just sleeping in cellars and

shelters, but always 'going without'. No fresh eggs, except perhaps
one a week for an expectant mother. No fresh oranges or bananas;
coupons for everything, from a bar of chocolate to a pair of shoes.
Of course this made running a 'sociable' voluntary organization
extremely difficult. 'Several societies', we read in *The Townswoman*,
'have asked if they can purchase milk for their meetings. We have
been in touch with the Ministry of Food which regrets that
societies like ours are not eligible for special permits under the
recent milk supply scheme.' Or, again, in 1940, 'If Guilds wish
to run their teas in the normal way they will need to obtain licences
from their local Food Committees, so that they may register as a
"canteen" and obtain supplies of sugar and butter. But they may
prefer to organize refreshments so that each member brings her
own butter and sugar.'

Women were naturally specially concerned with the food supply
—making the best of the skimpy rations and the strange new
foods which were imported from the United States. In 1943
Mrs Stella Houghton was writing for *Townswoman* readers:
'The enemy has failed in his efforts to starve us . . . we have lived
for the last two years on very much the same foods as we have
grown up on, cutting out the luxuries and substituting more of the
simple, protective foods. Now a new phase has been reached and
we are receiving foods which are in more compact if unusual form.
The heavy demands on shipping space mean that we must be
prepared to receive foods that take up less space in storing and
packing . . . . Four of these new foodstuffs are dried milk, national
wheatmeal flour, American bacon and salted cod.' In 1942
whalemeat was introduced but its meat-like appearance and fishy
taste made it unacceptable to almost everyone.

Very many Townswomen's Guilds took to vegetable growing
in a big way, and some of the accounts of their horticulture are
very inspiriting. A West Hartlepool member reported in 1942:
'We have a very large garden at the back of our house. After we
had a talk on gardening by Mr Grey of the Agricultural College
at Durham, my husband and I decided to let the Guild have a
plot for their own use. It had been a hen run. So we asked Mr Grey
to come and examine the land. He said, "You women should revel
in it." He advised us to grow potatoes and greens the first year.
We meet every Tuesday. It was a bit heavy at first. But after a cup

of tea we were quite ready for another go. We ran a few whist drives and bring-and-buys in the winter months to buy the tools. We have set two stones of potatoes and lettuces and onions. Well, our labour has not been in vain. Everything is sprouting through.'

A parks superintendent told Southgate Village TG, 'A garden in times of peace is a haven of rest. In wartime it is a munition factory.' Hounslow TG came to this conclusion in the spring of 1941 and seven members volunteered to 'dig for victory', as it came to be called. Mrs Miller 'who had precious little experience of vegetable growing' was their head gardener. 'Eventually,' the Hounslow women reported, 'we were able to get a piece of ground in our local park—grassland, where the children previously played ball, and mothers rested in the sunshine. Some members of the Guild started to dig it up for us, and as soon as the first piece of ground was ready we planted our first potatoes. But the soil got harder and harder and the grass longer and longer and the time that the Home Guard could spare from their other duties was less and less and there was still an awful lot to dig. We realized that if we wanted to plant anything that year we should have to dig it ourselves.

'By that time the grass was almost knee high and in the sweltering heat with the garden shears we cut the grass down and well and truly dug the rest of the ground. We planted almost as we dug. There were now only four really active helpers. The rest came when they could. We had no money for bean poles so we pinched off our plants (grown in our private garden) at about two feet and with the large quantity of hay we now had, laid this thickly along each row, after watering the plants well in with buckets of water carried from the Rose Garden tap some distance away. This conserved the moisture and kept the beans clean and we picked about 84 lbs. We also planted our first season sprouts, savoys and a sowing of winter onions, turnips and spinach. From the odd turves, old bricks, grass, etc, we have the makings of a fine marrow bed. We dug up nearly 100 lbs of potatoes.'

Despite all that hard labour and selling the produce to TG members every Wednesday afternoon at ruling shop prices, the gallant gardeners did not make a profit in their first season. They felt they started too late in the year for financial success. Nothing daunted they took on a second allotment in the park for their second season. This was already dug and they put it entirely under potatoes. The Townswomen gardeners deserve to be remembered. It was reported that one Guild actually kept twenty-two allotments going.

Not only growing food but collecting valuable herbs became a widespread contribution to the war effort. 'In response to an appeal for herbs a nettle party was arranged by Rosehill and Willington TG. It was a most enjoyable afternoon and 17 lbs of nettles were handed to the drying centre at Newcastle.' 'A collecting centre at Guildford was staffed daily by TG members in the afternoons to receive nettles, foxglove seeds and, later, rose hips and horse chestnuts.' A number of Guilds collected sphagnum moss for hospitals and Dalkeith was actually granted a petrol permit for this purpose. Keswick reported despatching 34 lbs of sphagnum moss, 60 lbs nettles, 7 lbs foxglove leaves and 665 lbs rose hips. Shanklin, Isle of Wight, organized rose hip and horse chestnut gathering rambles. Many thousands of pounds of jam must have been made by TG members. Thurso's jam-making centre was a great success. 'Although we were, maybe, getting tired of the chop chop of stalks of rhubarb the result was gratifying—1005 lbs of rhubarb jam, all of which we were most fortunate in disposing of locally, thus saving the expense of transport.

'On another occasion we staffed a centre to collect surplus fruit in the adult schoolroom, and people brought in their surplus rhubarb which we weighed and paid for at the fixed price. The people brought it in all manner of conveyances, including prams, barrows and horses and carts. But we were proud to help with this fruit, which would otherwise have been wasted. It was sent to the jam factory to go in with our rations.'

Of course the Townswomen knitted. Laurencekirk TG had a gas drill lecture from a member who was an ARP warden and did their knitting while they wore their gas masks for fifteen minutes. Make-do and mend went on everywhere. Corstorphine TG reported 'members are fashioning new costumes from old garments and don't care a hoot who knows it. Just to show what can be done with a little imagination they are going round other Guilds with samples of their work and have staged a mannequin parade.'

And of course, they provided 'comforts'—not only for the men and women on active service abroad. Quite commonly they adopted

balloon barrage sites. One Guild in fact adopted three. 'The first
was in a residential area and had a lot of its requirements satisfied
by its neighbours. All they needed was a very large teapot which a
TG member immediately gave. The other sites require small
things that are really scarce, such as ping-pong balls, darts, a clock,
playing cards, small tables, chairs and bits of old carpet. All centres
are short of these, but we are doing our best for them.'

'Make-do and mend' was almost an obsession during the war.
It gave a comforting illusion of being able to contribute something
of importance to the war effort even if one's life was in the home.
Clothing was, of course, rationed for several years after the war
was over, but it was first seen as an urgent problem during the
evacuation. 'It is more important than ever,' said *The Townswoman*
'that the clothing of children evacuated to the reception areas
should be kept in good repair. Some Guilds have long undertaken
this task for a particular school, or for the children from one area.
Could *your* Guild find out if there is a need for organized mending
for schoolchildren in your neighbourhood?'

The housewives of Britain had to take an awful lot of lecturing
about lessening their demands on our diminished resources.
Hugh Dalton, then President of the Board of Trade, addressed
all the associations represented in the Women's Group on Public
Welfare in trenchant terms: 'If every garment now in the homes
of Britain, every pot and pan, every sheet, every towel, is kept
used and kept usable until not even a magician could make it hold
together any longer, the war will be won more surely and more
quickly. Today when raw materials are brought to these shores
only at the risk of brave men's lives, every woman who throws away
a garment which is not completely worn out is guilty of sabotage;
every woman who spends the family's coupons when she could
make a wearable substitute from something else in the family
wardrobe is helping to lengthen the war. We must do our best
to make the whole nation conscious of the need to Mend and
Make Do.'

Some of the economies people were always urging upon one
another seem pathetically small now. The NUTG Homecraft
Convenor suggested that in order to save soap when washing up,
the crockery should be piled together and first wiped clean with
paper, which should be saved, dried, and used for firelighting.

Did this conflict with the obsessive urge to *save* paper? 'At our committee meeting,' one Guild wrote, 'the question was raised of the membership cards which are now full. It was realized that owing to the paper shortage you may not be able to supply new ones and our vice-chairman suggested pasting paper over the previous signature so that the card can be used for a long time to come.' Head Office could always spare a little time and a little space in *The Townswoman* to suggest to secretaries and other officials how they could be more helpful. In 1942 a Note to Secretaries explained: 'We have to punch a hole in all letters and reports to attach them to files and it is so difficult when the reports and letters are written right up to the top lefthand corner of the paper. Before the war we could get gadgets to fix on to such letters, but it wasted a lot of time fixing them without covering up any of the writing and they are not available now. If a spare 1½ inches could be left in the top lefthand corner of every letter and that space not written on behind, then a great deal of the NUTG's time (and temper!) would be saved.' And then there was the matter of the Lill pins, in 1944. Such a sad little note. 'We have carefully husbanded our stock of tiny pins called Lill pins, and seldom send them out of the office. But from time to time, as with this issue, we have to part with nearly 600 pins to attach the enclosure to the invoice. If each Guild secretary that has been collecting these pins would send them back gradually by pinning all enclosures we could then re-collect our stock. We have bought none since the war and now we need them we cannot find any to buy.' Only two or three years ago a WRVS organizer in Hampshire asking Head Office to supply some string was told sternly, 'Lady Reading [founder of the WRVS] always unpicked the knots and re-used the string.'

All this seems so trivial now, but 'Waste not want not' was fanatically preached right through the war. A Dunfermline town councillor declared that there were only two books worth keeping in any house, the Bible and the bank book. A writer in a popular magazine wrote 'Every woman who destroys a scrap of paper destroys the means of making British weapons as surely as if she helped to blow up a munitions dump. Every woman who keeps a store of paper in her home, old bills, old letters, unread books, finished periodicals, wrapping paper, cardboard boxes, is

automatically forcing a ship to make a perilous journey on the high
seas to fetch that quantity of paper carelessly ignored by her.'

It seems extraordinary now how such hyperbole could be directed at British housewives—not men, of course, for they were
supposed to be 'doing their bit' anyway—and how humbly they
responded. The headquarters staff also asked for 'any papers that
Guilds and Federations felt need not be kept for the purpose of
record, provided the paper was not written on both sides'. This
'waste' paper was used for making carbon copies. Old circular
letters on duplicating paper were especially welcome and the backs
were used for new circulars. But the HQ governesses went further,
in a comment in January 1943: 'We have noticed in the press that
several Guilds have had a demonstration of paper flowers. Now
surely . . . why do they do this in the face of a national campaign
to save every inch of paper, not only to save shipping space but
because paper is wanted for munitions? To complete the picture
it only needs a member of the Guild to arrive hot and bothered
because she was late round her last streets collecting for her town's
paper salvage drive!' (To that gibe the Paisley Guild did answer
back. 'The general opinion here is that in these days of substitutes paper flowers are contributing beauty and colour in hospitals
and homes which would otherwise be dull and bare. Can as much
be said for all the newspapers, books and circulars which are still
being circulated? Why single out the flowers? Won't they all
finish up as salvage?')

But generally speaking the Townswomen seemed positively
grateful for the lectures they received from 2 Cromwell Place on
how to run their affairs. Here is a typical stern admonition:
'Some people regard the war as an excuse for not doing the things
they have disliked in peace-time. Some members wonder if the
Guild should read its Constitution during the next twelve months.
At the present time many Guilds are unable to carry out all the
clauses of the Constitution and when considering a particular
proposal need to know how far it is something that is a main
principle or how far it is a matter of detail that is not so important.
Reminding members of the normal and making clear what are
temporary adjustments seem to us to be important in Guild work,
and indeed, in life generally.

'So we believe that studying the Constitution, probably in

sections during the year, even while we sew and knit, will be a help to the members, to keep them in a GUILD, and not let the Guild lose its special outlook, which distinguishes it from every other organization.'

A month later, Guilds were reminded sharply that 'everything that involves the receipt or expenditure of money, for any activity that is done in the name of the Guild must be handled as laid down in Section XIII of the TG Constitution. These rules affect sewing parties and all other activities. (Read the Constitution while you knit and p. 415 of the Handbook.) We hope that all groups are being run by properly constituted sub-committees, with terms of reference'. Even at this time of strain every nicety had to be observed. 'We notice from reports of Guilds' annual meetings in the press that in some cases the chair is taken by the president. This should not be. Those Guilds whose annual meetings are not chaired by the chairman, please read Paragraph 97 of the Handbook.'

Alice Franklin, who was for a time honorary treasurer as well as honorary secretary, was particularly concerned that Guild finances should be kept in order. She took two pages of the September 1943 *Townswoman* to set out for treasurers their duties and the way to prepare their accounts. 'In some Guilds,' she wrote, 'there still shows on the right of the balance sheet "Cash in Hand", which means that all money was not banked at the close of the financial year in October. The members should query this when it happens, even if it is a small amount. Perhaps all petty cash was not called in and banked on the right day in October; it sometimes means that one of the funds, usually a charity one, is not being managed in the right way, and all the money is not being banked without deduction. It is for the members to watch this point.

'Members may say "We trust our treasurer; we shall hurt her feelings if we scrutinize in this way!" Surely it is for the protection of the treasurer to know that she is working for those who share her responsibility. Writing as a treasurer I can say that there is nothing more deadening or disappointing than the members failing to show their interest or to raise any points on which they want information. It may be that everything is so clear they understand it, but it may equally well be boredom or failure to attempt to accept responsibility in a Guild for its management.

'THE TREASURER'

'There must be no apathy in our experiment in democracy. Women asked to be full citizens, i.e. have the vote, and finance is no longer a thing about which any woman should say "I don't understand about figures."'

Not all Guild members were always so serious and so doctrinaire, it is good to know. A Townswoman now living in Billericay, Essex, remembers how she joined a Guild in Grangetown, Sunderland, when she was only eighteen. Her mother and grandmother were members and she had been attending with them for several years as a visitor. 'In the war years,' says Mrs Arnold, 'women needed a social life, with husbands and boy friends away.' First, though, she was co-opted to read out the Ministry of Food leaflets. 'They were to help the housewife to make a wonderful meal out of very little, such as 1 lb of mashed potatoes, $\frac{1}{2}$ oz grated cheese and one tablespoon of reconstituted egg, baked in a moderate oven for half an hour. This, according to the Ministry of Food leaflet, made a lovely supper to warm you up before going into the shelter.'

Mrs Arnold's mother, a member of the committee, promised to provide refreshments for two tables at a Guild whist drive. 'We decided to have one round of corned beef sandwiches, one sausage roll and one cake. This would have been fine, but we had no meat coupons left and our butcher was rather strict and would not let us have the corned beef. So I stood at the greengrocer's two hours to get two bananas. These were duly mashed and a thin line of strawberry jam spread on the bread made very nice sandwiches and for 1s [5p] a most enjoyable evening was had by all.'

Miss Florence Goodyear wrote from County Durham to her mother in North Manchester about her difficulty with the rations—and this, actually, was in January 1946. 'I got my rations at noon—tea, pilchards, two boxes of matches, custard powder, two tablets of soap and all the other stuff. I called on the butcher and he will save me a chop tomorrow. Also I got some apple jelly. I've not had a spot of jam with Mrs W. She's just scoffed all my sugar and the extra pound. I told the girl about the preserve coupons and she said she'd cash them for sugar.' It is difficult to recall how long coupons were with us. Even in 1953 the Ministry of Food was still appealing for Townswomen and others to help their local officials with the distribution of ration books.

Women are always 'needed' in war-time, for all kinds of duties other than home-making. In 1942, for instance, they were told that at least 6,000 domestic workers were needed in hospitals all over the country, and because of the shortage the Ministry of Health encouraged the recruitment of part-time shift workers through local employment exchanges. Voluntary organizations like the Townswomen's Guilds were asked if they would undertake that their members would do the needed domestic work on certain days and times (e.g. weekends); would help to find girl workers, both paid and voluntary, too young to join the Forces; would provide shift leaders and organize rotas of part-time workers; and would organize transport to bring in the workers (subject, of course, to petrol being available). The Ministry warned that most of the domestic work would probably be heavy cleaning and kitchen work, though some young girls might be recruited for dining-room service and similar lighter work. It promised a 'Hospital Service Badge' for all workers undertaking regular full-time domestic work in hospitals. Was it, in fact, ever minted or issued?

Four Townswomen's Guilds in Heston and Isleworth tried out their own enterprising recruitment scheme. 'Realizing that shops and offices will find a great shortage of female labour under the new call-up of women, Hounslow TG felt that some arrangements could be made to use the part-time labour of Guild members locally. A questionnaire in the Guilds suggested that there was a sufficient number of Guilds to go ahead. The Ministry of Labour offered all co-operation and were willing to treat the Guild as an employment bureau for part-time work. The Guild set up a bureau, staffed by members, who were to arrange rotas and index the categories of jobs and potential workers. The same rate of pay was to be offered whatever the shop. The Guilds found that quite a high proportion of their members had some experience of "commercial work" and were prepared to volunteer to keep the shops going if they found themselves short of staff. Another idea for using the services of volunteers was floated by the Board of Trade—"mending clubs" which were to be based chiefly on factories doing urgent war work. Voluntary societies like the Townswomen's Guilds were to set these up in collaboration with the factory welfare officers. The "menders" were expected to provide a service for the "workers" for nothing, any payment being made to the needlewoman to go to charity. It seems unlikely that this idea really took root, though it was urged upon the willing horses of the NUTG by their leaders, like all other calls for unpaid voluntary work for the "war effort".'

Other kinds of appeal to the Guilds were regarded with a very suspicious eye by the NU officials. Alice Franklin read personally not only all the reports sent to head office by the Guilds, but all the newspaper reports forwarded by the press cuttings agency. In January 1942 she read 500 annual reports and studied their accounts in detail and sent to each Guild a separate criticism of its operations. 'It is a Herculean task,' she confessed. 'I wonder each year if I am mad to attempt it.' But she owned that she found it a fascinating job and assured the Guilds that she found the reports well written. 'Such interesting meetings have been held, so much

HRH The Duchess of Gloucester attending the NCM in May 1974 flanked by members of the National Executive Council.

Among the many sculptures of Dorothy Russell, a Townswoman, was a head of Mrs Jessica Moore, first chairman of the International Committee, and she is here handing it to Mrs Moore.

A national council meeting at the Royal Albert Hall with delegates from England, Scotland, Wales, and Northern Ireland.

Members of a Birmingham TG demonstrating support for the Keep Britain Tidy Group for Royal Jubilee year.

Some of the many activities and presentations mounted by the Guilds: (above) the 'Olde Tyme Musical' float arranged by Swindon Penhill TG for the Carnival; (below) 'Period Bathing Belles' presented by the Nene Valley Federation.

has been achieved on all sides. I do not believe that there is a Guild
that has not a National Savings Group; the garments made must
run into millions; and members are serving in increasing numbers
on war- and peace-time committees of their towns. Whatever is
up and doing seems to be done by Guild members.'

But some calls on Townswomen's time and concern were not
approved by the eagle-eyed officials at Cromwell Place. Seeds
of potential trouble were located and sternly commented upon.
'Many Guilds,' wrote Alice Franklin, at the beginning of 1943,
'have sent delegates to meetings of the Women's Parliaments
that are springing up all over the country. Did they stop and think
before they accepted their invitation? Have they thought whether
it was wise for the dignity of the movement for the Guild's name
to be given to something about which they presumably know little
or nothing? What is the constitution of this "Parliament"; how is it
governed? By whom are the rules made (if any) which are laid
down for its guidance? Is it educational? Is it democratically
controlled?

'Those who did go to these Parliaments will have noticed that a
series of highly contentious resolutions were passed, and at least at
one meeting TG members took part in the discussion, speaking for
their Guilds, and voted without any mandate from the Guilds.
Of course no mandate could have been given, because as an
educational body with the common meeting ground in our objects,
we could not have passed resolutions of that kind. The Press noted
that Guild members were there and that fact will be used by those
who promote other Women's Parliaments to entice other Guild
members to go—and to speak and vote. So we are in danger of
losing our common meeting ground. It is curious how many
moribund societies are now becoming vigorous, often under new
titles, with entirely new, propagandist programmes. We noticed
recently three quite different propagandist stunts appearing to be
from different organizations, but all from the same address and
from the same offices, using the same type of paper (with no letter
head).'

The old, well-tried manipulative techniques were naturally tried
on this young and presumably impressionable organization, but
the watchers at Cromwell Place were always on the alert: 'A Guild
recently consulted us about a request of a new member to get the

Guild to pass a resolution on a highly controversial subject, because the organization to which she belonged wanted it passed but could not do it itself; and so the members were joining Guilds and other organizations to carry out its propaganda. Some Guilds feel flattered at being approached; but if they would stop and think and realize that they may be being used as a pawn and the common meeting ground destroyed, they might not respond so easily.'

The preoccupation with maintaining the Simon Pure image of the NUTG in the midst of hostilities, when life in many of the towns and cities was at its least bearable, seems strange more than thirty years on, but of course normal activities did go on. People continued to look forward to a time when the war would be over and we could build up more than just the fabric of the blitzed cities. The surge of interest in 'social questions' was remarkable. In part it was stimulated by the Women's Group on Public Welfare, a liaison body drawing together all the major women's organizations which was set up in 1939 with the Rt Hon Margaret Bondfield, the first woman Cabinet Minister, as chairman. The National Union of Townswomen's Guilds has been affiliated to the WGPW since the beginning and its officials, both professional and voluntary, have played a great part in its work right to the present day, when it is known under the less cumbersome title of 'Women's Forum'. Without doubt the NUTG representatives were influential in drafting a 'common meeting ground' type of constitution both for the WGPW and for the local women's groups which were set up during the war as Standing Joint Conferences of Women's Organizations. The language is so familiar: 'To provide a common meeting ground for the exchange of information on matters of interest to women's organizations and to the city and the district; to afford facilities for co-operation between women's organizations in fostering specific proposals that may be agreed; to co-operate as may be agreed in schemes when approached by the local offices of the Government or by local authorities.

'It is important to note that specific proposals of national interest on which the societies wish to take action must be referred to the Women's Group on Public Welfare for its consideration, for it is in a position to advise SCOW's on problems, latest developments and the best way in which they can be approached,' said the official *Townswoman* comment. 'What is really needed is a constant reminder of the various clauses of the constitution—and who can do this better than the TG representatives who are in the habit of studying the TG constitution each year and checking up to see that they are keeping to the spirit and letter of their objects?

'TG representatives should always have their SCOW constitution with them, and if the conference strays, raise a point of order and read the clause concerned. If after that a Standing Conference persists in itself taking action, the NUTG should be informed, as it is represented on the sub-committee of the Women's Group on Public Welfare that is responsible for the recognition of the local conferences. We hope it will never be necessary for Guilds to withdraw from the Standing Conferences, and if all act as we suggest, the question will never arise.'

One can hardly believe that the local Townswomen's representatives really followed up this invitation to behave like barrack-room lawyers or teachers' pets, for relations have continued all these years to be close and harmonious. It is tempting to think that this reliance by committees and officials upon rules and forms of procedure is a particularly feminine vice, but it would not be difficult to find trade union delegates of the male sex who can always quote chapter and verse for their actions and who would fight almost to the death to maintain their rule book intact. However that may be, adherence to the rules and constitution certainly did not prevent the NUTG or any of the affiliated organizations from doing some impressive work on WGPW-sponsored war-time projects. Guilds studied diligently, for instance, the report of a committee of the WGPW on 'Our Towns'. This was a close-up of the conditions of life in towns as revealed by the evacuation of mothers and children. This study, Townswomen were bluntly told, 'showed a depth of poverty and personal degradation (in a certain percentage of townspeople only) undreamed of by any except social workers and social investigators'. 'There are two kinds of poverty,' wrote Dorothy Charques, 'one which leaves room and air for courage and endeavour and the other which is founded, perhaps, on physical defects, or which has existed for generations in which effort is all but impossible and hope all but extinguished. It is with the latter kind of poverty and the evils attendant upon it, the juvenile delinquency and want of discipline, the bad habits generally, the ill-health and skin diseases, the bodily dirtiness and almost entire lack of any idea of personal hygiene, with which the authors of "Our Towns" mainly deal.'

Dorothy Charques added, 'It is not the spoiling of someone's best bedroom which is important, but the misery and degradation of a large number of our fellow citizens.' Having had this shock to complacency the TGs were probably the more ready to study the question of family allowances, as they did from 1942 onwards. Not everyone, by any means, was in favour of this new scheme of social welfare, the special concern of one of their principal founders, Miss Eleanor Rathbone. The war-time Civics convenor, Mrs L. Keith Robinson, contributed some fine forthright stuff about social welfare problems to *The Townswoman* and clearly had a lively sense of humour. 'Some Guild members have raised the objection that if every shade of opinion is studied, the unfortunate Guild member will end up by having no views at all, but will be wandering around with a sick headache saying "I'm sure I don't know what to believe. It is all too complicated."'

Mrs Keith Robinson made a gallant effort to sort out the complications. She posed a dozen questions about the effectiveness of family endowment. Would it effectively reduce child poverty? How, to whom, and how often should it be paid?, and so on. At the moment, she added, 'family endowment seems to be a comparatively non-party issue . . . but it would be wise to get the prospective Opposition candidate to give his views and possibly a speaker through the Family Endowment Society'. (She pointed out a fact which in the 1970s has been quite forgotten . . . that some unions were still uncoverted. Opposition from trade unionists who thought that a family allowance would encourage employers to attack wage standards was originally quite fierce.)

Even more important than the family endowment debate, however, was the vast scope for discussion of the Beveridge Report published in 1943. There really could be no clearer indication of the fact that the British people as a whole never seriously considered for a moment that they might *lose* the war, than the publication of this blueprint for the welfare state, long before the tide had really turned in the western allies' favour. Mrs Keith

Robinson enthuses 'Many study or civics groups must be thrilled
at the opportunity to study a report of this kind, which touches on
old and new economic and social problems. We have heard that
Hounslow's reading circle of fifteen members has started to read
the shortened form of the Beveridge Report, has already had the
acting secretary of the TUC to talk and is arranging further talks
from a doctor and a representative of an insurance company.'
Mrs Robinson herself wondered how they had the moral fibre and
determination in the midst of ration book problems and worries
about menfolk in the Forces, for she admitted 'It takes a strong man
or woman to get through Sir William Beveridge's report. . . . The
copy supplied to me by the NUTG is now a wreck. It is dog-eared
from pages turned down for reference, battered from being carted
on trains as I travelled to and from the hospital where I have spent
so much time lately, and crumpled from having been fallen asleep
over. . . . But I have proved my ABC theory of learning to read. The
first fifty pages were Greek to me and I despaired of ever understanding it, and almost tried the summary to see if it were any easier. But I
decided that it made a fine counter irritant to more personal worries
and ploughed on. Suddenly the daylight dawned and the report
began to make sense and in fact became enthralling reading.'

Cynically one wonders now whether it was to take women's
minds off the fact that thousands of their homes had been destroyed
by enemy action, that the General Housing Advisory Committee
of the Ministry of Health launched in 1942 a questionnaire on the
design of dwellings that would be built when the war was over.
There is not a scrap of evidence that the Townswomen were
dubious. They were among a number of organizations questioned
and were regarded as a specially valuable cross-section of urban
housewives, and they joined in with a will. Just one sceptic wrote to
The Townswoman saying that ever since 'the post-war housing
questionnaire was plumped under our noses and we had to supply
the answers in about twenty minutes,' she had had it on her mind.
'It strikes me as the height of folly to ask middle-aged women—
or men—to plan post-war houses. No one over 30 should have a
say in the matter.' This Guildswoman must have been a lively lass,
in spite of writing herself off as middle-aged, for she thought it
high time that the planners should plan for the family plane.
'This is not a dream, but a very real thing for the youth of today

and an accepted fact to them as plane construction returns to civilian uses.'

No fewer than 343 Townswomen's Guilds took the questionnaire very seriously and practically. Did post-war planners and architects take any notice of what the thousands of women questioned in 1942 and 1943 said they wanted? Under the aegis of the Women's Group on Public Welfare there were 35,652 group answers and there was a very striking degree of agreement about their fundamental wants and needs, said the statistician who analysed the completed questionnaires. The women showed a strong desire for privacy, both for the household and for the individual—so open plan housing came in, ensuring that practically all activities of the family should be carried on in full view. They wanted space, enhanced by light and sunshine. Of the English women who answered the questionnaire, 78·55 per cent wanted to be able to purchase a house and 62·32 per cent preferred a house to a flat and 17·64 wanted a bungalow; only 0·98 per cent wanted a flat . . . and high rise flats were what a great many of them got.

How many planning departments faced with the actual problem of rehousing their local citizens after the war ever looked at this report, or the conclusions of the statistician who analysed it? How much follow-up did the TGs themselves do, with their local housing departments and the Ministry of Health? Of course, it is true that the ordinary housewife cannot always foresee what will prove best for her comfort and well-being—77·91 per cent of the women answering this questionnaire voted for an open fire, and 80 per cent wanted a copper. It was before the ordinary family had become acquainted with washing machines, much less gas-fired central heating, but in general the tastes and wishes of the ordinary homemaker have not changed all that much and their tastes and wishes have been given scant consideration by planners, architects, and housing authorities.

In its maturity the NUTG retained and developed further its deep interest in home planning as well as home running. A national conference on 'Your Home', in 1977 addressed by a panel of architectural and building experts included a fascinating description of an 'Eco house'—a house designed to use solar heating. It also launched a project for Guild members to work out on paper how to remodel a kitchen—their own or someone else's—to adapt a house for an elderly or handicapped person, or to extend a house to give more room. This was not intended as a competition but to provide a display for the Golden Jubilee celebrations of 1979.

The war years were not in the least a time of retreat, or even of standing still, for the majority of TGs. Music and drama flourished in an astonishing way, side by side with social studies, and those three dedicated advisers, Mrs Ruth Roper, arts and crafts, Miss Kathleen Merritt, music, and Miss Margaret Leona, drama, toiled up and down the country despite the blackout and despite the hazardous nature of train journeys. Lady Cynthia Colville's rallying call in September 1939 just about summed up the attitude of the Townswomen's Guilds, both nationally and locally: 'I believe it is tremendously important,' she said, 'to keep our cultural flag flying, to devote more, not less, energy to our study of drama and appreciation of art, to our choral singing and to our handicrafts. After the last war we talked of "Homes for Heroes" in terms of bricks and mortar but there are less tangible building materials that are every bit as important in the construction of a home and Townswomen's Guilds can take their part in welding and weaving these.'

4

The Whole Woman

Crafts

The essential difference between the Townswomen's Guilds and Women's Institutes and most other women's organizations is that the TGs and WIs cater for the *whole* woman—the whole range of her pursuits, domestic, cultural and 'social', in every sense of the word. They were formed at a time when almost all women did some kind of 'craft'—mostly needlework, crochet or knitting. Even entirely 'political' women like Margery Corbett Ashby and Alice Franklin were skilled needlewomen. Mrs Gertrude Horton still has in her Epsom home a chair whose seat was beautifully worked by Alice Franklin in *petit point*. Four years after its inception the National Union of Townswomen's Guilds had a craft exhibition at which its president, Mrs Corbett Ashby, was awarded a green star 'for a charmingly worked firescreen'. At that time she was taking part in the Disarmament Conference at Geneva. It is difficult to picture Margaret Thatcher or Shirley Williams finding time to relax in this way.

This craft exhibition was staged at the Imperial Institute, South Kensington, in connection with the annual council meeting. The strongest class was the embroidery, the largest was the knitting and crochet, but much of this was found to be disappointing in its finish. 'Some very good work was rejected because of the knots used,' said an adjudicator. 'It was, unfortunately, necessary to be very severe with the crochet, nearly all of which had the same faults. The design was poor and it was worked too loosely.' Even at this early stage of the TG's development, the concern for high standards was almost fanatical. Enjoyment always took a poor second place behind excellence as a motivating force. No one ever said, 'If a thing is worth doing it is worth doing badly. . . .'

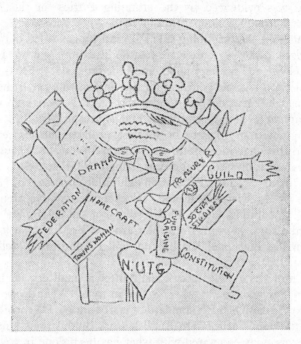

Adviser after adviser, tutor after tutor, hammered away at the need to produce original designs, and indeed the old-style 'transfer' is now really in retreat. This early adjudicator said more in sorrow than in anger, 'In spite of constant experience to the contrary I shall continue to hope that designs for pictures and tablecloths of "the herbaceous border" type, where the effect is produced by a mere trick of stitchery will some day cease to appear, just as I continue to hope that workers will some day understand how deadly dull wool work on canvas usually is, because the quality of the colours selected for it is so poor and muddy, or so crude and garish.' Pewter work was already an established craft, quite highly praised. Co-operative entries included a patchwork quilt copied from a quilt made by a member's grandmother, a complete outfit for a doll made by twenty-one members, and a doll's four-poster bed, with bedclothes, hangings, and occupant in nightdress, copied from an exhibit in the Victoria and Albert Museum. Dolls and other toys are still one of the 'crafts' at which Townswomen delight to show their skill, as was evidenced by the stunning entries for the *Townswoman's* Christmas competition in 1975, 1976, and 1977.

Right from the beginning NUTG craft judges ruled out marks and prizes, awarding only stars for the best work—in 1934 green for excellent, red for very good, and blue for good. Since then the 'top star' has become gold. About the time of this first exhibition the Carnegie Trust decided to give the NUTG £800, spread over two years, to develop its craftwork, and as a result Mrs Ruth Roper was appointed in 1934 to be its first professional adviser. She promptly began writing useful articles on crafts for *The Townswoman* as well as visiting Guilds and organizing exhibitions. Guilds were advised in 1936 to hold Federation exhibitions first so that NUTG experts could visit them and select representative items for national exhibition later. The result was an exhibition which received a support grant from the Carnegie Trust so that it could be shown in Blackpool, Darlington, and Edinburgh as well as in London.

The humbler fry did occasionally utter a small cry for understanding: 'A poor craftworker,' wrote in 1934, 'What do we mean when we demand a "high standard of craftwork by TG members"? When the whole of modern English work, both professional and amateur, is poor compared with what has been done in the great periods of craft history, is it not farce to continue this talk of "high marks", "proficiency" and petty distinctions between those of us who work a little less badly than the rest? Let us rather devote our energies to the establishment of TG handicrafts on the broadest possible lines, encouraging every member to use her powers to the utmost, not only because of the pleasure it brings to the individual but in the hope that when a living tradition of hard work is once more established there might spring out of it one of those unexplained creative impulses which do suddenly produce first-class work.'

Mrs Roper sometimes in her writings sounds austere and hypercritical, but she must have had real warmth and true perception. Here is her Credo:

'We are at a stage when we need some further organization of our handicrafts. First, however, let us be certain that it is worth building up an elaborate scheme which includes teachers, lecturers, loan exhibits, tests, classes, special courses, our own booklets, judges and all the other things that go to the provision of information about crafts. Handicrafts have grown by popular demand in the Guilds: Are they going to prove merely a fashion for a few years?

'In my opinion Handicrafts in some form are a necessary part of our life. Some craftswomen say they work to make a rug just for the use of their friends. This is true, but the underlying reason is that they want to—or they would be doing something else. Others do no crafts, feeling that it may be all right for the old or delicate, but not a good way for a normal adult to spend her time when she can buy things instead.' (How exactly Ruth Roper expresses the slight scorn which many well-educated and 'cerebral' young women have expressed in recent years for 'arty-crafty' pursuits undertaken chiefly, they think, to fill up time and escape boredom. Has television given a final death blow to this sort of work with the hands? And might not there be fewer tense and stressful women if crafts were more acceptable as a way of spending one's time?) As a matter of fact Mrs Mary Courtney, the then national chairman of the NUTG, put this point very well in a speech at a crafts exhibition at the London Tea Centre: 'I have seen it suggested that such craftwork is a wasteful way to use the time so dearly bought for our emancipation. Our answer is that this beautiful work shows the joy in craftsmanship which serves as a release and a recreation from the many present problems of family life. This work has been done by busy women in their leisure time. I have yet to hear similar criticism of what a man chooses to do with *his* leisure time.'

Mrs Roper was not quite such a total perfectionist as she often sounds for she has an illuminating comment about the people 'who care for crafts only when they are perfectly done'. She commented, 'They have had their eye accustomed to the exact, unvarying standard of *machine* work and do not understand the variations which are the hallmark of all human technique. Still less can they understand mistakes which people must make when learning, but for which a machine must be scrapped . . . but let us in our Guilds make for work showing personal thought and

experiment, else we shall soon have "mass production" of stools
or bags following a popular model.'

Later Mrs Roper expanded her view of the reason for the
dichotomy between 'machine-made' and 'hand-made'. 'When
machinery was brought into use by the invention of the steam
engine and used for mass production to pile up wealth for a few,
hideous objects and hideous living conditions resulted from this
grim competitive drive. The beauty-lovers, sensitive artists, made
a terrible mistake, with lasting results for us. They said, "It is
beauty and handwork against hideousness and mass production."
They turned their backs, fled the dirty stream of everyday life,
got into a quiet backwater and formed arts and crafts societies
to return to the past. Handwork, only. Simple cultured life.
Everyday life suffered for lack of them. Industry continued without
love of making; the critical help they might have given was not
there. If only they had seen that you can have machines *and*
craftwork in life.'

Perhaps one of the most important contributions Townswomen's
Guilds and Women's Institutes alike have made to society is in
keeping creative craftwork alive. Indeed in the villages the WIs
have undoubtedly preserved many crafts from extinction and both
rural and town women have kept alive the satisfaction of producing
artefacts for the enrichment of their own surroundings and their
own lives—and the lives of their friends and neighbours. As Ruth
Roper said 'Handicrafts are (or should be) a necessary part of our
life'—as tension-reducers, if for no other reason. Mrs Roper's
philosophy also included the firm belief that an appreciation of
Beauty was fundamental, not only in the things people made, but
in their surroundings generally, and especially their homes. She
was fierce about insensitivity to Beauty in Guild handicraft.
'It is no good blinking it or pretending that it does not matter. It
matters enormously and it is my job and responsibility to say so.
Grin and bear it. Fault-finding is necessary, but it is only a start.
Find the leak in the pipe, the hole in the tooth, the rot in the
flooring—but advise how to clear up the mess, repair the damage
and suggest a fresh line of action. Thus it is that I make no bones
about condemning those frightful afternoon teacloths stamped with
a mass of so-called michaelmas daisies, or the even more shapeless
cottage and herbaceous border. The majority of these designs repel

the trained and purified eye just as a sickly crooner is repulsive to
a musically educated ear. You can only see how bad they are when
you have done something on sounder lines yourself.'

She wondered, too, why women who were well-dressed could
not carry their good taste into their home backgrounds. 'Their
house looked vile,' she wrote of one poor woman's home. 'Its
colouring was repellant to me. The sitting-room carpet was obviously designed and coloured by a flock of muddy alsatians tram-
ping and rolling on a dirty dishcloth background. The result,
a "modern" design of 1939, is to be seen in a million British homes.
As to the rest of the room, the curtains were a thin, acid green.
The walls had a mottled, smeary paper, the upholstery was a
brown-like, pink-grey-brown affair. The cushions were acid
green. I hated that home yet thought the owner's clothes delightful.'

Like later craft advisers to *The Townswoman*, Mrs Roper was
very insistent on the importance of the design of their exhibitions.
It was to be a recurring theme throughout the years. 'The aim is
not to get the handicrafts done *for* a show, which is a false purpose,
making the show a reason for doing work when it should be the
outcome of what people have ordinarily been doing. Every now
and then it is *fun* to collect the things people have been making and
let everyone see them. We go, look and learn, and the showing is
the main thing and must be well done. We need beautiful arrangement; people want to see things clearly and at leisure. This
arrangement is a craft in itself. We want to aim at having it perfectly simple and simply perfect. Elaborate opening ceremonies,
teas, crammed stands, sideshows, hurried staging, crowds, judging
done on the day, all tend to make complications and confusion.
Keep it simple, not making a worry out of a pleasure.'

On another occasion Mrs Roper was telling the exhibition
organizers they did not take *enough* trouble—though in a different
way from the ceremonies she thought irrelevant: 'Do you have
songs by a choir,' she asked, 'and leave the contraltos in the cloak-
room and the pianist on the stairs? You do not have a dramatic
display and place half the players behind a backcloth or seat them
in the passage. Do you go to the Academy and expect to find half
the pictures stacked on the floor? Yet I see piles of knitting;
a folded counterpane balanced on a glass vase; an untidy row of
slippers placed on top of each other on a radiator grid when a

windowsill is available. Platforms where fine displays could be
arranged are kept empty for speeches. Do you go to see the
handcrafts, distinguished visitors, or tea-tables? Are members'
beds at home laden with shoes and their draining boards with
library books? No, but you might think so.' The therapeutic value
of crafts was especially important during the war years, for
ordinary harassed housewives as well as for hospital patients.
In 1940 Ruth Roper invited Townswomen to send to her their
own directions for working special pieces of handicrafts, and she
herself particularly commended patchwork 'as a craft well-suited
to co-operative work. You will also find that the papers can be
covered with great satisfaction to oneself during the hours of
waiting at any post if you are on National Service. In the little
village where I spend much of my time, members of my patchwork
class are to be found in the inn on most evenings arranging their
designs under a fire of criticism from almost the entire adult
population.' Some Townswomen helped servicemen in hospital to
make costume jewellery, especially bead necklaces, for their
mothers, wives or daughters.

Woolston TG, Southampton, was one Guild which was particularly successful in its hospital craftwork. Mrs Roper commended
their work but added the professional's caution: 'Occupational
therapy is a branch of re-education, requiring much skill and
experience, as well as adaptability and tact, and therapists receive
long training. At the moment there is such an overwhelming
demand for "things for patients to do" that non-specialist helpers
must take their part. These helpers have not always a basic
knowledge of many crafts nor practice in adapting work to hospital
patients' needs. Supply of tools and materials is very short. In
spite of these difficulties the work must never be allowed to sink
to the level of a mere pacifier and time-killer, a futile and tasteless
occupation without real creative activity. It says much for our
TGs' skill and understanding when, as in this Guild and others,
they make a success of this work.' Mrs Roper produced a set of
notes for some of the therapeutic crafts.

As the tide turned and the British people began to think of
'the shape of things to come' it had to be admitted that craft
standards had slipped during the war, and that it would be
necessary to remind Guild members that 'we shall need to help

younger women coming back from the Forces to see and understand what high beauty of workmanship really is. You can be of
so much more value to the community if you become skilled.'

An ingenious idea to help to revivify craft sections, started in
June 1945, was the handicraft box. 'Every box is not necessarily
a box; some are merely flat cases, like a war-time novel. Each box
contains instructions on and examples of some branch of some
craft. They are meant for the help-each-other handicraft groups
of Guilds. They not only provide information but show the high
standard of work that can be achieved. Only convenors of properly
formed Handicraft Sub-committees can send for them. They can
be kept for one or two weeks at a charge of a shilling a week or
1s 6d [7½p] a fortnight, Guilds paying the postage both ways.'
'I shall have two boxes ready by the time you read this,' wrote Mrs
Roper, 'embroidery and needleweaving. Soft slippers and patchwork are to follow. Send for a box and get an idea of quality of
work and design. Avoid those badly made slippers and "bobbly"
patchwork.'

Like all the officials of the NUTG, paid and unpaid, Mrs Roper
never forgot to emphasize the importance of efficient organization
and record-keeping. 'Organization Woman' could be as well
trained to be efficient in a handicrafts sub-committee as in any
other aspect of the Guilds' work. 'What happens when there is no
handicrafts sub-committee?' asked Mrs Roper. 'Mrs A. filled with
delight in patchwork and quilting forms a group quite uncon-
ventionally and happily. They just get together. All very nice.
Mrs A. possibly writes to me and receives back a long and labor-
iously jellied-off series of notes I have made. She gets several
booklets. The group works hard for three months and makes a lot
of "beginners' work". Naturally they aren't very highly skilled in
three months. Then some of them want to stop; or Mrs A. goes
away, or gets bored, or there is a quarrel. The class fades out.
There is no record kept of the work done; my written notes have
mysteriously disappeared; the names of the books are lost, no one
has troubled to keep the paper templates they made for the patchwork. There is a great ragged gap in handicraft activity.'

In the immediate post-war years the National Union of Townswomen's Guilds grew so fast that it might well have burst its
banks, but it never did. In Arts and Crafts, as in every other section,

progress was orderly and well-controlled. Arts and Crafts conferences were held at which experts gave stimulating lectures. At the 1951 Arts and Crafts conference, Federation chairmen were asked to supply answers to eleven questions about their Guilds' activities, and Miss C. L. H. Cowper, a former national secretary, opened up the subject of craft judges and judging, which was to become increasingly important to the movement. Ruth Roper would have approved the theme for the next year's Arts and Crafts conference, 'Interior Decoration'. Each Federation was asked to send for exhibition two portable articles of high standard connected with the exhibition theme, such as cushions, traycloths, table mats or pottery.

Meantime, many Guilds and Federations were putting on exciting exhibitions. For a handicrafts and homecraft exhibition in Darlington the largest hall had to be hired to stage the 2,000 exhibits sent in to celebrate the NUTG's silver jubilee. In Caerphilly, Glamorgan Federation set up an exhibit at the Welsh National Eisteddfod. This was a mock living-room, staged in a classroom of the boys' grammar school. Members of a small sub-committee had spent six to eight months travelling round the handicrafts sections of all the Glamorgan Guilds, selecting work as varied and distinctive as possible. With the exception of the carpet and a few pieces of furniture borrowed for the occasion, every item in the 'living-room' was the work of a Townswoman, and included a small settee, a long fireside stool, a draught screen and a coffee table, as well, of course, as table cloths, cushions, firescreens, painted glass and china, embroidered pictures and chair seats. At the Three Towns Show, Hornchurch TG gave an all-day demonstration of pillow-lace making. They had been taught by a tutor whose family had done it for generations.

In 1950 the Guilds in the Mid-Hants Federation began a linen panel, 9 ft by 4½ ft illustrating in embroidery the D-Day story. The first stitch was put in by the then Mayoress of Southampton, and two years and nine months later, another Mayoress put in the final stitch. An executive member of the Royal School of Needlework supervised throughout. When the Coronation of Queen Elizabeth was drawing near, the needlewomen speeded up the work. The Mayoress took it to the Royal School of Needlework to be pressed, stitched, and arranged for framing, and it was unveiled on

22 April 1953 by Princess Alice, Countess of Athlone. The panel was presented to the town of Southampton for hanging in the new art gallery.

It is pleasant to be reminded that not all the craft objects were of such a high degree of seriousness. Mrs Joy Arnold, of Billericay, has a lively memory of her mother, when a member of Grangetown, Sunderland TG, deciding in her handicraft session to embark on a wall plaque. 'Nothing so simple as painting it or embroidering in lovely silks,' recalls Mrs Arnold. 'It had to be made from the bones of a cod's head. This was duly purchased from the fish shop for three old pennies and boiled and boiled and boiled until the fish fell off the bones, and the smell . . . I can still see the five cats sitting at the kitchen door (and we did not even own one of them). The bones were then soaked in alum and dried. They were painted with poster paint and varnished. They were arranged and arranged until my mother could see some shape and then, there it was—an arbour. A pixie was then made with barbola and placed on the seat, which was the jawbone. It was hanging on the wall for over thirty years—until recently my mother knocked it off the wall while dusting.'

In 1953 one of the most distinguished advisers ever to serve the NUTG was appointed, not only as crafts adviser but to direct social studies. This was Miss Lucile Spalding, a highly gifted writer as well as organizer. After leaving the NUTG she devoted her organizing talent to the Association of Headmistresses, and her writing talent to documentary features, including a portrayal of John Bunyan, for BBC Radio 3.

It was inevitable that the NUTG should follow a similar path to the Women's Institutes in establishing firm national craft standards. At the National Arts and Crafts Conference on standards in 1956, it was decided to set up a system of tests in handicrafts in order to establish a national standard and to enable Guild members to qualify both as teachers and as judges. Miss Beatrice Briant, the Ministry of Education Adviser, who always sat with the National Executive Committee and kept a very close liaison with them, was very strongly in favour of this proposal. She was accustomed to advise on the selection of experts to talk at conferences and helped to recruit the aid of local education authority officials, organizers and inspectors, and the heads of art schools and technical colleges who judged crafts at NUTG exhibitions without fee.

The idea of the Townswomen training their own judges was discussed with enthusiasm. Miss Briant suggested that LEAs might arrange weekend courses for craftswomen who knew their own craft but needed to acquire the other qualities of a good judge; also that present judges might be willing for a 'trainee' judge to go along with them for experience. Members were also advised to take every opportunity of acting as stewards and judges' clerks, to gain 'know-how'. Miss Briant always felt strongly that the Ministry of Education's grant to the NUTG must be used to foster serious educational work, in crafts as in every other aspect of its interests. The Craft Scheme served the movement well but was discontinued in 1975.

And so preparations were made, under Lucile Spalding, for the first NUTG 'stand' at the Ideal Home Exhibition at Olympia in 1957. Between 1,700 and 1,800 exhibits were offered and had to be sifted—not only to choose those of the highest standard, but to ensure a well-balanced and interesting display. The first assessment was that the embroidery was as usual the largest class, with an encouraging number of original designs, and that the other offerings included more than might have been expected of paintings, modelling, wood-carving, carpentry, and silver and copper work.

Margaret Playle, NUTG press officer and features editor of *The Townswoman*, described the scene at Olympia vividly, and her description is worth quoting for its enthusiasm, and because exhibitions like this are less common in the seventies than they were in the fifties. 'The crowds press round, seeking somewhere to rest awhile. And there are two archways leading, it would seem, to a peaceful by-way. Between, and on either side of them, there are shop windows, brightly lit, gaily coloured, displaying toys and children's wear, silver and lace, and marvellous embroidery, of a gaiety that no machine has ever yet turned out. Written across the two centre windows is "National Union of Townswomen's Guilds" and projecting above an inviting little yellow door, the sign "HANDMADE".

'Leading through an archway are five windows and over each is the name of a craft; carving, leatherwork, metalcraft, basketry, weaving. On the other side of the archway is a display of toys, of which the centrepiece is a circusmaster with ringmaster, complete with whip, monkey astride a horse, seal, bear and clown. During this exhibition eighty-three members took part in demonstrations of crafts and skills.'

The Townswomen were rightly proud of their public image, but this was not achieved, of course, without some private heartache. Lucile Spalding imagined a typical monologue by a rejected would-be exhibitor: 'Well, I don't know, but my *friends* say my cloth was every bit as good as the one they showed. In fact I couldn't understand the judge passing that one. The colours were *terrible*.' Entrants had to be told remorselessly, as Miss Spalding put it, that 'a bedside lamp looking like a lighthouse was not acceptable'. But immediately after the 1957 exhibition she explained kindly and helpfully how the process of reducing all those hundreds of entries, to the 230 that could be accommodated, actually worked. The initial selection was on a description, and only 725 items were actually sent to London for judging. 'Here and there an exhibit which had ranked as a star piece in a Federation exhibition could not quite stand up to the best work from all over the country. In some cases the only fault found was that the exhibit had the slightly wilted look of a piece that has already appeared at several exhibitions.'

As always, the embroidery class was so large that judging had to be very severe. Judges encountered obvious faults of design, some work was criticized for attempting to imitate painting or nature too closely, in embroidery, 'a medium which is better used imaginatively and decoratively, with full regard for the texture of the different types of stitchery instead of competing unsuccessfully with paint brush or camera lens. In the choice of tone and colour, however, embroidery can pick up hints from photography and painting'.

Then there was the old question of hackneyed work. 'Craft judges, it should be remembered,' said Miss Spalding, 'suffer from the fatigue of seeing the same stool top or tablecloth at a dozen exhibitions. I myself have been confronted with six identical Jacobean firescreens in one show, identical, that is, except for their colouring, some variation of stitchery or the fact that more had been cut off the top or sides of one transfer than of the others.'

If Miss Spalding sounds hypercritical she was not so in fact. Recalling her days with the NUTG just after she had retired after many years spent as secretary of the Association of Headmistresses, she said 'Many of the Townswomen were so self-deprecating. I tried to encourage them to appreciate that if they couldn't design with a pencil, they often could do so with a pair of scissors.'

In 1959 the NUTG again exhibited at the Ideal Home Exhibition, and the National Union 'unpackers' inevitably asked themselves, as they set up thirty trestle tables, and coped with boxes, brown paper and string encircling some 750 entries. whether the exhibition would be up to 1957's. Miss Spalding was pleased that there were a number of entries for the less usual crafts, like silversmithing, metal work, jewellery, leatherwork, and pottery, but only a few of them were outstanding. Mr Grant, teacher of silversmithing, found the construction of some pieces inaccurate. 'Made by hand does not mean made cock-eyed' was Miss Spalding's brisk comment. 'Toys,' she added, 'were, not for the first time, outstandingly good, charming, sensible and safe. Judges of both sexes were charmed by this section. In fact, but for their strength of character and determination they might have stayed to play'—a comment that could equally well have been made by the editor of *The Townswoman* about the judging of the entries for the toy competition she ran in 1976. The 1954 annual report of the NUTG had reported that twenty-six of the dolls made by Bristol members for their 'Elizabethan Life' exhibition were sent to an international exhibition at Neuchâtel; and three dolls were sent for a Canadian national doll dressing exhibition at Toronto, and one, showing the Queen's coronation robes, won third prize out of an entry of 2,000.

Aiming still higher, the NUTG in 1964 staged a crafts exhibition at the Victoria and Albert Museum. This time *only* original designs were accepted in the embroidery classes, but fears that this would reduce the entry to a pitiful number were groundless. Not one 'herbaceous border' worked on to a transfer! How proud Ruth Roper would have been of the way her Townswomen had grown to maturity in their craft work . . . and it was not a matter just of new young embroiderers sweeping the board. Mrs Hilary Newton, the then crafts adviser, told how three pupils of a Mid-Surrey TG teacher of original design exhibited in the show. All three entries were from work on leaves and seed-heads, but all were completely different. And all were novices 'thus destroying the myth that beginners can't get anywhere'—and also the myth that Townswomen might be too old to learn new ways, for some of the exhibitors were in their sixties when they decided to learn how to use new methods and new materials. Their reward was that *young* visitors to the exhibition were excited and truly astonished by the quality of work, saying, 'We thought they were old fuddy-duddies.' It was sad for the National Union that less than half the work sent forward from the regional selections was considered by the judges to be worthy of the national exhibition, and no doubt, once again, there was heart-burning. Mrs Newton wrote 'Were the national judges too hard? We do not think so. They know that through the Craft Training Scheme we are striving for a new high standard; they know we are striving to give our work a look of the present day, not of the past. They helped us by believing that we wanted to show work only of the very highest standard.' Another factor in reducing the number of entries accepted was that the final selections was left to the V. and A. designer of the exhibition. Again Mrs Roper, with her strong views on the importance of exhibition layout, would have approved. This exhibition was felt to be a striking lesson in the technique of display, for it was simple, dignified and colourful and represented a great variety of crafts.

It was ten years before the NUTG put on another substantial national crafts exhibition and this time a working party was set up a full three years ahead of the chosen date. Three experienced craft judges who were also Townswomen sat with Mrs Mary Sobey, then national chairman, and set themselves three main aims: to produce a schedule which would show the best TG work to the best advantage; to encourage new crafts; and to profit by the experience of the Victoria and Albert Museum exhibition. It was the national secretary, Mrs Marjorie Erskine-Wyse, who thought up the intriguing title 'Designing Women' for this exhibition, held in the Kensington Town Hall. The lessons of the V. and A. exhibition led to the decisions to limit the knitting classes to those which needed particular skill; to omit dressmaking, because garments need to be *worn* to show their full effect; and to cut out homecraft classes, for in 1964 exhibits had been broken en route and became a great responsibility in re-packing and returning.

In the same year the exhibition 'It's a Townswomen's World'
at the Daily Mail Ideal Home Exhibition at Olympia covered a very
great variety of Townswomen's activities and raised the interest of
thousands of visitors. No fewer than 2,000 enquiries about membership were received. No wonder the large-scale exhibition came to
be regarded as the best recruiting agent the movement had discovered, or that it was tried once again in 1976, at a 'jamboree'
entitled 'Townswomen at Trentham'. This festival, exhibition
or whatever grew out of a Floral Exhibition at Syon Park and was
not intended to display the full range of Townswomen's activities—
indeed it excluded crafts as well as music, drama, and citizenship.
It concentrated on horticulture, floral arrangement, homecraft
and wine-making, and drew the crowds partly because of the
numerous 'side-shows'—exhibitions of parachuting, police dogs
at work, firework displays, and china decoration. It was a family
day out and those who came to enjoy it as such seem to have had a
very happy time and to appreciate the fact that something so
enjoyable had been arranged out of London! Others, who perhaps
were expecting a more traditional kind of exhibition expressed
disappointment. Probably Mrs Coram, national chairman, and
members of her executive were remembering the severity of the
judgments passed on TG craftwork at the V. and A. exhibition,
and were wanting to provide a happy experience for the many
women who could never hope to achieve 'gold star standard' in
their crafts. Were they thinking, perhaps, that too much emphasis
on the austere standards of the previous professional crafts advisers might discourage the sort of women the NUTG was now
very much wanting to recruit?

Music

There is little evidence that the Founding Mothers of the Townswomen's Guilds were passionately interested in music, but they
knew it was A Good Thing and an ingredient in the 'whole woman'
they cared about nurturing, so they fostered it enthusiastically.
In 1937 the Carnegie Trust made a grant of £500 a year to cover
both music and drama and by the most fortunate of chances Miss
Kathleen Merritt was engaged as music adviser. She was a fine
musician herself, a violinist and conductor, with much experience

of choirs, an excellent communicator and the friend of many distinguished musicians whom she was often able to draw into Townswomen's music-making activities. At seventy-five Miss Merritt was still conducting the Southern Orchestral Concert Society's 1976 season of concerts in schools, colleges, and churches in Hampshire and Sussex.

She began training choirs when she was only eighteen and despite being a violinist, she had a rare appreciation of the value of the human voice. 'Singing is such a *real* musical experience,' she said, 'the instrument being one's own voice.' This belief in the importance of the human voice was crucial to her success as Townswomen's Guild music adviser, for very few of the Townswomen had access to any other instrument, and choral singing was the essence of their musical experience.

One gets a picture of great gaiety on the music and drama side of the early days of the Townswomen's activities, to set off against the rather strict co-ordination of organizational activities: Kathleen Merritt and Margaret Leona, the first drama adviser, were both very attractive, spirited young women, popping in and out of No 2 Cromwell Place with all sorts of ideas, reporting to Alice Franklin and Gertrude Horton, and finding out from the education secretary, Anne Elias, what Guilds wanted visits, and what possibilities there were for organizing 'schools'. What these two meant to the life of the movement during the war years can hardly be over-estimated. Though they were paid only for 'half' or 'quarter' time they seem to have spent endless hours in the NUTG service, writing excellent monthly notes, advising Guilds on choice of music or plays, and spending endless hours travelling the length and breadth of the land in very uncomfortable war-time conditions. Miss Merritt remembers being sent off to Newcastle, where she stayed a night in an hotel and then was sent on to 'some obscure place on the north-east coast where I was to deputise for the music convenor and heard that "the new music adviser" was going to *speak*. This was nerve-wracking, for I'd never done it before. But I survived the ordeal and after that experience I always spoke on the spur of the moment, with only a few notes, for this seemed the best way of making contact with the members.' Miss Merritt obviously shared the rare gift of communicating about music with the people she admired like Walford Davies, Alec Robertson, and Eric Robinson. 'If you talk down to people, whether children or adults, it is no good, but really first-class music always makes contact. If you have real performances by first-class artists people realize something is hitting them.' Miss Merritt *always* went for artists of top quality for NUTG events, as she still does for Southern Orchestra concerts, and she always worked on the principle that practical experience of music-making—as in singing —was necessary to music appreciation. 'Just putting on records,' she said, 'often means that the music goes over their heads.'

By 1942 Kathleen Merritt could say 'We may be proud of the fact that there are now very few Guilds without a choral group' and bombs did not stop them singing. 'In Plymouth the other day an enthusiast came to me saying "We have lost our hall through enemy action and our present meeting place has no piano, but we want to start a choir." I explained that many choirs are temporarily practising in members' houses and suggested that rounds and folk songs provide excellent material for unaccompanied singing. Do not hesitate to begin, even if you have only six or eight singers. If you can find a good leader who is willing to learn and who can make the practices interesting and enjoyable, your numbers will gradually increase. Try to find an accompanist who is modest and willing to work to improve. There is probably hidden talent in every Guild.'

On another occasion she wrote 'Often on visiting a Guild I am told "Our members are quite unmusical, can you do something to make them interested in music?"' Kathleen Merritt regarded this as an enjoyable challenge because she simply did not believe that so many members were really unmusical, and was sure there was a way to convince them. She was unfailingly enthusiastic. 'On a summer evening madrigals sound lovely in the open air. And when not in the open air I know of no better way to make one unconscious of the distant noise of guns and bombs.'

In Miss Merritt's monthly notes in *The Townswoman* there were frequent references such as 'Hull and Southampton, two of our most badly blitzed cities, have both managed to organize concerts for their choirs.' 'In spite of suffering severely from enemy action Sunderland produced no less than seven TG choirs.' But what was almost more remarkable than the persistence of local TG choirs was the enthusiasm for music schools held actually at TG headquarters, in the heart of London. 'I was given a very good piano,' Miss Merritt recalls, 'which was housed at 2 Cromwell Place and enabled us to hold schools there for conductors, pianists etc.' Miss Merritt persuaded that excellent pianist and teacher James Ching to take several of these. One was announced for 'solo piano, piano duet, piano and other instruments and/or impromptu playing of an accompaniment for singer or choir (singers provided). Only a short break for luncheon, for which candidates should bring their own sandwiches. Black coffee available at 2d per cup.' In March 1944 a school for conductors 'filled the meeting room to capacity, with a demonstration choir of twenty-seven voices and about fifty participants from far and near. The school included song after song and practical conducting and choir training. The afternoon was given to sight reading.' A year later Miss Merritt wrote of another conductors' school at Cromwell Place: 'We had a demonstration choir, formed spontaneously from among the near-London Guilds with whom I had personal contact. I made it a condition that not more than two members from each choir, plus the conductor and accompanist if they happened to be singers, might attend. My appeal for singers met with a quick response, though for most people it was an hour's journey from home. There was a demand for the choir to remain in being, so we had fortnightly rehearsals until these had to be suspended on account of the flying bombs.'

The response to the call to make music was indeed astonishing during those war years. Announcements of schools were usually made only through *The Townswoman*, yet the places for students were always all taken up. New choir leaders often emerged as a result of these schools, which were sometimes held in the provinces as well as in London. Miss Merritt was never put off by a student's admission that she could not read music. 'I confess I have often said,' she admitted, ' "Never mind if you can't sight read; just come along and sing. If you follow the music you will see when it goes up and when it goes down, and later, whether you must leap or move step by step." I do not retract those words—to *begin* is important; knowledge comes with experience, and with knowledge, a deeper understanding of the music. In the time of Queen Elizabeth I people could read music as easily and naturally as they could read poetry, because music was the recreation of the people.

Townswomen have given ample proof of their capacity to defy difficulties. Perhaps our choirs will form a vanguard to raise the prevailing low standard of sight-reading in this country.' It is amusing to note that at a very recent Townswomen's Guild music school at Birmingham a similar comment was heard: 'The people who can't sight-read are better at keeping their eye on the conductor than those who can. The sight-readers keep their noses in their copy.'

Like many other serious musicians, Kathleen Merritt was always opposed to the competitive element in music festivals and hoped that the Townswomen's choirs would in time be willing and able to try for a high standard without the impetus of competition. Very much in the same vein as Ruth Roper (who, incidentally, was on the staff of Bedales School when Miss Merritt was a pupil there), she wrote 'Many TG members associate the word "festival" with a stupendous and often exhausting effort in which music and drama compete for attention. I hope this kind of festival will soon die a natural death. It originated through the goodwill of Federation executives who, wanting to do something for both music and drama decided to kill them both off with the proverbial stone, and through lack of advice from specialist committees often launched ventures without any clear idea of their purpose.'

She was by no means opposed, though, to every type of festival. Her first, at Petersfield, was a lifelong inspiration. As a small child she was taken to hear the massed choirs rehearsing at the Petersfield festival. 'The conductor had renounced his place on the rostrum in favour of an aged man in a white linen coat who seemed to be in some difficulty about a stick he was waving in the air. He was tall and stooping, with a bald head and a pink neck that seemed to become even pinker as I heard him say "I don't care how many beats there are in the bar. I want it to sound like this."

'Sir Hugh Allen who used to bring his orchestra from Oxford every year was standing by, trying to help his friend Sir Hubert Parry [the composer of *Jerusalem*] who had come to conduct his own work *The Lotus-Eaters*.' That was the beginning of a long association with the festival. Sir Hugh was succeeded by Sir Adrian Boult, who became a close friend of the festival. Kathleen Merritt loved it all, except the competitions. 'Of course they did much to stimulate effort, but for my part one or two marks this way or that way seemed always invidious and out of tune with this fine enterprise!' Miss Leona, her contemporary as drama adviser, felt exactly the same way.

Naturally Miss Merritt tried to stimulate the playing of other instruments than the piano, but without lasting success. (She herself played in an all-women string quartet.) In 1943 she reported that a Townswoman, having accompanied a choir in Mill Hill, bought herself a baton and set about building up not a choir but an orchestra. She first gathered together two or three string players and a pianist. A few more players began to come along. One was a good violinist, to act as leader, and one a good cellist 'to form a foundation'. When the music adviser first heard the group she had to admit 'there were painful sounds as well as pleasant ones, but the right spirit was there'. The following spring she visited this orchestra again, in a large room in a private house, containing little besides a piano and chairs. 'The first session was called "the beginners class" and was directed by the leader of the orchestra who sat at the piano and accompanied pupils in unison and two-part pieces. There were five members. Each had succeeded in finding, buying or borrowing an instrument, and all, including my friend the conductor, had begun to learn the violin from scratch. One member told me that by careful planning she was able to practise for half an hour a day. She tried to find a time when her husband was away and her neighbours were out shopping. When the more advanced players arrived the beginners and I settled down to enjoy listening . . . There was rhythmic precision and this derived from the baton, which by this time had become part of the conductor.' It is not recorded what happened to this fascinating experiment, and in later years Kathleen Merritt had forgotten about it.

Because of Kathleen Merritt's extensive contacts in the world of music remarkably fine concerts were put on in the immediate post-war years. It was hoped that Benjamin Britten would write a work for the NUTG's twenty-first birthday, but this fell through, as indeed did the whole concert, cancelled because at that time the movement was going through a financial crisis. Concerts given in connection with the National Council Meeting in 1950 were noticed favourably by *The Times* music critic. These included

Purcell's *St Cecilia Ode* and Gustav Holst's *Rig Veda* hymns
performed by a choir drawn from the Southern Federation choirs
and Miss Merritt's own orchestra. This was one of the last events
she organized and conducted before moving on to other fields,
and giving place to a young singer, John Carol Case, who was to
play an essential part in one of the movement's finest cultural
events. Mr Case's avowed aim was to make music enjoyable, and
that he and his successors undoubtedly did. Taking a quarter-
century leap forward—a Townswomen's Guild residential music
school that was undoubtedly the most stimulating kind of fun,
is worth recording here, to show how much in line present attitudes are with those held by Miss Merritt and Mr Case. This
school, held at St Peter's College, Saltley, Birmingham, alongside a
drama school, explored the theme 'With What You've Got',
under a charming tutor, Mrs Veronica Jamset. Every student had
been sent a copy of Pergolesi's *Stabat Mater* which had been
performed by two previous music schools and was fully enjoyed
by this one. The members took the Latin text in their stride and
not many of them were badly thrown by the discovery that the
copies were in a transposed version, which in one chorus meant
that the singers were singing a major third above the printed notes.

What the members wanted to do was to *sing*—the Pergolesi, a
carol from Britten's 'Ceremony of Carols', the Thomas Morley
madrigal 'Since Singing is So Good a Thing' or just rounds and
simple part songs which gave volunteers a chance to try their
hand at conducting. But Mrs Jamset had a fascinating innovation
to try on her students—free composition on some theme from
Shakespeare's *Tempest*. Everyone came armed with a copy of the
play and most were probably terror-struck at the idea of composing
anything until they saw the splendid array of instruments the tutor
had set out . . . glockenspiels, xylophones, chime bars, triangles,
tambourines, every size and kind of drum. Some never did conquer
their nervousness. A few were a little scornful of free-style
'mood' music. One Manchester woman took herself off to the
college chapel with a companion or two and returned with a very
pleasant voice-and-piano composition. Another produced a vocal
trio which was almost professional. But most happily banged and
rattled and blew. A charming little Welsh woman with a figure
rather like a cottage loaf, incredibly light on her feet, with a very

good musician from Derbyshire concocted a delightful *entr'acte* with a xylophone for nymphs, a drum scraped with a whisk for reapers and a French horn for the barking dogs.

Mrs Jamset very much doubted whether her regular students at the college would have achieved as much as the Townswomen. But was it worth the expense, they asked themselves in discussion later. 'I am worried about so much money being spent on *me*,' said one anxious participant. 'I have enjoyed every minute and got a great deal out of it, but how will my Guild members benefit?' Said another, 'Our choir would laugh at me if we played with instruments such as we have here, and would call it a waste of an evening—even if we could afford to buy things like glockenspiels and chime bars.' Dr Joan Waters, chairman of the NUTG education sub-committee which organized the sequence of 'cultural' schools, had some trenchant answers for the doubters. 'The craft exhibitions and cycles of schools are to raise standards. If we do here the things you do already and don't try to encourage you to do something different we ought to stop spending this money.' And then 'If you say you can't afford to buy chime bars and other musical instruments, how is it you can raise so much money for causes like the League of Hospital Friends?'

Through the enthusiasm and devotion of their music advisers, the Townswomen had some remarkable opportunities of music-making. John Carol Case actually composed all the music for *With This Sword*, a documentary that needs to be described in full later, since it was a shining achievement which united so many aspects of the Townswomen's interests; Armstrong Gibbs composed *The Gift*, and Imogen Holst composed *The Sun's Journey*. Surely no other women's organization has had such riches lavished upon it. Miss Helen Anderson, the music adviser who followed John Carol Case, said that *The Gift*, a mime to music, presented in 1959, with Alison Graham Campbell, the drama adviser, was perhaps the most interesting thing she worked on. 'It wasn't exactly a successful work if you looked at it dispassionately from outside,' said Miss Anderson, 'but it was an extremely interesting work to produce and work on, and it taught all the people who took part in it a lot because they had never worked in this medium of miming to music before. We got Geraldine Stevenson to do all the dancing and mime and she did very well for us—I think it opened people's

eyes quite a lot to their possibilities.' Alison Graham Campbell
admitted after the performance in the Scala Theatre that some of
the audience found the meaning obscure. It was devised by Dr
Armstrong Gibbs and Benedict Ellis for adaptation to the limited
forces of Federations, and even Guilds, and it was the London and
near-London Federations who first presented it. The theme was
concerned with the world and man's life here on earth—the
whole family of man, looked at not from the angle of any one
country but of mankind itself—'or perhaps better,' said Miss
Graham Campbell, 'to say womankind, for it is what women *give*
to life that the work deals with. We see women as mothers giving
life and tending the young and sending them out on life's great
adventure. Later women are shown as the gloriously capricious
element in life, fickle, fresh and beautiful as the month of April.
Then we take a peep into family life, a comedy scene in which
mother and daughter plan a glorious carefree holiday while father
has a nightmare of unpaid bills. We see the loneliness of an old
woman who is brought to join the feasting. We see a woman as
hostess and homemaker, a picture quickly followed by semi-
satirical sidelights on the housewives of today. What comes out of
this? Woman's life is a life of giving. Is that enough to give existence meaning? No, there is something else . . . the gift of grace
which only God can give. So the climax of the work is the well-
known prayer "God be in my head, and in my understanding."'

The singing was the important factor in this work, for the choir
needed to have exceptional clarity of diction to get the message
across. Helen Anderson found that there was excellent musical
'material' in the Townswomen's Guilds. As she later became
warden of Denman College, the adult education centre of the
National Federation of Women's Institutes, she was in an in-
comparable position to compare the two organizations and she
stresses that in choral work the Townswomen's Guild had the
great advantage of numbers. Institutes which function in small
villages have less chance to build up the fine choirs than the
Townswomen have. 'The TGs' music was very strong, awfully
good,' she said, looking back. 'It was particularly good in different
parts of the country where there was very good leadership. I found
especially good choirs in the South-East and in the North-East.
It was fascinating to go round the country and realize how the

quality of the voices changes in the various regions. The whole
style changes. The Home Counties were musically more sophisticated and sang with refinement but not particularly beautiful
tone quality. When you got up to the Potteries or the Nottingham
area you found they sang very strongly and easily, not with as much
background knowledge, but with a lovely quality, a pleasure to
listen to.'

Miss Anderson also made a very interesting discovery about
leadership. 'I found that leadership, in the WI as well as the TG,
often came from someone who moved from her own area to another
area. The leadership in the Colchester area came from a Yorkshire
woman. Up north the leader would be someone who had moved
from the south. It seems that being uprooted from your own home
area is very stimulating and makes you do something. It brings
out your potential in many ways. I find this is the same wherever I go.
You have got to make a life for yourself, to go out and do something.
Perhaps you may not have succeeded at anything in your own
home town. Perhaps you haven't even tried.'

Miss Anderson thinks that her most interesting experience with
the Townswomen was the National Music Festival she organized
in 1965. She persuaded Imogen Holst, daughter of Gustav
Holst, to compose a work for it, *The Sun's Journey*. All the choirs
all round the country worked on this for two years. 'I took Maurice
Jacobson around with me and we did the whole nine regions,
adjudicating amongst the choirs. We brought all the winners to
London in May 1967 and had an orchestra in the Kingsway Hall.
Imogen conducted the work herself, and it was quite an experience
for everyone. It was only a half hour work, quite difficult, but very
skilfully written, and was a great experience for the Townswomen.
I don't think Imogen quite realized how difficult the work was
rhythmically, or that rhythm may be more difficult for amateurs
than the notes. There were some hazardous moments but they all
learned a tremendous lot by doing it and they got a tremendous
thrill through coming to London to take part.

'There was one delicious moment in performance—not really
anybody's fault. It was something Imogen herself hadn't realized
was a possible hazard. In the middle there was a solo which ended
in a way which meant that the tonality wasn't quite settled. After
it there was an unaccompanied twelve-part round. This some keen

member started, picking up the wrong note. I saw Imogen's eyebrows shoot up when she heard it. It didn't matter during the round—they sang all through the round, but then the great question was whether the soloist was going to be able to get back on key. Luckily she was a good musician; she did get back and it was OK. That is the sort of thing that can happen with an amateur choir when you haven't envisaged all the snags. It never happened in rehearsal. They were supposed to memorize that entry and pick it up from the final note of the solo, and one realized too late it was something they should have practised.'

Drama

Music and drama have always gone in hand, and Townswomen's music and drama advisers have always co-operated on projects, from the first advisers, Kathleen Merritt and Margaret Leona, onwards. Margaret Leona's energies, however, were always directed chiefly to creative, documentary drama, especially towards enacting themes which had relevance to the lives of the Townswomen. Right through the war, even after she was called up into service with the Admiralty and could only spend a quarter of her time with the NUTG, Margaret Leona was indefatigably travelling the country, exhorting, encouraging, stimulating. 'A week with the Tees-side Federations brought me into touch with twenty Guilds; two sessions a day with members of drama groups and members keen to form drama groups. This was followed by a fortnight with the Wearside Federation adjudicating six non-competitive festivals at five centres during the first week and following this in the next week with two schools at which I amplified the written criticisms of the plays and acting points and rehearsing the detail as much as possible in the time with the original casts.

'The schools and festivals were held in the afternoons because of the blackout but in spite of this drew quite large audiences. The one evening festival, at Sunderland, drew crowds, people standing several deep.' Miss Leona commented that this showed the great need during the war for entertainment. It also showed her dedicated energy. She was always suggesting themes for the drama groups to work on. A typical 'scheme': 'The discovery that the world was round; the reaction and persecution for such an outrageous idea. The Industrial Revolution. The Chartists. The Tolpuddle Martyrs. The Trade Unions. All this up to the present day. The growth of knowledge and the abuse and distrust of knowledge. The ignorance of "society" and the struggle against conventional power for a more enlightened viewpoint leads to the Nazi persecution of culture, of scientists, professors, artists and students —all done in the name of "heavenly" vision.'

This was pretty ambitious stuff for ordinary, untrained members of local Guilds, as Miss Leona realized—so she devised more homely themes for them to work on: 'the billeting office; our allotment; Christmas Day; the unexpected visitor; in the shelter; the waiting-room; waiting for the bus; reading the constitution; the canteen.' The idea was to divide the meeting room into groups, each group to choose one of these headings. 'Talk over a story that might illustrate it and allot characters. See that there is a good beginning line and a good end line, and a surprise in the situation or atmosphere at the end. You will find this a good way of recruiting new members by developing dialogue and character.' Some might think this a very intimidating introduction to Townswomen's activities, but Margaret Leona had no doubts about her methods. 'All of us have to allocate our time more directly to the war. Much energy is wasted by not using recreation to the fullest capacity in the most suitable way. War demands refreshment, strong meat, strong comedy, illumination of present problems. Make use of them.'

Is there anything really comparable today with this widespread fostering of creative, experimental, home-made drama? Some social studies groups use this method, and with the young, street theatre seems to be a spontaneous expression of the impulse to dramatize experience. Miss Leona did not, however, encourage her 'students' to run away with the idea that what they could achieve was comparable with the work of the professional. 'The scope of the professional,' she said firmly, 'is wider and clearer than that of the amateur. She is a "trained instrument" and can obviously interpret and sustain expression through the difficult acrobatics of technique required in burlesque, comedy of manners or classical tragedies, with greater ease and assurance. The amateur attempting a major emotion of classic dimensions has not as great a command of her instrument and only interprets in "flashes". But develop these "flashes", this spontaneity; link the flashes all in sequence. It won't come all at once, but come it will and if you relate it to material connected with your own experience, you are creating in a way that cannot be destroyed. And you cannot be defeated. The more you relate your work to the expression of things you know, the greater the command you will have of emotional expression.'

Miss Leona did not at all care for the kind of 'sketches' and historical playlets, and the sort of run-of-the-mill acting material which was commonly offered to all acting groups, with a cast list specifying how many 'm' and 'f' were needed. 'They always wanted to dress up and be in costume,' she says, 'and to do the impossible. They loved doing historical drama but they couldn't approach it. They didn't know how to walk, they didn't know how to speak, the furniture was all wrong. You couldn't begin to find what to praise. It needed a lot of work to help them. Of course what they wanted was a "Big Show!"' The time would come, ten years or so on, when the Townswomen got their Big Show and triumphed in it, but under Miss Leona's direction they were learning a technique of presenting documentary material which developed in a very impressive way under later drama advisers, and has certainly left its mark upon the sort of drama that Guilds still undertake.

Like her colleague the music adviser, Miss Leona bitterly opposed the competitions with marks that most of the Guilds seemed to want. 'Then they could say "Well, we would have got the prize but we failed by one mark", and not realize that the reason for their failure was various points. You really can't measure performance in marks.' Miss Leona didn't much like play-readings, either, and it displeased her that many universities encouraged play-reading rather than performance and didn't pay their tutors for taking acting classes. 'Everything had to be read and explained, rather like a university course, which upset numbers of the tutors who were drama minded.'

A typical creative documentary approach was based on a BBC discussion concerning ideal housing 'for the youth of tomorrow'. This fitted in admirably with the questionnaire on housing which the Ministry of Housing had circulated among women's organizations, including the NUTG. The members of the Friern Barnet and

Whetstone Guild listened to a twenty-minute recording of Elizabeth Denby talking with a group of youth leaders from all over England who were keen on house planning. Hardly had the recording finished when the Townswomen rushed into discussion, with very little prompting from Miss Leona. After about half an hour she gave out headings to various groups, such as 'The New Kitchen', 'Moving', 'The Family Row', allowed the groups ten minutes to agree on a plot and then called on each group to enact its sketch. The result was a striking melting of the problems of housing into the interest of the characters, developed as the actors talked about their theme. 'I think many members were taken by surprise,' said Miss Leona. 'They said they would try this in their Guilds, and thought they would listen to BBC programmes to get ideas for their own sketches. Others wondered what this kind of thing had to do with drama. Others commented how the sketches had enabled people to express strong feelings about the houses they would want. Some illuminating remarks were made about the husband's attitude to the new home.'

It was not until the end of the war, and after her marriage, that Miss Leona resigned from the NUTG, and started giving solo programmes all over the country, from Cornwall to Co. Durham... as indeed she still does, looking remarkably youthful, vivacious, and elegant. It is not surprising that when the NUTG was looking for a successor to their first drama adviser they asked the candidate they finally appointed what experience she had of documentary drama. Whether Alison Graham Campbell knew much or little at that point, she was soon up to her ears in it, along with the music adviser, John Carol Case, and the Social Studies and Crafts adviser, that brilliant writer and organizer Lucile Spalding.

One of the most exciting passages in the history of Townswomen's cultural activities was a joint effort by these three. The story opened in 1952 in a railway carriage somewhere between Plymouth and Paddington, with John Carol Case and Alison Graham Campbell talking over their first collaboration, a joint school for choir and drama members. Two years later the NUTG would be celebrating its silver jubilee. How? Their minds were blank except for one thing on which they were completely agreed. 'It' must be the Royal Festival Hall, or nothing. When the drama adviser met the NUTG drama sub-committee she was asked to outline the subject for a pageant. Instead of asking for time to consider this she rashly offered a half-planned coronation pro-gramme she had been turning over in her mind, rapidly refurbished as a TG celebration pageant. She even suggested the title, *With This Sword*, and explained that the main emphasis should be on women and social conditions today, getting right away from the hackneyed historical pageants of tradition. The drama sub-committee wholeheartedly approved and the very next day Miss Graham Campbell had to put her idea to the Central Council. The subject and title were accepted on the spot and recorded in the minute book.

The 'sword' was double-edged . . . several Guilds protested against the supposedly militarist symbol, and when the script came to be written there did not seem at first to be scope for 'the sword' —this was later overcome and it appeared as the symbol of justice and mercy. At this point the Social Studies adviser came into action and by April 1953 had ready a two-page synopsis based on three narrators. All that summer the three collaborators were in con-tinuous contact, sometimes working on music and words together, sometimes at the end of three telephones. John Carol Case played his musical settings loudly down the telephone and in one case the script writer was expected to compose words to fit the tune and phone them back only two or three hours later. 'Not being trained to take musical dictation,' commented the poor Social Studies adviser, 'I did my best with an improvised musical shorthand to capture the tune and rhythm, the verses were churned out and read over the telephone and then were sung back by the music adviser.'

It would be untrue and unjust to suggest that *With This Sword* was the absolute peak of the Townswomen's achievement in the sense of a public display of all they stood for, but it probably was the peak of the achievement fostered by the movement's system of having professional advisers. And however you look at it, the Festival Hall performances were a remarkable feat of organization and training. Also, it is the best documented of all the Towns-women's 'big shows' and so is worth recounting in some detail as yet one more piece of evidence of what women organized in a voluntary movement can achieve.

The masque was dedicated to 'Those fearless women of days

gone by who resolutely fought for us and won for us the privileges and duties of citizenship; giving us for the first time the right to follow whatever employments, careers or professions we might choose', but the 'plot' was by no means confined to the movement for the emancipation of women. It was more in the nature of an exploration of the growth of the Welfare State and of social concern. There is an Auditor whose job is to obtain a progress report. Various scenes are put before her, opening with a big 'musical' of life in the eighteenth century, immediately offset by a scene showing women and children working in the coalmines. From the Victorian era the scenes show life in the drawing-room, in the servants' hall, and in the sweat shop . . . 'and then suddenly everyone realizes that Judy O'Grady and the Colonel's Lady are partners in the new demand for emancipation'. Using the pattern of 'the seven ages of man' the contribution to human well-being of the Welfare State is depicted, followed by seven 'nightmares' showing twentieth-century commonplaces of cruelty, callousness and crimes of violence. In the final reckoning the players come to realize that 'the margin between credit and debit in our life today is perilously small. And so the Auditor, taking leave of the audience, says "Look to it with vigilance, for you are all share-holders in this enterprise. May your work prosper. Go your ways."'

Not revolutionary dramatic fare, perhaps, but the techniques were brilliant. Using mime and music the masque blended the technique of a modern revue with that of a documentary or living newspaper. There were three narrators, all Guild members, of course; one Welsh, one Scottish and one, presumably, English. There were three monkeys interrupting the action; six 'house husbands' also intruded. The RFH cast totalled 600 women, all amateurs; they had to be selected, of course, as well as trained, and they could not be brought together in London to rehearse together until the eve of the performance.

The actual production was in the hands of a professional, Warren Jenkins, an actor with an experience of life, as well as of acting and producing, which must have qualified him to deal with any conceivable emergency in the production of the NUTG masque. During the 1939-45 war he served with a Quaker medical unit operating in China, starting by driving a truck on the Burma

Road. He was on the last train out of French Indo-China when a bridge was blown up, and with members of the unit he constructed rafts and floated down river to the Chinese side. There he organized and accompanied supplies by air, by sampan and then by single-line rail over bamboo bridges, finally travelling by charcoal-burning truck up roads which were no more than a narrow ledge on the mountain side. Later he was lent to the Chinese Industrial Co-operatives, buying supplies and trucks in Burma and in charge of convoys which drove from Rangoon to the Gobi desert. So doing the rounds of the Guilds wishing to participate in *With This Sword* must have seemed child's play to him.

Back to the writing and plotting of the script: 'The problem of exits and entrances, "business", quick changes, sound effects and other mechanics of production now loom large. Up to eight hours a day are devoted to scripting, and outside these hours revisions have to be dictated to the secretary, who patiently types and retypes the script at top speed. The delightful part of the work is the patience, good temper and co-operation of the seven people working on the masque. None of them apparently minds either their hard work or their favourite idea being scrapped in the interest of the whole.

'The scenes are subject to many changes, and the drama adviser is feverishly trying to allocate them to Federations and to map out the producer's tour. At last, nearly distraught, she issues an ultimatum. She states the number of players offered by each Federation and demands that the remaining scenes be written strictly to fit the available actors. No extras allowed. Galley proofs and page proofs occupy a good deal of December. Our editorial adviser helps heroically until the not-so-early hours of the morning. Christmas holidays for the scriptwriter are spent correcting the last proofs for the printer who throughout is as good as his word and delivers the Play's "Strictly Confidential" advance copies just in time for the producer's first tour.' The music adviser (John Carol Case) was meanwhile enduring his own nightmare—finishing the composition of the music in time for the producer to take it with him. As for the head office staff, they were in danger of going quietly crazy as Federations withdrew their offers of participation, right up to the eve of the producer's tour, so that not only had 'parts' to be reallocated, but train journeys reorganized.

A crucial section of the masque was the intervention of the Three Monkeys. For instance, they sang on their first entry

'We're the optimistic flunkeys
We are madly happy monkeys
Wearing blinkers
We are wishful thinkers
Hear no evil, See no evil
Speak no evil too
For everything is lovely in the garden.'

Auditioning them could not begin until they had had time to rehearse the music written for their songs. There was naturally tension within the rank and file members as well as in Cromwell Place. This is how one member described it, 'Years ago (or so it seems) the Federation announced there would be a pageant in the Festival Hall and in blind faith about sixty members sent in their names to take part, not knowing what lay ahead. A mime class was formed. We had been allocated a small episode for six women but in view of the fact that so many were enthusiastic we were now to have two small episodes needing twenty-three women and some under-studies. There was great excitement then and the first mime class was for us mainly concerned with our chances of being chosen to go to London. Were there twenty-three women younger and more glamorous than us? Only thirty-six have turned up. Perhaps we *shall* get to London, even if only as understudies. We had a mime class a week under an excellent teacher. Then came the great night when the Federation chairman brought the scripts. How eagerly we bought them. It would mean a mime class a week until June and four days at least in London. Could we make it? Had we trained our husbands so that we could leave them for four days? We struck a sticky patch. Some members couldn't possibly get away in June and so our numbers fell below the required twenty-three. There was much heartburning among those left. The producer was due the next week and we could muster only twenty-two and no understudies. Should we all be turned down? Could we tell him we should have the number somehow by June? Would he regard us with scorn and a "How like women" look and say "It won't do; you'll have to revert to the original episode for six"? But oh, joy of joys, on the day of Mr Warren Hastings's visit more members came and we were twenty-four. Saved, with one to spare, and Mr Jenkins, so kind and friendly, just said "Try and get some more for understudies if you can."

'After that things seemed to go well. We booked accommodation in London, we worked out the cost, with the Federation paying expenses so that no one need be debarred through inability to pay. Then came props, when the stage manager studied her script. We had to find warming pans, coal buckets and what's this? A *hip* bath. At the next class they came with their silver trays, warming pans and coal buckets but no hip bath. By the time Mr Jenkins comes we do have a foot bath, which is something, but the search for the hip bath goes on. We imagine ourselves being subject to queer remarks as we make our way to London, but like the suffragettes of old we shall march bravely forwards, heads held high . . . and our hip bath not too prominent, we hope. At his next visit Mr Jenkins calls us "darlings" and we all feel twenty-one again. We are told we shall only be on stage for a few seconds, but does that sadden us? Not at all. We are thrilled to be even small cogs in the wheel, and we know that the whole will be something we shall talk about to our grandchildren.'

This, of course, was the sort of thing that was going on all over the country. There were thirty-eight mimed scenes, with music written by John Carol Case; performers came from twenty-one Federations, as far apart as the North-East coast and Plymouth; choir singers were from thirty-seven widely separated Federations. (The singers wore peacock blue capes and threw them back in the finale to reveal sashes of the Townswomen's Guild colours, red, white, and green.) Warren Jenkins's memories were often deeply moving. 'I was amazed by the quality and quantity of work done by the local producers and actors during my absence. . . . Suddenly the monkeys bound into my thoughts: monkeys, praise the gods, who thought rehearsals only begin with producers' tea and whose maternal activities had not diminished their agility one jot . . . chaotic memories of stranger hermaphroditical figures with female forms and black beards; of maternal figures being squeezed into girlish corsets; of the Composer's frightening frown at wheedling prayers to add illicit bars to concluded scores; but most of all of that amazing moment when through glass I saw three gentle ladies with hands on hips and hats on heads, swooning to a mike, recording blues, and then without warning clutch their noses and slap their thighs to shriek an abandoned jitterbug.'

The performers were only the 'front women'. Up and down the country scores of Guild needlewomen were busy. The wardrobe mistress, Gillian Armitage, provided workmanlike drawings and patterns of the costumes she had designed to guide the TG seamstresses in their work of love, and travelled up and down the country to see how they were progressing. She combed London shops for the right materials—right in colour and texture and right in price. She selected what hired costumes she could, but they were only a fraction of the 750 needed.

With This Sword was taken very seriously by leading journalists and men of the theatre. For instance, Kingsley Martin, editor of the *New Statesman* wrote, 'As a whole the performance was quite brilliantly written and staged; full of surprising and excellent twists and its music both delightful and ingenious.' An Oxford Playhouse producer, Oliver Wilkinson, went further, in complimenting the creators of the masque not only on a production that was 'bold, courageous and pointed', but on 'a really tremendous achievement not only in size and complexity, but in breaking new ground. You have achieved a tremendous step forward in drama for such widespread organizations as the NUTG. You have made history. I can't say how much I admire you for taking this great step. It is quite staggering.'

Big public presentations were only one aspect of the devotion of the Townswomen's Guilds to the performing arts. *With This Sword* was presented on a smaller scale by a number of Federations in the Midlands, North East and West Country, and there were many plays, documentaries, pageants and festivals from 1950 onwards, but drama was a subject of serious study as well as entertainment. Miss Graham Campbell set up a four-year study plan which combined lectures by distinguished people in the world of drama, and follow-up competitions. The first-year conference was concerned with introducing the Study Plan, the first over-all subject being on the various approaches to drama. The later phases covered play-making, play-presentation and theatre appreciation. In the play-writing competition the best scripts were published by the NUTG and some runners-up were accepted by outside publishers. Other competitions were for synopses for documentaries, with indications of the music, scenery and costumes; scrap books of local or Federation drama activities and group critiques of theatre visits. A National Drama Conference in 1955 on 'Women in the Theatre' brought together 500 TG members from seventy-eight Federations, eleven county drama advisers and representatives of the Ministry of Education, the BBC and twenty-two women's organizations. Two years later a National Drama Conference brought together 900 delegates and visitors, and the guest of honour was Dame Edith Evans. There was never any difficulty in recruiting distinguished men and women from the world of the arts and education to Townswomen's events. It was at this conference too that Mrs Norah Lambourne described the ingenious 'Adaptable Wardrobe' which proved such a stimulus to Guild drama sections right around the country.

'It may seem extravagant to you that a set of basic garments should be the aim of drama groups, but it pays, giving the actors a feeling of theatre and relaxation in costume on the stage. A stage costume should not be fancy dress.

'One of the worst sins in making period costumes is to use too little material—too skimpy dresses, too few petticoats, the wrong kind of material for the period. Use the right weight of material, no matter how cheap. It can be sacking, calico, old sheets, so long as it has bulk and is not skimped. If your basic garments are to be a really practical set they must be made of fairly tough material which will stand up to constant use. The material should be bulky and self-coloured. If the wardrobe is very well designed and made, a great many component parts can be used in performance.'

Mrs Mary Harrison designed an actual set of adaptable garments which were made by members of the North Middlesex Federation. Using some of the members as models at the National Drama Conference, Mrs Harrison showed how a standard basic costume could be adapted to different periods by changes of sleeves, collars, front panels, trimmings, etc. The basics were: A large, long, semi-circular skirt in heavy flannel, open at the front, with a big waist and adjustable hooks and eyes. This is useful also as a cloak and a Roman toga. It should not be hemmed; if it is a fraying material it should be doubled-sided, with the edges seamed; a straight skirt gathered on to a waistband open at the front, made of cotton—an invaluable peasant's skirt or petticoat; a similar straight skirt suitable for wearing over an Elizabethan patterned petticoat (can be made out of furnishing material of appropriate design) and matching sleeves; a T-shaped, long-sleeved tunic with wide sleeves for the mediaeval period, which can be worn over a skirt for a woman or over bound leggings for a man; a sleeveless fitted short jacket for either man or woman, to be worn over a skirt or with added sleeves fitted into the bodice with ties and loops; a fitted pointed bodice with a stiffened front (back fastening makes this more adaptable for different periods); sleeves, hoods, ruffs, and a cap headdress suitable to the Tudor or Elizabethan periods complete the basic wardrobe—Mrs Harrison was even able to contrive a Victorian costume from it, with a neat white collar and tartan trimmings.

The NUTG's advisers always put special emphasis on documentaries, feeling that they linked so much of the special interests of the members in their four 'sections', music, drama, arts and crafts, and social studies. In 1956 Lucile Spalding, under her pen name of 'Marion Jay', devised a documentary 'Pleasure and Pain in Education' which was written and performed at a National Social Studies Conference. It was a series of scenes, from Queen Elizabeth and Roger Ascham's widow, to a modern schoolmistress deeply distressed by the large size of her class and the grottiness of her schoolroom. It was published in 1960 by the Oxford University Press as part of a little volume 'Why Not Write a Documentary Play?', in which the other two advisers, Alison Graham Campbell and Helen Anderson also contributed ideas suitable for documentary themes. Miss Spalding always had grace and wit as well as clarity and sound sense. In her introduction she gave a tart warning: 'The crude technique of an old-fashioned pageant should be avoided, as (*enter a character in Elizabethan costume carrying a scroll*) "Hearken, Oh Gentles, to ye words of Roger Ascham." The narrator at this point is likely to produce a pair of modern spectacles and read us two pages of textbook.'

Alison Graham Campbell wrote delightfully on the same theme: 'Unfortunately the language of pageants and pseudo-historical plays cometh, oft-times, more readily to ye pen than doth ye real thing. An archbishop of our day is quoted as saying he does not care "two hoots" what people say to him on a certain issue—one of Elizabeth I's archbishops cared not "three chips". What talk there is has to be thoroughly dramatized. Chunks of textbook scattered through the dialogue never sound convincing.'

It would be a pity not to give an idea of the fun and enterprise that were to be found in grass-roots drama sections . . . the Guild who having performed a small play which had just one 'prop', left it on the bus . . . and it happened to be a *bus stop*. When, cold and weary, they collected it from the returning bus they were smitten with giggles, but the bus inspector seemed to find nothing either odd or comical about this bit of lost property; or the young Grangemouth member who was 'outlawed' from Guild plays for many years because in her very first walking-on part she walked out of the door about three seconds before the maid offered to show her into the garden. This same member was very impressed by 'fantastic fruit head-dresses made of papier-mâché by a young man at the Art College'—so impressed that twenty-three years ago she married him!

When the NUTG decided to bring all the 'cultural' sections under one heading, with one education officer instead of separate advisers for music, arts and crafts, music and social studies, there was a good deal of anxiety in the Guilds and Federations as to whether the interest would not flag, without the 'professionals' to stimulate and organize it. The most effective answer was a very remarkable performance of *The Miracle* at the Royal Albert Hall in May 1969. The producers were three leading Guild members, Councillor (later Alderman) Mrs Clara Thubrun, who was chairman of the National Education Sub-Committee, Mrs Hazel Helder (guilds North of the Thames) and Mrs Greta Raikes (South of the Thames). Choirs from near-London Federations were trained at area rehearsals by Mrs C. Brooksbank and Mrs Winifred Thompson. The Pro Arte Orchestra, with sixty players, was conducted by Graham Garton . . . orchestras of professional standard have always been beyond the reach of Townswomen's Guilds' accomplishment.

The Miracle, a vast spectacle to music by Humperdinck, was first produced in this country by Max Reinhardt in 1911, but the production which is still talked about by people who never saw it was by Leonid Massine in 1932, with Lady Diana Manners (daughter of the Duke of Rutland, who became Lady Diana Duff Cooper), as the Madonna. Her beauty was known around the world—in our times the only famous beauty who was not a star of stage or screen. Lady Diana was astounded when she heard that the NUTG were to produce this mammoth show on the platform of the Royal Albert Hall. It was the restriction of space that astonished her, but many professionals must have been even more startled by the enterprise of a collection of amateurs venturing to stage a production most professionals would fight shy of. The fact was, of course, that the professional stage could not *afford* to put on *The Miracle* with its huge cast and expense for costumes, scenery and so forth. A very large voluntary organization like the National Union of Townswomen's Guilds could draw on hundreds of unpaid actors, and hundreds of unpaid needlewomen. The logistics were even more frightening for *The Miracle* than for *With This Sword*. The cast of 400 monks, nuns, courtiers, soldiers, and townsfolk had to be dressed in costumes of the late fifteenth century designed by Harry Vaughan. The sets had to be erected immediately after the close of one National Council Meeting Session and removed before the next. The designs were mobile and made use of the tiers of choir stalls at the rear of the platform, and also incorporated the great organ and its mass of pipes. The moving masses of miming players had to be drilled with the precision of the Royal Marines.

The choir singers came from all the near-London Federations and it was no easy matter to track down rehearsal halls central enough for all to find from outlying areas and big enough to hold 500 singers and still give space for acting. Because of the difficulty of getting hold of vocal and piano scores and other problems, rehearsals could not begin until the end of January, so the call was 'come who can'. Whatever misgivings this 'open house' policy stirred at first it paid off handsomely in the end, revealing a streak of musical or dramatic talent even in the most retiring members. Three producers were rehearsing in three different places, but there was a remarkable degree of team spirit and co-operation. The actors *never* rehearsed with the orchestra, until the eve of performance, and had to rely either upon a piano accompaniment or on tape recordings made by the musical director and a friend on two pianos, singing the vocal parts. By the end of the rehearsals the tape was worn out—and at that one and only full rehearsal the cast hearing the full score with strings, woodwind, brass and timpani were apt to think that they were faced with a quite different work.

The leaders of the Townswomen's Guilds knew the Royal Albert Hall well, of course, from annual national council meetings held there. They knew that under the platform the whole place is a maze, a labyrinth of platforms at three levels. The building being circular, it is difficult to orientate oneself. 'The battle plan' was worked out with the utmost care. It was necessary not only to organize a traffic flow of nearly 600 persons, including the orchestra, but to improvise dressing-rooms for nuns, choristers, male singers, boy actors, girl and adult actors, soldiers, principals of both sexes and also arrange some seating accommodation for the groups who would be off stage at various times and who would be wanting to take the weight off their feet.

Some ingenious Organization Woman solved the problem by re-labelling the eleven entrances leading to the stage from the various points with letters of the alphabet and allotting corresponding letters to each section of the cast from the very beginning. Beneath the auditorium TG stewards with totem poles labelled A,B,C, and so on, had the task of herding gipsies, courtesans, nobles, peasants or whatever, to their correspondingly labelled entrances. All this averted the catastrophe of traffic jams . . . although it is recorded that one frustrated figure clad in surplice and cassock was desperately trying to join an ecclesiastical procession and hurried along a passage-way crying 'I've been told to go to H. Where the hell is H?'

As with costuming the masque *With This Sword*, there was a nation-wide sewing bee to provide the clothes for *The Miracle*. Masses of material of plain and gorgeous hues was donated by Courtaulds and by Mr Winstan Wykes, the husband of a former national chairman of the NUTG. The bolts of material were deposited at 2 Cromwell Place and the committee room was turned into a wholesale cutting room, whence the cut-out garments were distributed in bulk to the three rehearsal areas. 'As so often happens,' an observer commented, 'quite a few actress-seamstresses had to be urged not to look so lovely . . . peasants and beggars in particular.' After this lecture, one member returned with her peasant dress looking as though she had slept rough in it for months. Asked how she had achieved this effect with brand new material she said she had made a bundle of it and stuffed it up the chimney. When a theatrical costumier failed to provide a 'Virgin's Crown' a gorgeous diadem was designed and made by a Townswoman. Councillor Clara Thubrun caused consternation when she buttonholed an eminent physician at the hospital of which she was governor, saying she urgently wanted a baby. Her explanation 'It's for *The Miracle* you know', perplexed him still further and he was only restored to the world of everyday things when it was explained to him that Mrs Thubrun wanted a dummy such as is used in ante-natal teaching, for the Madonna to cradle in her arms.

The Miracle was indeed something of a miracle—but those who were responsible for it were convinced that even the boldest venture presents no insuperable problems given the enthusiasm, the ingenuity, and the dedication of the ordinary Townswomen's Guild member. The same music drama was produced, with the same kind of courage and enterprise, in 1974 by the Newcastle-upon-Tyne North Federation with a cast of 200 before an audience of 2,000.

Individual Guilds and Federations tended to be inspired to greater efforts by these large-scale national efforts which were so much praised. Many entered British Drama League festivals. What top-class amateurs some of these Guild groups were is instanced by the South Norwood Afternoon TG who in 1967 made history as the first all-women group to reach the British final of the British Drama League Festival of Community Drama, winning on the way three cups and a shield. The play they chose was *A Tragedy Rehearsed*, an excerpt from Sheridan's *The Critic*. They journeyed to Edinburgh, but failed to win. In 1971 they presented García Lorca's play *Dona Rosita the Spinster* and were invited to perform it at the English final in York. Unfortunately their coach broke down and having arrived two hours late they missed their lighting rehearsal, had too little time to settle down, and were beaten by a team from the West of England who later won the British final also. This was not South Norwood's lucky day—their coach broke down again on the return journey and they had to wait on the hard shoulder of the motorway from 2 a.m. to 4.30 a.m. and reached home at 9.30 next morning! This gallant group has disbanded now, but the South Norwood secretary cherishes the hope that new recruits will achieve the same standard as the earlier group . . . and indeed, have better luck.

The interest in drama survives to the present day and very many groups are active. The monthly journal *The Townswoman* keeps a 'Play Bank' which consists of plays written by Townswomen which have been successfully performed by TGs. Three reading copies at a time may be borrowed from the Play Bank in return for a stamped addressed envelope but they have to be returned after seven days. Then acting copies can be ordered for 35p each, plus postage. But there is no acting fee, for the Townswomen authors offer their plays to all other Guilds for their enjoyment. Some of the plays are 'strong drama' or mysteries, some comedies, and some just short sketches to entertain the company for the 'social half hour' . . . but all have the advantage of being written with a cast of amateur actresses in mind. One can hear echoes, though, of the voices of the exponents of documentary drama, Margaret Leona, Alison Graham Campbell, Lucile Spalding, urging the members to create drama out of their own experience of life and their own social studies and concern with 'public questions'.

This Play Bank is typical of the way the current *Townswoman* fosters the essential activities of the Guilds, just as it did through the Advisers' Notes in the early days. The Play Bank, in fact, grew out of a 'Write Your Own Play' competition, for which 137 entries were received and two were published commercially. There have also been a 'Write Your Own Guide Book' competition which produced some beautiful illustrated compilations in Architectural Heritage Year, 'Write Your Own Cookbook' and 'Write Your Own Song', in which some entries were astonishingly professional. Kathleen Merritt and Margaret Leona, first music and first drama advisers, would be proud of these descendants of the early TG members they inspired.

5

Acorn into Oak Tree

How *does* an organization grow from a handful of enthusiasts, a handful of local units, into a national network involving scores of thousands? There is no sure-fire recipe for growth. All one can say is that there has to be a need, felt but hitherto unidentified, and dedicated persons willing to try to meet it. Since the end of the 1939–45 war, many new organizations have burgeoned in response to a clear need, like the Pre-School Playgroups Association or the National Association for the Welfare of Children in Hospital, but all these have started on a completely voluntary basis. The National Union of Townswomen's Guilds from the word 'go' had an efficient, paid, chief executive officer, clerical help, and an office to service the movement, though of course it would not have grown as it did without precisely the kind of devotion that got the post-war voluntary societies off the ground.

The relationship of paid and unpaid officials has always been tricky, as many a large women's organization has found. The NUTG was exceptionally fortunate in that its first chief voluntary officer, Alice Franklin, and its first paid executive, Gertrude Horton, became close personal friends and worked together most amicably in the formation of the NU and right through the testing war years with the then chairman, Miss Joan Loring, and with the executive which, with the agreement of the Guilds, stayed in office until after the end of hostilities. Everyone realized that plans would have to be made for expansion when peace returned— indeed, a special Council Meeting was called for May 1944 to discuss this very subject, but the 'doodlebugs' began to fall on

London and it was called off. People thought that the women coming out of the Forces and out of the munitions factories would need some kind of fulfilling organized activity and companionship of the kind the Townswomen's Guilds provided, but no one could have foreseen the positive hunger for Guilds that would be displayed.

To be part of a rapidly expanding movement is gratifying for everybody . . . but expansion does need a lot of money, and by 1945 this had become a real worry. Although it was announced at the 1945 special Council Meeting at Southport that the Ministry of Education had decided to make a grant to increase the NUTG headquarters staff so as to expand its work 'in the promotion of liberal education for adults', Miss Franklin felt impelled to plead with the Guilds to make a supreme effort during 1945 and the two following years to raise enough money to sustain the expansion programme. The delegates agreed to the expansion programme and they agreed, too, to recommend to the Guilds that they should raise £10,000 in 1945 and again in 1946—or £20 per Guild of 100. But at the 1946 Council Meeting there was quite a lot of opposition to the call to Guilds for £20. Some delegates thought the salaries paid to the officials were too big. Surely the leaders in London could run the movement on 'a little less financial basis', as one delegate put it. 'What does London do for us?', asked another. Watford moved to halve the 'colossal' budget of £20,000, but this was comfortably defeated. In 1947 the call for yet another £10,000 was agreed, but because there were by then more Guilds, the contribution from each was reduced from £20 to £15.

The NUTG has always presented a carefully calculated budget to its annual Council Meeting. In the three post-war years the anticipated revenue was expected to cover easily the expected increase in expenditure . . . and did, except that in 1947 dry rot in the basement of 2 Cromwell Place involved a lot of unforeseen expense. Mrs Hilda Christian, then the national treasurer, had to admit to the 1948 National Council Meeting that instead of starting the financial year with a balance of £7,011, as had been hoped, they started in fact 'minus £250'. It is extraordinary that in such a lively movement, filling so many diverse needs, the Expansion Fund target was never once met. In the 1970s the national chairman,

Mrs Eileen Coram, who was previously national treasurer, had to
say just the same kind of thing as Mrs Christian said in 1948.
'Very many Guilds have always given generously,' said Mrs
Christian. 'Others have sent quite small contributions quite out
of proportion to their membership. Others, well able to do so,
have made little or no effort to raise their share of the sum agreed,
although during the year those same Guilds raise many hundreds
of pounds for other charities. Some Guilds hold the point of view
that as their own delegate was not instructed to vote for these
budgets, they take no responsibility for the amount agreed. This
is surely a negation of the fundamental principles of democracy.
Furthermore, to dishonour agreements is a form of social dis-
honesty.' Blunter words than Mrs Coram would use in 1977,
but her sentiments echo Mrs Christian's, and no doubt those of the
leaders of many other organizations. Why is raising money for
charity so much more satisfying than raising the money needed to
keep afloat the organization which makes these charitable efforts
possible? No one yet has solved this mystery.

The unpleasant fact had to be faced in 1949 that there was an
overdraft of £1,625. This must have been very upsetting for
conscientious officials quite unused to being 'in the red', but the
situation was much more serious because two of the guarantors
of the overdraft, Alice Franklin and Joan Loring, gave notice that
they were about to withdraw their guarantee. This was the outcome,
it seems pretty clear now, of an explosion in the central control of
the NUTG which resulted in the end of the long reign of the
triumvirate of Loring, Franklin, and Horton. A bursting of these
bonds was probably inevitable sooner or later, for the movement
was mushrooming in an extraordinary fashion. New methods of
organization were probably necessary, and a firmer financial
structure. However that may be, Mrs Mary Courtney was the
catalyst, a Scotswoman living in Bristol with her doctor husband.
At the outbreak of war she had been more or less thrust into the
chairmanship of her Guild and very soon was co-opted on to the
national executive—on the suggestion of Alice Franklin. She was
not only an able and experienced voluntary worker, a national
vice-president of the YWCA and so on, but an inspiring orator
with a natural instinct for leadership. Right through the war
years she went up to London regularly, spending two or three

days at a time in the office. When Miss Loring resigned the chairmanship in 1948, Mrs Courtney was elected. When the financial
and organizational difficulties of the movement became plain,
the paid staff organizers asked for a meeting with the National
Union officers. Many of these staff organizers were old suffrage
organizers, experienced and capable but naturally accustomed to
their independence, and not always easy to handle by newcomers
who had not been through the mill of the old suffrage campaigns.
They didn't like their duties being put down in black and white,
they didn't like taking instructions from the NU staff, and most
of all they disliked the proposal that they should be attached to
groups of Federations, for they preferred to be based on 2 Cromwell Place. The meeting of the organizers with the chairman,
Miss Loring, achieved very little and the officers themselves
disagreed.

So at the executive meeting of June 1948 it was agreed to set up
an organization sub-committee, which again met the paid organizing staff. It was over the chairmanship of this committee that the
breach with Miss Franklin came. Mrs Courtney felt that she, as
the new national chairman, should take the chair of this special
committee. Miss Franklin felt that she should be chairman, as
organizing secretary—as the treasurer was chairman of the
Finance Committee. It was put to the vote and Mrs Courtney was
elected by fourteen votes to seven. Miss Franklin resigned and Mrs
Horton was clearly *persona non grata* in the new set-up and after
some miserable weeks asked the executive to terminate her
contract.

There must have been a good deal of 'shock and horror' throughout the movement, for Miss Franklin was popular all over the
country. A contemporary tribute from Mrs A. A. Mitchell described
her in glowing language. 'Since time immemorial Nature, perhaps
tiring of a monotonous lack of variety, has sent forth a genius,
someone with natural ability and special mental endowments.
Such individuals create their own aura and as a rule it is not until
their activities are withdrawn that their influence and achievements
are fully realized and appreciated. Alice Franklin has helped to
lay the foundations of a national movement so securely and has so
guided its growth and vigour that the edifice no longer needs
props and scaffolding, but will increase its strength by its demo-

cratic self-government, for which she so strenuously laboured. Miss Franklin never sat back and said "That's all right, that will do", but ever from her brain ideas evolved for expansion, experiment and development which she urged with characteristic patience upon her fellow-workers.'

Alice Franklin's chief creation was the Common Meeting Ground, which she defended fanatically from erosion and during the sixteen years in which she worked practically round the clock, indefatigable and unpaid, the movement grew from 108 Guilds to more than 1,000. But Mrs Mitchell's heartfelt tribute may give a clue to the conflict which led to her resignation; 'Risk of unpopularity never deflected her from the course that seemed right to her. Her courage, sincerity and never-failing sense of humour enabled Miss Franklin to cope with open opposition successfully and to gain the confidence of her opponents. She often threw open a choice of opinions or action with an ingenuous or provocative "I don't know". Her strong personality will be greatly missed throughout the national movement. Her name will be spoken with affection and respect by those who laboured with and sometimes differed from her over the years. Her words will often be quoted and the result of her Herculean work will continue throughout England, Scotland and Wales and even, as our not infrequent visitors tell us, will reach the other side of the world.'

Looking back across the thirty years since Miss Franklin's retirement, a member of the Head Office staff, Anne Elias who worked with her, emphasizes the clash of personalities that led up to the breach. 'She could be very stubborn, very obstinate,' she said. 'I think she antagonized many people. If she had reached a certain opinion she wouldn't give in.' Nor did her sense of humour please everyone. Long after her retirement from the NUTG she grinned at one of the staff advisers whom she met at a function of another women's organization and said under her breath, 'Be careful. You had better not be seen talking to me.'

Naturally Guilds up and down the country felt Miss Franklin's departure acutely, and some asked that the minutes of the executive meetings leading up to it should be made public. Mrs Courtney wrote a formal account of the affair to chairmen of the Federations but they had to accept it as it was. 'Members of Federations will appreciate the impossibility of making available the minutes of the

Executive Committee,' she wrote. 'It was after the fullest consideration of the relevant information that the decision was reached,
in the belief that it was in the best interests of the movement.
Federations will appreciate the inadvisability of entering into
further controversy when once a decision has been reached.'
Miss Franklin was evidently not the only NUTG leader who,
when she had reached a certain opinion, would not give in.

One or two Guilds suggested a presentation fund for Miss
Franklin but she would have none of it. Typically she referred the
proposal to the Constitution as it applied to present and retiring
officers of Guilds. 'The NU has never given a lead on this subject,
but as Function 2 of the Constitution includes the phrase "encouraging the members to equip themselves, as individuals, for
service to the community" the privilege of being chosen to serve
ought to be enough. There has never been a presentation to an
NU officer, so there is no precedent, but I feel that having been
allowed the privilege of helping to build the movement for so
many years is something that does not call for a presentation:
it is the other way round. I feel I should thank those who allowed me
that privilege and who have given me fifteen years of happy
memories which are mine for keeps.'

And so the two pioneers who had practically created the
structure of the NUTG departed. Call them nannies, call them
governesses, call them what you will. They were very remarkable
women. Though Miss Franklin lived until the age of seventy-nine,
dying in 1964, her name never again appeared in NUTG annual
reports, nor in any accounts of events in *The Townswoman*. Mrs
Horton became secretary of the Fawcett Society in succession to
Miss Philippa Strachey, and when she was living in retirement in
Epsom, at the time this book was being written, members of the
Epsom Guilds had not even heard her name. The structure these
two and their committee members had created and cherished
proved to be very long lasting.

In Mrs Courtney the movement had found a leader quite different
in style but equally dedicated to the cause. The 'New Plan'
for organization, adopted in 1948, widened the democratic control
and was, in fact, a pretty thorough shake-up. A Central Council
was to be elected, with two delegates from each Federation, to be
responsible for the policy of the National Union. The intention

was that this should meet at least two or three times a year. It has sixteen members, half elected annually for a two-year stint. The Council nominates and elects the National Executive, of whom eight have to be members of the Central Council—whose meetings, therefore, are a shop window for those who would like to take on further responsibility. Four other members must already have served at least a year on the NUTG executive, so that continuity is assured. There is no proviso that the elected members must be drawn from various regions of the UK, so there may at times be a preponderance of members living in the Home Counties. The *members* are predominantly in the Home Counties, too—an estimated two thirds of the membership.

The annual meeting at which this new plan was adopted covered two whole sessions and twenty-nine resolutions, with many amendments, were debated. Everyone who is involved in organization conferences knows that the one area of debate calculated to heighten interest and arouse really strong emotions is procedure, rules, constitution. When this marathon discussion of the NUTG's constitution was completed an outsize copy of a coloured chart depicting the pattern of the movement's organization was hoisted above the platform. It is not reported that there were cheers, but one can almost hear them echoing across the years. All this was in aid of 'democratizing' the movement. It was also necessary to put its finances on a better basis. In 1949 it was decided to replace the voluntary contribution to the National Union by a definite national affiliation fee and to increase the subscription of the individual Guild member from 2s [10p] to 4s [20p] a year. The head office was to be reorganized 'under the expert guidance of a business consultant, in the hope of achieving substantial economies', though nothing seemed to come of this. After Miss Franklin and Miss Loring withdrew their overdraft guarantees, an urgent appeal was made to every Guild to send £5 urgently. By 25 May of that year 541 Guilds had donated £3,087 and the NUTG was solvent again . . . but the twenty-first birthday concert due to be held in the Albert Hall that November under Kathleen Merritt's direction was cancelled, even though the Guild choirs had been practising for some time. It was also agreed not to hold the first new Central Council meetings until 1950. All this retrenchment must have been sadly disappointing, but the 1,000th Guild had been opened—at

Bath, in November 1948—and the Ministry of Education and
Scottish Education Department were now between them making
grants of £3,500.

Right from the beginning the Scottish membership has been very
important to the NUTG. Very early in her presidency Mrs Corbett
Ashby toured the Scottish fishing villages and other centres. Mrs
Mary Courtney was equally enthusiastic—she was, of course, a Scot
herself. In the very first issue of *The Townswoman*, April 1933,
there is an account of a tea party at 10 Downing St, where the
Prime Minister's younger daughter, Miss Sheila MacDonald, was
hostess to Lady Cynthia Colville, Mrs Corbett Ashby, and about
250 other guests, invited to support an appeal to extend the Townswomen's work in Scotland.

Many were the mass rallies and festivals organized by the
Scottish Regional Committee. Members came from towns in the
far north right through to the Border country—an International
Co-operation Year pageant in 1965 drew 2,000 Guild members to
Stirling.

Devolution, by way of a separate 'Scottish Office' was specifi-
cally rejected in 1955, and the NUTG is proud to be the one large
women's organization which covers the whole of the United
Kingdom, though it has representation on all the Scottish advisory
bodies in addition to the NU representation on the similar 'British'
bodies.

Reorganization of the movement's finances in 1948 made
possible expansion right throughout the country. This was
achieved, of course, by a balance between the enthusiasm of
volunteers and the trained skill of the professionals, and it was
crucial to NUTG thinking that the volunteers themselves must be
trained. This was chiefly done in 'TG Helpers' schools. Even in
the immediate post-war year the Guilds budgeted for three
residential schools and £600 was allocated for this, to cover
residence, transport, fares and tuition other than by the TGs' own
staff and voluntary officers. The first school of which there seems
to be a record was held at High Leigh, Hoddesdon, in December
1947, with thirty-nine students from Guilds as far apart as Buckie
and Banffshire and Saltash in Cornwall. The students had
indicated beforehand in what subjects they would like to qualify
as helpers, for they were to be trained for specialist duties, not as

women of all work. The specialities were secretarial, finance,
programme planning and TG reconnaissance (a method of getting
members to participate in research into questions of social and
public importance). Everyone was given a chance during the
school, though, to volunteer for other subjects. Miss Franklin
and Mrs Horton were the first tutors, with the husband of a
Guild member who was an accountant. He deputized for her
because she had been taken ill. The day the school ended the staff
organizers went into conference at 2 Cromwell Place, and every
student's attainment and first test was considered in detail, just
as if it had been a college 'business studies' course. Seven poor
ladies failed to pass this first test, but a few did so well in the
finance section that they were accepted with no further training.
The rest went on to a further test under a staff organizer 'in the
field'.

One of the students wrote illuminatingly about the way this
school was run: 'One day we continued the lines of "make-believe"
begun in our homework, and became an imaginary Guild, "Any-
town Evening Guild" with a chairman, "Mrs Leader" (taken by
Mrs Horton). In this way we learned how to run an ordinary
Guild meeting with speed and interest and even the financial
statement came alive.'

The TG Helpers, important as they continued to be throughout
this expansion period, worked within a framework of paid professional organizers. By 1952 there were eleven of these, covering
all areas of Great Britain. During their three months' intensive
training, these officers were paid at the rate of £300 a year. This
rose to £350 and then by annual increments to £450. The training
was concentrated on working alongside visiting organizers and
being given work to do under their supervision. They were all
allocated to given areas and their chief function was the formation
of new Guilds.

'Sometimes there are sufficient interested people for a Guild to
be formed at once,' members were told, 'and the staff organizer
has only to assure herself that these form a cross section, so that
the common meeting ground is provided. At other times the
organizer has to pay three or four visits and see personally a large
number of individuals before even a preliminary meeting can be
held. She must try to make a good impression on these people,

who are usually complete strangers to her, and waken their interest in the TG movement, of which they may be hearing for the first time. The amount of help from the Federations varies greatly.

'The staff organizer has to attend six formation meetings, "public" "full" and "committee". The sixth, the programme planning committee, may be taken by TG Helpers. All this may take from six to ten weeks. Staff organizers have to plan their work so that they have several Guild formations at various stages at the same time. This almost invariably results in a good deal of overlapping and the organizers frequently find the pressure of work exceedingly heavy. The organizers also have to spend a good deal of time on clerical work—often far more than on meetings—for detailed reports have to be sent to the NU at every stage, lists of members made out, subscriptions handled etc.'

The complexity and thoroughness of this recruiting operation is quite startling to us in the seventies. It can only be compared with the selection and training of the voluntary workers for the Citizens Advice Bureaux and Marriage Guidance Councils. It seems obvious that there was a need for organizations like the Townswomen's Guild and in many places women were queueing up for help in forming Guilds according to the correct pattern, but it is hard to avoid the feeling that there was a kind of missionary zeal which was almost obsessional. TG Helpers came to be trained in 'formation work' to meet the great need, but this was to supplement the staff organizers, not to lighten their load. 'The work of the TG Helpers covers the first and second meetings only, and though there may be another TG Helper in the neighbourhood able to conduct the programme planning meeting, this still leaves the Staff Organizer with all the work in connection with the first Guild meeting.'

'Organizer' was a job, a very demanding and not specially well paid job. One rather wonders how it came to attract so many lively-minded women in the fifties when there was no dire shortage of employment. The TG organizers had not only to set up the new Guilds but to conduct schools in Guild management and procedure and attend all sorts of Federation functions, rallies, festivals, exhibitions, and so on. This was the organizer's only real opportunity to see the fruit of her labours, the Guilds she had formed busily and happily at work. There are hints that things were not always serene and jolly for the organizers, and that they were sometimes regarded with suspicion—the old story, which seems to run right through big organizations, that voluntary workers are apt to be suspicious of those who get a salary for doing very similar work. 'It is difficult for a staff organizer to get regular and adequate meals. This is increasingly so now that the cost of meals on trains is prohibitive. Staff organizers receive 25s [£1.25] a day maintenance allowance and not 30s [£1.50], as with the voluntary members of the movement.'

Were there complaints of slacking? An article in *The Townswoman* shows that there must have been rather pointed criticisms from time to time. 'The staff organizer,' members were assured, 'often spends a large part of the week-end on clerical work and is never free of the telephone. It often happens that a staff organizer is seen doing her shopping or taking her recreation at a time when a member considers she ought to be working. This has resulted sometimes in remarks about the free time staff organizers appear to have. Nothing can be more hurtful to conscientious and hard-working organizers than to have such things said about them, when they have more than likely been out until midnight the day before and may have another meeting that evening. The staff organizer's greatest encouragement and reward is the appreciation of the movement of what she is doing. Unkind criticism, based on what may be incomplete knowledge, can have a very depressing effect on her work.'

Some of the complaints must have been pretty vigorous, for the article goes on 'The National Union will always supply information or investigate legitimate grievances and does at all times keep a watchful eye on the work they do. The organizers report fully to the National Union. They are doing a very difficult job with courage and enthusiasm.'

'The difficult job' never had much future in it as a career. Miss Dorothy Milnes, a former ATS driver, became a staff organizer for Kent immediately after the war, was later responsible for Sussex and East Anglia, moved to Cromwell Place as an organization officer and then was appointed national general secretary. But she did not stay very long. Her successor, Miss C. L. H. Cowper, a graduate in public administration had learned to know the movement and the executive committee as Ministry of Education assessor. (The Ministry still sends a representative to national executive meetings—presumably to make sure that the grant is being well spent!) The then chairman, Mrs Mary Courtney, was much impressed by Miss Cowper's academic qualifications and her approach to the work was very much in line with Mrs Courtney's own. Indeed she set a pattern of social studies conferences which made a lasting impact on the movement. Her 'Woman in the Changing World' study conference plan was seminal for a number of years. In 1976 Mrs Courtney said 'The stamp of Miss Cowper is still on the movement', despite the fact that she had had to retire in 1951 because of the illness of her mother.

There tends always to be a conflict between concentrating all possible resources on an efficient headquarters which can service the 'branches' properly and extending the work of volunteers. Members round the country are apt to question whether it is really necessary for so much of their affiliation fee to be spent on the headquarters staff, and unless the national general secretary can communicate very intimately with the Guilds, this unease quickly grows. Mrs Lillias Norman, the quiet Scot who became national secretary in 1954, found her own means of communication, in her editorials in *The Townswoman*. One or two colleagues said later that they thought her a 'cold' personality, but her writings suggest that she was not at all cold, only very reserved and very shy in face-to-face encounters. She was the only national secretary after Mrs Horton who tried to give the ordinary members a feeling of what life was like in 2 Cromwell Place and what kind and quantity of work went on there. In her New Year issue of 1958 she wrote rather sadly 'I feel I am in danger of becoming a rubber stamp—a name at the end of a circular which evokes no feeling except perhaps of boredom. And I aspire to something more personal. Perhaps if I passed on to you from time to time a few words about my sallies into the midst of Guild members at work and play it might serve this purpose.'

She must surely have been right? The awareness of belonging to a great *national* organization is not easy to maintain. Mrs Winifred Clark, then a national vice-chairman, referred in 1975 to the distance between the ordinary Guild member and 'That lot at the top' when announcing plans to revive an idea from the

NUTG's early days, of 'At Homes' at headquarters once a month from March 1975 to March 1976.

Mrs Norman described for *Townswoman* readers what it actually felt like at the head office in the busy months of spring. 'Despite the longing all good housewives have to indulge in a thorough spring-cleaning the NU decided to wait until summer because the thought of having cleaners and painters with all their paraphernalia in the office during the next month or two is almost too much to bear. The tempo is increasing fast in the preparation for the NCM, the National Elections, the rehearsals of *The Gift* and the Salzburg tour.

'We have just had the builders in, making a telephone booth on one of the staircase landings. This gives us much needed space in the general office, as well as providing quiet for our telephone operator. She is quite pleased to have an office of her own and sit in splendid isolation. We feel we are becoming like the Old Woman Who Lived in a Shoe—there is always room for just one more. And now for the moment we have cheated the confines of material walls with a little ingenuity and have gained a little elbow room. Also I must tell you we are becoming quite up-to-date, having acquired an electric floor-polisher. It has been on our conscience that we should ask anyone to go down on her knees and polish these wide expanses of linoleum. But now the Committee Room floor is looking as it has never done before and throwing back reflections quite in the style of the well-known advertisement.' The staff enjoyed equally the refurbishing which took place in 1977. Lady Henniker Heaton, administration secretary, chose the elegant colour scheme—pale dusty pink walls, mushroom brown paint and bitter chocolate carpeting.

When representatives of fifty Guilds—drawn at random, Federation by Federation, so as to ensure that two from every part of the country could be invited—came to Cromwell Place in 1976–77 it was all delightfully homely. Probably the outstanding impression most of the visitors took away was of the four flights of stairs, getting steeper and steeper to the top of the tall narrow building. Any member who had the idea that 'that lot at the top' lived in luxurious ease must have lost it for ever as she panted up the last flight of stairs to the small offices where the chief organizer, Mrs Bessie Hall, the education secretary, Miss Julia Nicholson, and

the oldest member of staff, Miss Elias, have their small rooms.
As the visitors toured the building and met staff and NEC
members they were able to compare notes with other Guild
members. Two NEC members prepared a buffet lunch . . . a
typical female way of saving time and money. Can one imagine
executive members of any exclusively male organization thinking
this a worthwhile contribution to the success of a visit from
provincial members? (Even if they knew how to begin to set about
it!)

The benefit was, of course, two-way. Mrs Hall wrote 'We at NU
are tremendously encouraged and stimulated when we realize
how many difficulties are overcome in order to visit us. Some have
baby-sitters to find (including Dad) for very small children.
Some must leave home in the early hours and travel home the
same night. One wrote to thank us on arrival in Scotland at nearly
midnight after her long day, but I think the reward for enthusiasm
goes to the lady due to move house at 8 a.m. after arriving home
very late at night after her London visit. We had our usual obstacles to overcome, of course, such as "go slows" and train strikes.
Once we had a sorrowful call on the morning of the "at-home" to
say "I'm at the station all dressed up and nowhere to go." No
trains! (There was a happy ending to this one—she came to the
next "At-home".)'

Summing up, Mrs Hall hoped that 'by this close contact with
Guild members we can begin to narrow the gap which still exists
between NU and Guild members. It seems to come as a surprise
to some of our visitors that we are TG members who are just as
proud of belonging to our Guilds as anyone else. These At Homes
are occasions when we can be frank with one another and when
we all realize we have to contend with the same problems.'

In May 1955 Lillias Norman gave to the members a very detailed
guide to what kept a staff of twenty-three busy every week, all
the year round. It is worth recording as evidence of what a
complicated operation a voluntary organization becomes as it
grows in numbers.

'The General Office: Mail is sorted and distributed, morning
and midday and collected, franked and dispatched in the afternoon.
Here all the filing is done. Each Guild and Federation has its own
file. The General Office attends also to duplicating, and our

Roneo machine is kept in nearly constant commission. The telephone switchboard is in this office and the increasing traffic on our lines has made it necessary to appoint a telephonist to handle it all. A packer in the basement sees to the despatch of parcels. At the peak period of several weeks in the autumn up to 100 parcels a day leave the office and voluntary help is again given by Guild members as well as by other members of staff.

'Organization Department: This is the basis of all the rest of the work—the formation of new Guilds, committee schools, speakers, interpretation of the Constitution and Rules and the answering of a large number of questions on the general management of Guild affairs. The work of all organizers and TG Helpers is kept under review. Index cards are made out for each of the new officers by the General Office, for the treasurer by the Finance Department, and for the secretary by the *Townswoman* department. A parcel of stationery is sent to the new Guild, containing a membership book, membership cards, writing pad, annual report form and samples of other items. A visit by a member of the National Executive is arranged. Last year 143 new Guilds were formed. Half a dozen letters come each week to this department wanting to know where the nearest Guild meets. We are delighted to answer, though we may have to spend quite a time studying street plans.'

At that time the NUTG still had three professional 'advisers', Miss Lucile Spalding for social studies and arts and crafts, Miss Alison Graham Campbell for drama, and Miss Helen Anderson for music. These advisers had two full-time typists and another assistant kept the minutes of the education sub-committee, handled conference ticket arrangements and scanned minutes from the Federations, Guilds, and outside bodies.

In the Finance Department the Chief Clerk had '4½' assistants— one of the ledger clerks spent half her time getting estimates for stationery supplies, interviewing salesmen, and issuing stationery. During the financial year the busiest times were when the books were closed for the annual audit; the stock-taking at the beginning of the year, and the balancing of books; and from November onwards the checking of the Guilds' own audited accounts. The operation of the fares pool at the National Council Meeting was always a time-taking and complicated operation.

The Townswoman, another hard-worked department, was at this time in the hands of the national general secretary herself. She had one clerk to see to the collating of the material for publication and from autumn 1954 onwards she had Miss Margaret Playle as 'editorial consultant' as well as NUTG publicity officer. As for her own role, Mrs Norman described it thus: 'The National General Secretary must be available for consultation at all times and this means that at the end of many a day there is nothing concrete to show for the hours worked. More tangible is my responsibility for the agenda, minutes and reports of the National Council Meeting once a year, the Central Council Meetings twice a year, about seven meetings of the Executive Committee and meetings of various sub-committees.'

No paid chief officer of a national voluntary organization can have an easy life. To maintain a balance between being an efficient secretary to her immediate employers, the national executive, being a good controller and trainer of the head office staff, giving leadership to the whole movement and being available for collaboration with other organizations and able to answer questions from the media (newspapers, radio, and television), must be of nightmare complexity. Unless she goes out and about among the rank-and-file membership the paid national secretary is losing a great deal of her potential value to the movement, because she provides continuity, and is not liable, like elected executive members, to disappear after three, four or five years; she has probably met every organizational, and even ideological, problem many times before, and she has imbibed her organization's basic policy almost with her daily cups of tea and coffee.

If the national secretary is a good speaker she will be doubly welcome—but if the national chairman is also a powerful orator it is less important for the paid secretary to move about the country, and the elected chairman is subject to the temptation to think that this is almost exclusively *her* role. One great satisfaction of top office in voluntary movements, compensating for the tremendous demands on time and energy and loss of home life, is being able to travel all over the country, to be met, entertained, welcomed and honoured as a VIP by nice women whose admiration and gratitude shine from their eyes. It can be heady stuff, and not every woman whose talent for inspiring leadership is expressed from the platform

Imogen Holst, conductor and composer, wrote a cantata, *The Sun's Journey*, especially for the Townswomen, and conducted it at the Kingsway Hall, 1967, as part of the National Music Festival in which 511 choirs took part.

The interests of Guild members are indeed diverse:

Leslie Crowther and Glenda Jackson with entries for *The Townswoman* toy competition auctioned for handicapped children;

(*left*) HRH Princess Alice, The Duchess of Gloucester admiring lace making at an Ideal Home Exhibition;

(*top right*) A basketry class;

(*right*) A group of landscape painters from Bangor, Co Down.

The Brides of Begerin
presented at the National
Drama Conference.

A rehearsal of *With this
Sword* on the terrace of
the Royal Festival Hall,
1954.

is anxious to share the glory with her 'professional' colleague. Not every woman elected to high office in an organization really thinks of even the top paid official as a 'colleague'. Often, possibly too often, the paid chief executive never ceases to be regarded as an employee. Many professional women working for voluntary associations will privately assert that committees, even very experienced committees, tend to treat their professional staff rather as middle-class Victorian housewives treated their maids, cooks and governesses. Almost inevitably the voluntary workers tend to think of themselves as slightly superior beings because they are doing for nothing but love what the paid staff do for a salary. But that leaves out the factor that the professional *also* works for love, and often works extremely hard and for very long hours.

When Lillias Norman retired as national general secretary through ill-health in 1965, after fifteen years in various capacities, she said, 'It was enormous fun and enormously hard work. But one did it with a will, because one believed in its purpose and had faith in its members.' Most of the former staff advisers to the NUTG said the same—'I never worked so hard'. When she retired, also after months of what proved to be a terminal illness, Marjorie Erskine-Wyse said sorrowfully, 'It is my fond hope that I will be permitted to serve the movement in some way, however minor.' And this after twenty years of hard slog and internal battles that were sometimes painful.

It almost seems as if there ought to be a training course for the professional Organization Women. They need to be able and enterprising, but above all things tactful and patient, for their job is to ensure that the voluntary workers really run the show, or at least appear to do so, for without this opportunity for service at the top level, the supply of volunteers might very easily dry up. Women come into this form of paid service in so many different ways, with such very different qualities and qualifications. Dame Frances Farrer, for many years the general secretary of the National Federation of Women's Institutes, must have fitted into the job as the hand into the glove—she was essentially a Surrey villager by upbringing, one of the 'landed gentry' whose dedication to public service was instilled from their childhood. It must also have helped that she was an earl's daughter. Dame Caroline Haslett, director of the Electrical Association for Women from 1924 to

1956, came from the Women's Engineering Society to *found* the 'Electrical Women'. Mrs Kathleen Kempton, general secretary of the Co-operative Women's Guild, was practically born into the co-operative movement and had been actively associated with it since childhood. The National Association of Women's Clubs rejoiced in the energy, ebullience, and efficiency of Baroness Phillips for many years.

These leading ladies have not much in common in background, or perhaps in temperament. The same certainly applies to the women who have served as national general secretary of the NUTG. Miss C. L. H. Cowper who had a sadly brief reign in the early fifties, had been a Ministry of Education assessor on the NUTG executive; Lillias Norman had, so to speak, trained in the movement, for she was staff organizer for South-eastern Federations before becoming secretary of the organization sub-committee and then assistant secretary before being appointed national general secretary in 1954.

Marjorie Erskine-Wyse could not have been more different, either in experience, in temperament, or in background—she was an Australian. One thought of her primarily as a journalist and, indeed, she came to the NUTG from the Women's Institutes' journal *Home and Country*, to become conference secretary. She then went off to Beirut to be features editor of a new English daily newspaper there. She came back to edit *The Townswoman*, and perhaps it remained her first care in all her NU duties. But she had been a schoolteacher with a diploma in domestic science, a verbatim shorthand writer who won a gold medal, a PRO with the Australian Broadcasting Commission, a programme and presentation officer with the Foreign Office, attached to All-India Radio. When she was with a Middle-East news agency with its headquarters in Cairo she had many hair-raising adventures in Palestine. During a brief return to London she helped Basil Dean with his autobiography and the Festival of Britain production of James Elroy Flecker's *Hassan* at the Cambridge Theatre. After a return home to Australia she worked in the administrative division of the United Nations Food and Agricultural Organization in Rome.

However did such an adventurous and restless woman settle down to such a long stint in a staid office in South Kensington with a

rather staid organization of women? She *must* have found deep
satisfaction in the job. She herself said that no years had been so
rewarding as those she gave to the NUTG and what she said she
most deeply enjoyed was going out and 'meeting the people'—at
which, agreed every observer, she was extraordinarily good,
stimulating, challenging, amusing. Marjorie Rice, former national
chairman, on her resignation contributed another thought: 'She
inherited, perhaps from her Australian background, an almost
fanatical concept of hierarchy, discipline, and authority which
those who worked with her sometimes found uncomfortable and
always unassailable.' So perhaps there was another strong satisfaction for this remarkable woman, being indisputably boss, being
totally in command of a complex organization. An Organization
Woman of a rare kind and quality?

Marjorie Erskine-Wyse was commonly known as 'Tommie'.
She was tall, very elegant and gifted in many ways—her handbook
on music for the use of the NUTG was a surprising triumph to
those who knew her less well. To quote Marjorie Rice again:
'I shall always remember her wearing some stunning hat, projecting her unique and fascinating personality to the topmost
balcony of the Royal Albert Hall as she wittily quizzed the annual
report with those elegant lorgnettes. What panache.' The grief of her
death soon after her retirement was acute for those, like Eileen
Coram, the national chairman, who had worked most closely with
'Tommie', and the more painful because her high courage ended
in defeat. She had often boasted of her splendid health; she refused
to accept for months that she could not conquer her fatal illness
by a sustained effort of her powerful will. Probably what Townswomen will remember best about her is her gallantry. It is too early
yet to assess her contribution to the movement's development.
Certainly its organization was simplified in her time, but though
her own speciality was communication, and though in her farewell
message to the Guilds she stressed that communication had been
her major concern, she left less of her philosophy on record than
did her predecessor Lillias Norman. Mrs Norman retained the
editorship of *The Townswoman* and wrote all its leading articles.
Mrs Erskine-Wyse handed over the editorship to Michael Leslie
when she became national secretary and it was he who wrote the
editorials. Michael Leslie is Michael Erskine-Wyse, Marjorie's

husband, but they kept their relationship private except to their friends. (A young journalist who worked for a short time on *The Townswoman* with Michael Leslie, only learned after Marjorie's death of their relationship.) So it would be impossible—and unfair—to attempt to guess how much he spoke for her.

Mrs Erskine-Wyse's successor was no less a lively and enterprising personality, Mrs Rae Campbell Tanner. They shared a love of music—Mrs Campbell Tanner has trained WI choirs and produced and acted in WI plays, but her most unexpected passion is for flying. She has totted up more than 300 flying hours and is a member of the Women's Pilots Association. Her previous jobs have included being personal assistant to the managing director of a large store, conference secretary to an industrial association, estate management, and work with a transport company engaged in flying farm breeding stock and race horses to all parts of the world. No doubt, however, what especially appealed to the Townswomen's Guilds committee who appointed her was the fact that she was a highly successful 'mature student'. She left Cheltenham Ladies College with only 'O' levels, but studied for 'A' levels when her third son was already at school— for three months her study was done in hospital, lying on her back. She then went to Bristol University and took a degree in psychology.

What the general public sees of the work of the big women's organizations is the rallies, conferences, demonstrations, festivals which do indeed take up an immense amount of the time of the voluntary and professional officials, but a lot of the thinking of the executive committees has to be spent on balancing the books, working out what can be afforded, steeling themselves, too often nowadays, to unwelcome economies. The National Union of Townswomen's Guilds has always been insistent on the keeping of immaculate accounts. Local Guilds have been carefully drilled in keeping track of all money that comes in and making a faithful return to their own members and to NU. They know what their Guild can afford and that if the rent of the room for the monthly meeting and the fees and expenses of speakers and tutors rise above what can be afforded out of the subscriptions, ways have to be found of raising extra money. A bring and buy, a jumble sale, a series of raffles or coffee mornings. But one of the really serious problems of all large national organizations is the difficulty of raising money quickly to cover increasing national outgoings. A decision to raise the affiliation fee can only be made by the Central Council and the benefit from that will not be felt for another twelve months.

All the time the NUTG executive have been faced, like all similar executives, with the disagreeable task of making a sort of cost benefit analysis of the programmes it fosters. With the NUTG the cost of training their TG Helpers was an example of this kind of anxiety. In 1955 it was recorded: 'TG Helpers have come to be regarded as an integral part of the NUTG. They have performed a very great service in keeping the wheels of the movement turning smoothly by explaining to those in doubt the constitutional path out of many a difficulty and by drawing on their experience to give advice. But the National Union considers that the time has come to achieve a greater degree of uniformity not only in the standard of training but in the availability of Helpers. Some Federations have many, some none at all. It is therefore the desire of the National Union to devise a scheme which will trim the loose ends of the past and accord to the TG Helper the honoured place in the movement which she deserves.

'It is obvious that to be effective a TG Helper must have knowledge and experience, must be keen and kind, must have time to devote to those in need of help and above all must have unwavering faith in the worthwhileness of the movement whose foundations she is helping to strengthen. There are many valued Guild members who will qualify under all these headings, but the number who can be effectively trained is limited, firstly by the money available for the residential schools which are the core of the training, and secondly by the number of those available to run the schools. It is planned to hold two schools in 1955 which will provide the movement with a new body of freshly trained Helpers. These schools have been made possible by the generous gifts of the Guilds and Federations to the National Union Extension Fund. One point of difference from the old schools is that all those attending must qualify in general Guild management, whatever other subject they wish to specialize in.'

Two years later, Mrs Mary Courtney in her chairman's address to the National Council Meeting at the Royal Festival Hall announced that at that point no further schools were planned to train TG Helpers. There were already 107 of them, working along-side thirteen area organizers. Petrol rationing (imposed at the time of Suez) had hampered the organizers' activities but they had helped to launch 128 new Guilds, bringing the total up to 2,028. (The 2,000th Guild was formed on 17 November 1957.) A review of the NUTG's financial position explained why the decision had been made to suspend the training scheme. For far too long, Mrs Courtney said, the movement had been trying to work on a budget that was insufficient for its ever-growing needs, so that it had been faced with the choice of strangling that growth or appealing to the membership to raise a substantial sum of money which would give them the necessary security. It was not a 'cosy' security Mrs Courtney envisaged but a relief from the nagging worry which would release energy for developing plans and programmes that would match the aspirations of the membership.

An 'envelope' scheme was commended to Guilds to celebrate their silver jubilee and the response to this amounted to £14,545 presented in purses to the Duchess of Gloucester at the National Meeting. But this was nothing like enough to form the capital fund for which Mrs Courtney and her colleagues had hoped. It was one of the last major events of her long and lively 'reign'. She was one of the most notable 'platform personalities' the NUTG ever had, eloquent, forthright and challenging, and very much admired from the north of Scotland to the south-west corner of England. From 1948 to 1960 she had been elected unopposed as national chairman. When Mrs E. M. Diamond, a vice-chairman, accepted nomination Mrs Courtney decided the time had come to stand down.

Obviously the most influential member of the organization's hierarchy is its chairman. The 'president' (in England) is often an imposing figurehead who plays little part in its affairs. The NUTG has been more fortunate, for it started off with Lady Cynthia Colville, one of Queen Mary's ladies-in-waiting, and apart from Dame Margery Corbett Ashby, one of the founders, this office has been filled also by Hilda, Duchess of Richmond and Gordon and Mary, Duchess of Roxburghe, both of whom liked to sit with the Central Council as well as the National Council Meeting. The NUTG also likes to have a leading woman MP or two on its list—they have included Mrs Joyce Butler, Mrs Sally Oppenheim, and Mrs Shirley Williams.

At the 1958 NCM the national executive put forward an emergency motion to raise the subscription. This was carried, but instead of the increase of 7s 6d (37½p) for which the executive asked, or any of the amendments suggesting 6s (30p) or 5s 6d (27½p), the delegates voted for 5s (25p), of which 3s (15p) was to go to the National Union, 4d (2p) to the Federation and 1s 8d (8p) to the Guild.

The question of the cost/benefit of the TG Helpers went on nagging at the collective leadership. The annual report of 1958 said 'Because of the difficulty of finding funds to provide adequate and systematic training or refresher courses, it was seriously considered whether it would be wiser to abandon the scheme. But this prospect was approached reluctantly and with misgivings because it almost seemed to break faith with the Carnegie Trust which financed the original experiment. It was also recognized that the TG Helpers performed a useful function in an unobtrusive way and it would be a loss to the movement if they ceased to exist. The opinion of the movement was sought through the Central Council and the desire to continue the scheme was expressed in the strongest terms.'

Even in 1964 it was recorded that for any TG training school that was announced there were as many as ninety applications. And many of these applicants were as 'nice, kind and human' as Lillias Norman had hoped they would be. She wrote a charming note on them: 'Much of my time lately has been spent with TG Helpers' test papers. Reading them has been a most interesting experience and once again I am struck by the diversity of TG personalities, as reflected in the way the questions are answered, combined with a solid substratum of common knowledge about matters constitutional. At the end of some hours of reading and correcting, it all began to feel a bit solemn, when at the bottom of the third foolscap page of one set of answers I read, *Oh Mrs Norman, my hand is so tired.*' The 1964 annual report noted that of the 132 fully trained Helpers many were Federation officers, eight were members of national sub-committees, many acted regularly as stewards at national conferences and National Council Meetings. There were similar warm tributes to the TG Helpers in 1966, and indeed an extra effort had been made to train more of them, and the total at the end of the year was 186. The 1967 report recorded simply that a Working Party had been set up to review the TG Helpers scheme 'with the idea of forming a pattern which would be more in accord with the present trends and growth of the movement'. And in the 1968 annual report the termination of the TG Helpers scheme was announced in a paragraph which gave no explanation and recorded only a brief tribute to their work.

By this time an even bigger change had taken place in the pattern of growth. The leaders had gone on to make a mental cost/benefit analysis of the employment of professional specialist advisers. Since the early days of the movement local authority and extra-mural educational opportunities had increased immensely. When the NUTG started it was a pioneer in many adult educational methods and the Ministry of Education has always recognized its value with substantial grants. It seemed best to the pioneers to channel activities into four main sections, arts and crafts, music, drama and social studies, but their successors in the sixties began to wonder whether the 'sections' were not strait-jackets. There were fields of study and enjoyment which could not be easily fitted into any of these categories, and also there were Guilds who, loyal to the letter as well as the spirit of the Constitution, felt they had to set up activities in the four sections with four sub-committees even if there was no demand for them among their own members. And there was, of course, the financial problem. This was not only due to the cost of the advisers' salaries. NUTG salaries were never in the top bracket for professional women. A more serious cost was probably the expense of having the advisers go constantly round the country, organizing regional schools and conferences. Even the great national events, splendid though they were, did not justify themselves either in hard cash or in a great influx of new members whose affiliation fees would greatly swell the national funds. In fact the more successful in terms of prestige and publicity the more expensive they were likely to be.

In 1965 the National Executive decided to dispense with the four professional advisers. The decision was taken at a three-day policy conference and members of the executive went away and thought about it for two weeks. They met again in December and confirmed their decision. That meant that their national general secretary, Mrs Erskine-Wyse, had to draft letters of dismissal and despatch them so that they arrived on the eve of Christmas. It was not well done and left painful scars in the minds of more than one of them. 'Why', asked Miss Helen Anderson, several years later when she had completed a very happy term as warden of the Women's Institutes' adult education centre, Denman College, 'did the Executive not take us into their confidence and warn us that this change of policy was being considered?' Because, presumably, the committee was not used to this kind of operation.

In the long term, all the NUTG's specialist advisers made their mark in other ways—naturally, for all were women of great quality. Lucile Spalding, who had resigned early because the set-up was no longer congenial to her, became general secretary of the Association of Headmistresses, and Miss Graham Campbell became secretary of the Women's Group on Public Welfare, now Women's Forum. (An earlier assistant secretary, Miss Bilbie, became warden of Crosby Hall, the residential centre of the British Federation of University Women.)

The National Executive reported their decision to the Federations, the Federations reported it to the Guilds and many of the Guilds, very taken aback and sad, wrote to the National Union. Not one of these protests was printed in *The Townswoman*, and the members had to be content with verbal explanations from their officers, with a brief statement in the annual report presented at the 1966 Annual Council Meeting. This explained that 'the basis of the decision was the need to broaden the educational programme and make it flexible enough to take in subjects more in line with modern trends in adult education'. The criticism must have been pretty widespread, for Mrs H. M. Wykes, then national chairman, had to prepare a carefully thought out defence for the February 1966 Central Council meeting. 'Never at any time have we been insensitive to the thoughts of our own Guilds and Federations,' she said. 'In arriving at major decisions regarding the NU educational development every one of the executive had been through a heart-searching time and it was now her duty to say that these decisions must be implemented without allowing sentiment or sentimentality to intervene.' In accommodating themselves to the trends of the modern world, Mrs Wykes claimed, they could not remain cribbed, cabined, and confined within the

NUTG's main subjects. 'Thus we were faced with the unpleasant decision of dispensing with our advisers. Even so the decision was not immediately taken. We gave the matter two weeks' private thought. When we reassembled every one of us was confident the right decision had been made and that we would be failing you, our electorate, if we did not face up to the realities of the situation. The co-ordinating and broadening of our activities to accommodate the needs of today's world required a new look at our movement's regeneration of our activities.

'On the Executive's concern to discharge justly its obligations to its advisers, it was really anxious to fulfil those obligations. The sole object was the widening of the scope of educational activities. We have no intention of discounting arts and crafts, drama, music, and social studies programmes at any level in the movement. Indeed, we expect the new NU Education Officer when appointed to bring new ideas, a new and modern approach to these subjects and to encourage their development along lines most suited to present and future conditions. The National Executive Committee was within the authority awarded it by the movement. There was nothing in the Constitution which laid it down what salaried staff the movement shall employ. The Constitution merely says who shall employ them.'

As to the suggestion that the movement should have been consulted before the change was made, Mrs Wykes said that such a course would have produced an intolerable and humiliating situation for the advisers themselves. 'If you had been an adviser how would you have liked your future to have been discussed up and down the country? The NU could not have placed members of the staff in such an invidious position. We could not have behaved so shabbily. The advisers' appointments were terminated on the best possible terms that could be accorded.'

Does this apologia have the ring of conviction? The chairman of the education sub-committee at the time, Alderman Mrs Clara Thubrun, has never had any doubt at all that the decision was the right one and was justified by later developments. She would entirely endorse what Mrs Wykes said about local authorities now retaining highly qualified advisers on the subjects with which TG sub-committees were concerned and the availability of these facilities *freely* to Townswomen. 'From their schooldays onwards,'

Mrs Wykes said, 'women now have had wide educational opportunities and demand higher standards of intellectual stimulation. Women want, too, to improve their personal skills whether in embroidery, acting, gardening, music, painting, foreign languages or any other subject. The younger woman can only be attracted by a lively, up-to-date programme flexible enough to embrace everything from gardening to computers, and from keep-fit to the study of politics and population problems. Now that your Executive has realized the danger of resisting change and having had the courage to accept what it entails, I hope and trust you will rally to our advance into the future and make the change as smooth as possible.'

The NUTG's annual report for 1966 had to announce that despite strenuous efforts and many interviews, the Executive had not filled the post of Education Officer. It was not until September 1967 that the first holder of this post took up work—Mr Rodney Barnes who had been a teacher, WEA tutor, lecturer in Liberal Studies, and TV freelance contributor. He obviously co-operated fruitfully with his chairman, Mrs Thubrun, and in the spring of 1970 they set out jointly in *The Townswoman* their idea of the new pattern of educational activities in the movement, the key change being, of course, an organizational one, the establishment of an *educational* sub-committee in each guild, instead of sub-committees for each of the four sections. In the summer of 1968 the NU had urged Guilds to find out what activities their members really wanted to pursue by means of a questionnaire. It was a very complicated exercise for it had many divisions and sub-divisions. 'Arts', for example, included music, drama and the crafts as before, but also literature, the graphic arts, architecture, applied arts, homecraft and domestic science. 'The Sciences' covered social science, science and technology, philosophy and religion. There was a section labelled 'Recreation' which included indoor and outdoor games, hobbies and skills, and one labelled 'Miscellaneous' to take in such important matters as current affairs, visits, investigations, brains trusts and debates.

Did the programmes begin to reflect this diversity of interests? It would be hard to say, but there seemed little doubt that by the seventies the NUTG could draw on a great number of highly qualified and experienced 'Organization Women' to keep its activities going. There were, indeed, just as many educational projects as there had ever been. Doubters questioned whether the quality was as high, but overall the work certainly did not flag.

Early in the 1970s, though, the overall membership began to show signs of a small decrease. In 1971 the total number of Guilds, in 115 Federations was 2,781 which was reckoned to mean a total membership of at least a quarter of a million. In that year, 44 new guilds were formed; the movement had now taken a sufficiently firm hold in Northern Ireland and the Isle of Man for Federations to be formed. But the closures were on the increase—33 in 1958, 49 in 1969, 41 in 1970, 51 in 1971. The total number of Guilds at the end of 1975 was down to 2,694. Everyone knew what was wrong—it was not that the Townswomen's Guilds were failing to provide happy, fulfilling experiences for the existing members; it was that these members were growing older and were not being supplemented by new younger, more energetic and newly enthusiastic members. The predominant reason for Guild closures was the difficulty of getting officers and committee—too often many good members tended to feel that they had done their stint in various offices and did not want to go through the same routine again. If young women didn't come forward, there was nothing for it but to close. Yet how could really young, or young-middle-aged women be expected to join a group whose average age might be well over sixty?

There was no lack of leadership at the top, or difficulty in recruiting energetic and able women for the National Executive. Guilds were fostered in the Isle of Wight and Jersey as well as in the Isle of Man and Northern Ireland. Morning Guilds were tried out and some young mothers found this an excellent time for meeting together. Most young women who had jobs naturally preferred evening Guilds, but the older women, nervous of going out alone after dark, stuck to, or even changed to, afternoon Guilds. The time had come to question whether the NUTG pattern of employing field organizers should, or could, be continued. In 1970 there were fourteen area organizers, of whom four worked only part-time. The following year, two organizers retired and the opportunity was taken, said the annual report, to revise and streamline the duties of the other nine full-time and the part-time area organizers, so that the Federations were re-allocated between them. And then a very stern look at the finances of the movement led to a harsh and difficult decision . . . to suspend the formation of new Guilds entirely from 1 January 1972 for two years. So from that date, the post of area organizer became, in the word of the annual report, 'redundant'.

This could be seen simply as a story of nearly forty years of expansion and then the onset of decline, but that would be an over-simplification. No one who studies the year-by-year working of the National Union of Townswomen's Guilds can doubt that it was in part at least an *evolution*, a progress, not without painful traumas, towards democratization and self-determination. The old constriction of the watertight structure, the insistence on the Constitution, the reference to the Rules in every small difficulty, suited the raw recruits of 1928 to 1938. They were very unsure of themselves, and were liable to flounder with no clear direction from head office. This was not at all the case with the women of the 1970s. The younger ones were pretty confident of their ability to manage on their own; the older ones had learned, through years of training schools and of Guild and Federation committee work, to rely much more on their own judgment. Looked at in this way, the shrinkage of the NU staff can seem not alarming, but quite encouraging.

The chief link between Cromwell Place (under the National General Secretary) and the Guild and Federation officials is a woman who has been rooted in Guild work for many years, and was herself an area organizer, Mrs Bessie Hall. Mrs Hall's story is rather special, because she is one of the very few people still working for the NUTG who came into a professional job of some importance from her own local Guild experience. 'My interest in the NUTG grew from my first visit to a national conference,' she says. 'It was at Blackpool, fortunately for me, because my father lived there. I had two young children at this time, and my husband said, "You go to the conference and I'll take two days' holiday and look after the children." But his job changed and he was moved away. "It doesn't matter," he said, "I'll come back and take these two days as holiday." But three days before the conference he told me he had to go to London for a promotion board. So there I was, with the two children. How was I going to get to the conference? I made up my mind to take them with me. My father had just been left a widower and he was one of the old-fashioned type who had never even lifted a duster. As for caring for children, he didn't know where to start. I don't think that he had been on the beach at Blackpool for fifty years, but he did take the children to the beach most of the time I was at the conference.

'My interest stems from that time, which is why I think every Townswoman should be encouraged to go to a national conference. Until you do, and have only seen your own little Guild with perhaps fifty members you don't realize what a power the movement can be.' Mrs Hall's experience is much more like that of the current leadership of the National Housewives Register than is that of most head office staff of most traditional organizations, Her experience of being filled with enthusiasm by the first national conference she attended is in fact remarkably like that of many young women who are astonished and delighted to find at their first conference of the Women's Liberation movement that they are among sisters.

Mrs Hall became an organizer, for areas of Yorkshire and

Lincolnshire, in 1968. After the area organizers ceased to function, she headed the Organization Department at 2 Cromwell Place and dealt by post with the sort of queries that area organizers had been accustomed to handle. She also still keeps a careful eye on the range of activities in the movement, by means of the annual reports sent by Guilds to their Federation Secretaries, of which a detailed digest is sent to her, as Organization Secretary. From these summaries of the Guilds' annual reports, the officers and Executive can quickly discover each Guild's total membership and whether it is an increase or decrease; how many meetings are held a year and what is the average attendance; how much halls cost for full meetings, and how much rooms cost for committee and sub-committee meetings; what help the local education authority gives, in supplying tutors or rooms for classes; what activities the Guild engages in, and what members, if any, hold public office in the town.

When the NUTG started to form Guilds again, after the two-year suspension, a new method was put into operation, more informal and flexible so as to reduce paper work and take into account local conditions. Six one-day schools were held in various parts of the country to train two representatives from each Federation as 'Voluntary Formation Officers'. It was also agreed not to start a new Guild with fewer than fifty members in the light of the experience that smaller groups were apt to fail after a while. The Voluntary Formation Officers got off to a good start in 1973, with eighteen new Guilds, representing more than a thousand new members but Mrs Hall did not regard the experiment as altogether successful. Quite a high proportion of the Federations had no new Guilds to report. She was loath to believe that there was no potential for a new Guild in these 'barren' areas, and wondered if some of the Formation Officers were as energetic as they might be.

By the mid-seventies it was evident that there was a ferment in the movement which might well produce lasting change, especially in the way of loosening the organizational structure of the move-ment. (Self-questioning had been intensified by a remarkable document, a survey by two members of the Centre for Applied Social Research of the Tavistock Centre, published in 1970, which will be considered in the last chapter of this book.) A letter to *The Townswoman* in November 1975, headed 'Let's Cut the Cackle' over TG Elections, from Mrs Sheila Spence of Aberdeen, led to a long and lively controversy. 'There is no justifiable reason,' said Mrs Spence, 'why every member of every Guild should be given a nomination form and an envelope before the annual election for officers and committee. Guild members can be asked to confirm or deny their willingness to stand for election openly, so giving the less talkative (who would probably never be asked otherwise) a chance to be asked to stand for the ballot; those prepared to stand for nomination would then be listed on the appropriate number of forms, to be signed by any paid-up members, so saving dozens of forms, especially in larger Guilds. Indeed there is no reason why one large composite form couldn't be designed so that only one sheet of paper would be needed for each Guild—think of the saving that would mean in paper alone, to say nothing of printing.

'I hear howls of "But it's SECRET". Rubbish. If we are honest we know that everyone in a Guild has a fair idea whose names will appear on the ballot sheet. The secrecy comes in the voting. If nominations were handled in this way returning officers would have a much easier task, knowing from the outset that anyone on the nomination form had really consented openly to stand and would be spared the embarrassment of standing up in front of a strange Guild to be confronted with the awkward situation where Mrs A "hasn't said she'll stand" and "doesn't want to be on the committee anyway". This kind of thing can "throw" even the most hardened and efficient returning officer.' It must seem strange to members of many less rule-bound organizations that the NUTG still retained this time-taking and expensive procedure in the 1970s. The returning officers' expenses have to be paid by Guilds where one would have thought there were plenty of equally experienced and competent women able to count votes and see that all went according to rules.

The majority of correspondents to *The Townswoman* agreed. Typical comments: 'At our last Federation AGM at Southampton the returning officer drove over from Bournemouth in a raging blizzard (her car broke down on the way) just to tell us the officers were returned unopposed and no ballot was required for committee members.'

'So far as I hear very few Guilds have more nominations than they need and getting the bare minimum usually entails arm-twisting, so why the high-powered techniques? For goodness sake stop all this empire building and realize that for the average TG member TG provides a meeting place where she can make and develop friendships, full stop.'

'Yes, "cut the cackle" and don't frighten potential committee members away by red tape.'

'I've always thought what a lot of time and energy is wasted in TG elections. When I was secretary the committee decided to simplify the election and I brought only enough nomination forms and envelopes to the October meeting for the number of people needed for a full committee. Unfortunately our returning officer, a very knowledgeable lady, made me go home and bring nomination papers for every paid-up member.'

The whole question of 'over-organization' was interestingly analysed by a Bristol member: 'The constitution was probably 100 per cent workable in the days when ladies joined the TG to fill their leisure hours, but not in our pressurized age. Eight of my Guild executive have paid jobs and all but two have also family and home commitments. I joined my Guild in 1971 and in 1974 was asked to be chairman (which proves how hard up they were!). I had no experience, no knowledge of the Constitution, Federation was some remote body which held meetings on a Monday morning, of all times, and National Union—well, I had no idea at all what "they" did.

'I spent hours studying the rule book and came to the conclusion that it wouldn't be possible to abide by all the procedures with the limited help available from my committee, particularly in the area of finance—our treasurer was also new to the job, and inexperienced.

'Why, in heaven's name, does a tip to the driver on an outing have to "go through the books"? And why does every member issued with petty cash have to note down every telephone call and postage stamp? Surely we trust our ladies with 50p? (They have to do a fiddle anyway—how does one have any sort of a telephone conversation on a 3p call?) I recently organized a questionnaire to try to obtain some guide lines on what members wanted from the meeting. One question was "Do you find the business interesting?" Of the 52 replies so far received, 27 said "No" and four said "Only sometimes". They gave various suggestions for shortening the proceedings, most of which I can't implement because the constitution won't allow it.'

The implications of unquestioning obedience to the rule book are one of the most fascinating aspects of women organized in large groups. What sanctions could be invoked to prevent rule-breaking? No one ever seems to have answered that question.

6

Towards the Common Good

Can any organization ever have been so anxious to learn in order
to serve, as the National Union of Townswomen's Guilds? In
the very first issue of the first volume of *The Townswoman*,
dated April 1933, Margery Corbett Ashby wrote 'We realize
we cannot serve the common good unless we first educate ourselves.
We must pull ourselves up to a new standard of intelligent knowledge and experience.'

In their formative years, the Townswomen's Guilds were in-
hibited from taking strong positive views on subjects of public
concern for they were deeply anxious to preserve 'the common
meeting ground' by avoiding controversy. But apart from this
preoccupation one senses a very strong feeling of inadequacy.
Mrs Corbett Ashby herself declared 'We know we are behind in
education and experience.' So at their annual council meetings
the Townswomen never formulated 'demands' as other women's
organizations, like, for instance, the Woman's Co-operative Guild.
But the Co-operative women had already half a century of self-
education behind them, when the Townswomen had barely five.
So in the motions on public matters that came before the NUTG's
national council meeting, they nearly always adopted a safe formula:
'Guilds should study', or 'Guilds should be asked to study'.
A typical way round the difficulty of too-positive commitment was
a resolution adopted in 1935: 'The NUTG in annual council
assembled calls upon Guilds to give earnest consideration to the
question of maternal mortality, to study the report of the Chief
Medical Officer to the Ministry of Health and to take steps to

investigate local conditions; and calls upon all Guild members to pledge themselves to combat this high rate of mortality.'

Compare the impact of the more experienced Women's Institutes at their annual general meeting in the same year: It begged WIs to 'urge local authorities where necessary to carry out the Minister of Health's recommendations for the provision of specialized obstetric advice and an improved midwifery service. . . Further, this meeting is of the opinion that the opportunity of anaesthesia should be within reach of all expectant mothers.' In fact ten years earlier the NFWI had carried an even more forceful motion urging Institutes 'to do what may be possible to create an informed public opinion, without which no substantial progress can be made' (towards reducing the maternal mortality rate, which had remained almost stationary since 1902).

That kind of call to action was not in the Townswomen's book, but they laboured very earnestly and diligently to inform themselves, and in doing that they must often have prepared the climate of public opinion to accept needed reforms. In the thirties a preoccupation of all women's organizations was the necessity for women police. It seems extraordinary now to recall that in 1920 it was actually recommended that 'the Geddes Axe' (as tough economic measures under the Chancellor, Sir Auckland Geddes, were called) should fall on the women patrols working under the Metropolitan Police. (These patrols had been set up during the 1914–18 war to work mainly among women and girls living near camps and recruiting stations.) The National Council of Women was the spearhead of protest and called a meeting of sixty-four societies. A deputation went to see the Home Secretary and there was a Commons debate. Finally twenty of the patrols were retained as a nucleus and became the women police as we know them today. The National Council of Women still treasures a letter from the Metropolitan Commissioner of Police at the time, which ends 'I need hardly say that we owe you and your committee a very deep debt of gratitude for the work you have carried out, from which has sprung the officially recognized women police.'

This campaign preceded the formation of the National Union of Townswomen's Guilds, but for quite some years after there was still need to put pressure on Chief Constables to appoint women to their force—especially, and one would have thought obviously, to ensure that when women and girls were required to make state-ments, the questioning should be done by women, either police officers or specially trained and responsible substitutes. Opinion among women's organizations during the thirties solidified into a strong united front. The Townswomen went so far as to recommend that Guilds should not only discuss the position with regard to women police but should 'urge through the Chief Constable their provision where necessary'. It was one of the very few instances in these pre-war years when the NUTG actually urged action rather than study. But a surprising variety of topics came before the delegates to the annual conferences. Townswomen were troubled, for instance, about the health hazards of the door-to-door delivery of unwrapped bread, about the methods of hawkers and pedlars (who probably proliferated at this time of high unemploy-ment); they concerned themselves with the supply of domestic electricity at a uniform voltage throughout Great Britain and were ahead of their times in urging the use for household apparatus of interchangeable plugs and sockets.

Three subjects remained of basic concern . . . and still do, these were the care of the mentally defective and ill, film censorship (now extended to anxiety over television violence), and pensions. An important resolution passed in 1937 read: 'That members of Townswomen's Guilds interest themselves in and use their influence upon all possible occasions to protect the interest of all dependent women who are adversely affected by anomalies in the National Pensions Scheme and that information bearing upon this matter shall be circulated among Townswomen's Guilds.'

For some unexplained reason, there were no public issues debated at National Council Meetings in 1938 and 1939. There was no Council meeting during the war, and in the immediate post-war years the Townswomen were mainly involved in sorting out their own structure, organization, and finances, so that there can have been little time for motions of general interest. But in 1953 the NUTG entered a new era by passing two motions which radically altered the agendas for National Council Meetings for all the years to come.

'The time has now come when the National Union of Towns-women's Guilds which represents a large body of thinking women in Great Britain should, while preserving intact its non-sectarian and non-political character and the idea of its common meeting ground, express its view on National Affairs, especially on matters concerning women and children, provided that these views do not conflict with the policy laid down by the national Council Meeting.' The second resolution was: 'That the executive committee of the NUTG be given mandatory power to approach Government Departments and other public bodies on matters that have been the subject of resolutions passed at National Council.'

The enterprising member who opened up this debate was a Mrs Thorpe, for the Sussex Federation, and she had also the backing of the East Kent Federation for a simple motion: 'That at future National Councils less time shall be devoted to matters of internal organization and more opportunity be given for matters of public interest.' There were one or two speakers against and in fact Mrs Thorpe's motion got a majority of only twenty-nine votes. It was Stourport-on-Severn, seconded by the West Midland Federation, which put forward the important Public Questions motion. The executive opposed the last phrase about 'not conflict-ing with N.C.M. policy' and there was a keen debate before it was finally carried in the amended form. The mandate for the executive to approach Government departments on behalf of the movement was also carried by an overwhelming majority, but there were some strong doubts. Miss Beatrice Briant, the Ministry of Education assessor (who sat with the national executive at its regular meetings) replied to an anxious questioner that no conditions were attached to the Ministry's grants and they would not be affected by the passing of the resolution. Miss M. Craigie, the vice-chairman, speaking for the executive, sounded rather anxious herself, while seeking to allay anxieties of delegates nervous about the effect on the 'common meeting ground' policy: 'If this mandate is accepted the executive must sift every resolution which comes to it with the greatest care and satisfy itself that the resolution is in order accord-ing to the known facts. No resolutions will be sent forward or any action taken until they have been carefully scrutinized by the executive commitee.' 'This,' commented the annual report, 'is a fitting step for the movement to take on the threshold of its majority.' It is odd now to note that the second day of the annual conference at Blackpool which took these forward-looking deci-sions closed with discussions on 'Has the busy housewife time for the finer arts?' and 'Were fashions more attractive in Edwardian days than today?' In this last debate the speaker wore Edwardian dress and 'two members of the Wirral Federation paraded in the hall elegantly attired in costumes of that period, to the immense amusement and enjoyment of the delegates'.

A Public Questions sub-committee of the executive was set up in 1956. The first chairman was a very notable Guildswoman, Councillor Mrs C. G. Kettle, JP and her successors were equally outstanding in ability and energy—several became national chairmen including Mrs H. M. Wykes and Mrs M. E. Rice. The balance of interest and importance in the NUTG's educational programme was undoubtedly increasing in favour of 'public questions' and away from artistic and cultural preoccupations, and the study themes, though they never excluded the arts, were dominated in the sixties and seventies by matters of public concern. Certainly during the post-war years, more and more Townswomen were becoming involved in civic life.

One of the strongest claims the women's organizations have to being a vital strand in the fabric of our national life is that they train people for public service. A high proportion of women councillors, magistrates, and members of board and official committees have been—and often still are—members of a Townswomen's Guild or similar organization. There is a sort of innocent charm about a few of the stories of how Townswomen were first elected to their local authority. It was not so simple for all, and as political conflict has intensified, it is very seldom as simple for *any* woman aspiring today to serve on a council.

Once upon a time, for instance (actually this was written about as recently as 1969), the Mayor came to talk to a Pembrokeshire TG about the work of the Council. He hinted that he would like to see more women on the Council. So the chairman of the Social Studies section let her name go forward for election and all the members of the Guild helped in her campaign. 'The night of the election while the votes were being counted I think all our members were gathered outside the small Town Hall. How they cheered and applauded when our candidate's husband came to the window and gave the thumbs up sign. She had topped the poll. A few years later she became Mayor, with her 12-year-old daughter as mayoress.'

It was the same sort of pattern at Biggleswade, in 1964. The Social Studies group of Biggleswade Evening TG seemed to be falling into abeyance. Discussion at a member's house centred on the forthcoming local elections and all agreed that they ought to have a member on the Council. There were no women members at that time so 'we could see that it would be a lonely business at first for any volunteer. Two would be better than one, we thought. They could stand together as "Townswomen". We were able to get two volunteers where there would have been little hope of one. At the next meeting we studied all the old election leaflets members had been able to find to see the sort of things that were supposed to appeal to the voters. As a non-political and non-sectarian body we felt that we should be able to appeal to all shades of thought.

'The candidates each supplied an outline of her own (they were amazingly similar) and from these we were able to build an impressive and, we hoped, persuasive, joint appeal to the electorate. Each candidate belonged to a different church, so each congregation could be appealed to for support of the joint candidature and this lent weight to the non-sectarian nature of our views. The vicars of the two churches were asked to propose the nominations and women of responsibility in the town were asked to second them. For the supporting signatures the whole of the Guild would have liked to oblige, but we thought there should be the signatures of some men, as the candidates would be representing the whole town, if elected, so the Guild signatures were carefully rationed.

'The candidates were given lots of assistance at the Council office. The husband of one of the candidates was willing to act as election agent. Within a fortnight of our first suggestion nomination papers were completed and accepted and the order for the leaflets was at the printers. Two copies of the Electoral Register were divided up to give sheets to hand out to those addressing leaflets, keeping one to cross off the streets as completed. The Guild was magnificent. In two days the leaflets were all addressed and Guild volunteers delivered more than half of them. Our sister Guild, Biggleswade Afternoon, helped with the delivery, as did other organizations to which the candidates belonged, and the candidates' families cleaned up the areas for which there were no other offers. It was all so easily done and there was so much goodwill that it was worth doing even if we got no results. Every member did her share of canvassing—not a house-to-house canvas, but a "talk-about-it-wherever-you-are" canvas.

'Election day arrived and members who had their own transport saw to giving people lifts to the polling stations. It organized itself. The candidates made their tours of the polling stations during the day, not really knowing the ropes but bravely smiling at the electors. The counting of the votes was a new experience for those of us who were able to be present—a help for budding TG Returning Officers—and we were very tense. *We* wanted women councillors, but did the rest of the town? As the names were called out we seemed to hear those of our candidates all the time, but those were the names we were attuned to. Were we deluding ourselves? And finally, the result. We are an Urban District and vote for all twelve councillors at once. Our candidates were second and fourth with only a few votes between them. They were IN.

'Our councillor members proved worthy and have been elected for a second term of office. Both are now chairmen of committee. The town is glad of their services and the Guild is glad to be kept informed of how the town is being run. The candidates are agreed that their Guild training has helped them a great deal in their work. It is our aim to keep the Council well supplied with members for many years to come.'

These success stories are proof that 'ordinary' women can enter public life if they have some training in a well-run organization to give them confidence and some backing from the supportive women's groups, but it was only in the smaller local authorities that Townswomen had much chance of being elected as Townswomen. Councillor Mrs Catherine Kettle, JP, a vice-chairman of the NUTG and later mayor of the borough of Croydon, wrote in 1956: 'As this movement grows in age, experience, and numbers it is producing members who are trained in business procedure, conduct of meetings and organizations who are willing and able to assume responsibilities and it is natural and right that they should sometimes look outside for opportunities to use this experience. One field of opportunity lies in local government. All Councils need capable women and the National Union should be, and in some measure is, supplying this need. Some Guilds are well aware of this and advice has been sought on what part

Guilds can play in supplying this need while still observing the
Common Meeting Ground.

'Many Council elections are conducted on a party political
basis, and if the Guild put up a candidate she would have to stand
as an Independent (or as a Townswoman) and such candidates
stand very little chance of being elected. Election expenses are
heavy and the Guild would be responsible for these. This proposition should not be entertained, as in a party political election
votes cast for an Independent are very often wasted. Where
elections are conducted on a non-party basis (e.g., Ratepayers, or
Electors v. Labour) Guild members might feel they could stand in
such a category and be supported by the Guilds, but this is not
possible, as it would be bound to cause a division in the Guild
and upset the Common Meeting Ground. This need not, though,
deter any member from seeking election. She should join a local
organization responsible for nominating and (generally) financing
candidates and if she takes an intelligent interest it should not be
difficult, by working for the organization, to secure a nomination.
Suitable candidates are very hard to find, for many people nowadays
are not willing to give up the necessary time, voluntarily, for this
important work.

'Any Guild member who is accepted as a candidate can state in
her election address her TG office and/or her other claims for
support. She cannot say she is supported by her Guild, though all
members may as individuals give her any help they wish.'

One of the NUTG's best known and most admired city councillors was one of its pioneers. Mrs Ethel Wormald helped to form
the Childwall and Wavertree Guild in 1934 and became its first
chairman. Later she became chairman of the Liverpool Federation
and then chairman of the Liverpool Standing Conference of
Women's Organizations, and was elected to the NUTG Executive.
Her public service began with her appointment as a magistrate
in 1948. In 1955 she was elected to the Liverpool City Council
and two years later was the first woman chairman of its education
committee. Then she became the second woman Lord Mayor of
Liverpool in 1967, and a Dame of the British Empire in 1968.
In 1970 she was appointed Deputy Lieutenant in the County
Palatine of Lancaster—a very rare honour for a woman. She has
never lost her interest in the Townswomen and she said in 1970

that she accepted invitations to talk to Guilds whenever she could because 'It all started with the TG movement when I found the stimulus to emerge from suburban seclusion into active citizenship.'

Townswomen councillors and magistrates have been and are numerous and mayors and lord mayors are not scarce. But Townswomen MPs? In the Parliament elected in October 1974 there were only 27 women in a total of 630 MPs—though more than half the population of 56,000,000 they represented were women. A columnist, Corinna Adam, commenting in the *New Statesman* in March 1977 wrote of this situation that it 'betrays a contempt for women, a disposition against them which will take more than the discrimination laws to change. It also betrays a contempt for women of *themselves*. We don't put in and fight.' Would Townswomen fight for one of their number standing for Parliament? Are there women trained in the Guilds who have the confidence in their training and experience to enter the real political battle? These are questions to which no one seems to offer answers. Michael Leslie, when editor of *The Townswoman*, threw down precisely this challenge to the Organization Woman: 'Without the slightest qualification I may say that the NU Federation and Guild events that it has been my privilege to attend have been organized and conducted with unsurpassed forethought and precision. The organizational ability of all sorts of women who have found a common meeting ground is remarkable; their capacity to improvise in drama presentation and arts and crafts and social studies displays is as admirable as it is astonishing. Research on various projects is so thorough as to excite the envy of professionals. The foulest weather, transport strikes and breakdowns never seem to prevent TG members being where they want to be—and on time.

'Why then is this thoroughness, this ingenuity, this pursuit of one increasing purpose not so evidently manifest in all things that affect women as citizens? As housewives do they think themselves too busily occupied? If so they are surely subscribing to the subservient role man, for his own convenience, would assign to them. Nationally, the NUTG seems to lack a collective voice.'

It is all the more surprising because in *local* affairs Townswomen have often been outspoken and firm in action. In 1959, for instance, Morden Evening Guild became so interested in plans to develop a site to provide a department store, shops and an office block of seventeen storeys that they invited the Town Surveyor to a meeting. He brought a model "and though some objected to the height of the office block, all thought it a wonderful design". The secretary wrote to the local MP for his advice on their objections to the office block. He said few had objected in writing to the plan. She then telephoned the County Planning Office to find out if anything could be done to moderate the height of the office block but was told it was too late.

'The following February we learnt that a supermarket was to take the place of the much-needed department store. At the Guild meeting the members strongly disapproved of the Council's choice of store and the Town Clerk was asked to send someone to a Guild meeting. A councillor came who had been actively concerned, as did the local press. From the councillor we learned how bitterly disappointed the Council had been to hear from the developers that none of the big companies had been interested, because they did not think Morden a commercially sound proposition. The discussion went on keenly all evening. We did not achieve our aim of getting a department store, but did show the Town Council and people of Morden that we are really concerned with the future of the town.'

So did some irate Townswomen in Camberley, when local businessmen objected to the invitation sent to Camberley Evening Guild to send a representative to the local consultative committee for Town Planning. This committee consisted of three representatives from Camberley Council, three from the Chamber of Trade, and one from Camberley societies. 'The retiring president of the Chamber of Trade maintained that a woman representative would not be a good idea at all because the committee was started by traders and professional men in the district to meet the council and plan redevelopment. The Chamber voted to vote against our joining the committee. With 150 members we are the strongest women's association in the town and part of a national organization of a quarter of a million members. It is amazing and deplorable that traders should be unwilling to discuss a new shopping centre with women, when those women will be the main customers and be greatly affected by the new centre. This is to treat women as second class citizens *to be decided for*.'

Some of the successes local Guilds achieved were quite surprising. For instance, Darlington District Federation reported in 1957 that the Housing Committee had instructed the Borough Treasurer to include in the capital programme for the coming financial year a sum for the building of halls in the Cockerton, Haughton, and Firth Moor housing estates, after Guild representations; a Bristol Guild complained to the Margotsfield Urban Council that the screening round the local mortuary was inadequate and it was decided to replace plain glass by frosted and to plant a six-foot-high privet hedge round the southern boundary of the buildings; Upton TG campaigned for two years to get rid of the unsightly pill boxes erected after the evacuation of Dunkirk. (This meant contacting the War Office, the land agents, and the MP for Birkenhead.) 'Eventually,' said the local newspaper, 'they triumphed, and the sound of the explosions was like music in their ears. On 20 May 1959, the last of the seven pillboxes was destroyed by a hundred blows from a three ton ball dropped by a crane from 30 feet.'

Most men might say that they had better things to do with their time than inspect the state of public lavatories. Some women, whose husbands have told them stories of the objectionable state of men's conveniences, might say it is a pity that they are not as public spirited as women. Either way, it is a curious and notable fact that in the late fifties and early sixties a great deal of attention was paid to public lavatories, not only by the women's organizations but by local consumer groups. Quite suddenly there was a conviction that something ought to be done, and many Towns-women did it with a will. In 1956 the NUTG annual conference passed a resolution calling on the Minister of Health to make it compulsory on local authorities to provide facilities for free hand-washing in public lavatories. This set off thirteen Guilds in the South-west Herts Federation on a tour of inspection. They reported that although some women left them in a dirty condition, all were regularly cleaned. They urged Watford Council to provide all conveniences with running water, soap, and hot air drying machines or paper towels, and for policewomen to pay regular visits. They had 'a long and satisfactory reply' from the borough engineer. At Edmondsbury a good number of Townswomen attended a council meeting where the inadequacy of toilet facilities was discussed and the only woman on the council, a Townswoman, said she was grateful for their backing. As a result, free hand-washing facilities were provided and a chair for nursing mothers or 'anyone feeling ill'. Bury St Edmunds TG approached the Medical Officer of Health, with success, when they found that local public halls had no sanitary towel machines.

But of course, the great Public Lavatory Scandal, which produced complete unity among women's organizations, was the installation of turnstiles at the entrances. This battle may have a faintly comic ring now but the campaign did show how much persistence is needed to remove a grievance which affects only the female sex. The National Federation of Women's Institutes was probably the first organization to call for action to secure the abolition of the turnstiles in all women's conveniences, and to seek the co-operation of kindred women's organizations—and this was 1956, the year when the Townswomen had begun to take up this sort of subject. It was not until 1961 that the organizations really began to put on the pressure. The NUTG then joined in a powerful deputation organized by the National Council of Women to the Minister of Housing and Local Government and he was impressed by the stories of hardship; he was told about women who were pregnant, women with cumbersome shopping bags, and women with very small children and prams or pushchairs. As a result of this deputation, a new Minister of Health a few months later announced that he was making a permanent ban on loan sanctions for public conveniences which included turnstiles, and shortly afterwards he wrote to local authorities asking them not merely to refrain from installing any further turnstiles but to remove existing ones as soon as they could.

In 1963 a Private Member's Bill became law, as the Public Lavatories (Turnstile) Act, and made it compulsory for local authorities to abolish turnstiles within six months. This Act could not, of course, apply to private bus companies' premises, and the NUTG, NFWI and other organizations continued their campaigning. Even in 1969 they were still keeping up the pressure and an all-organization deputation went again to the Ministry to complain about turnstiles in lavatories at private companies' bus stations, car parks etc. The Parliamentary Secretary, Mr Arthur Skeffington, thought that action might need another Private Member's Bill—this has not materialized as yet, but no one can doubt that in this small matter the united front of women's organizations had a very considerable success. This reminder of what power they can wield when they unite does make one wonder, with Michael Leslie, why they do not exert it more often—and in more important matters.

The first 'public question' discussed at a National Council Meeting after the important decision of 1953 was on litter. 'The movement deplores the amount of litter deposited on roads and open spaces in Great Britain and urges that the NUTG shall support the endeavour to awaken the public conscience on this matter.' Alas, for all their splendid efforts, the national conscience remained pretty quiescent, but they certainly tried very hard and often with ingenuity. When Marlborough had an anti-litter campaign inaugurated at a public meeting addressed by Sir John Betjeman, the Townswomen not only took full part in the committee's work but contributed a thousand badges lettered, in black on white, 'Marlborough Anti-Litter Club'. These were distributed to children who promised to stop dropping litter themselves and to make others stop. The Townswomen's Guild chairman, Mrs F. B. R. Browne, visited every school in the area to explain 'the club' and said that TG members would be on the look-out for children wearing the badge. Those seen putting paper in bins or otherwise helping the campaign would have their names noted, and prizes would be awarded on these notes.

Sileby TG, Leicestershire, had a very keen look at their area. They appreciated the tidiness around the fish and chip shops but were not at all pleased by the trail of greasy papers in neighbouring streets, even in people's gardens, and thought that the state of 'King St from the station to the junior school, was shocking'. Hordes of pupils came off the train from Barrow and deliberately scattered bits of paper, sweet papers, etc, leaving a long trail of litter on a previously clean street. Itinerant ice-cream vendors threw big empty cartons into the village streets and dustmen left a trail of litter. The Sileby TG by no means confined itself to criticizing the behaviour of others—they praised the staff at Sileby Station, the playgrounds of village schools and the work of the Sileby Allotment Society in the Memorial Gardens of the park. Best of all, TG members and helpers themselves cleaned out Sileby brook.

In 1955 a Keep Britain Tidy Campaign was formed with more than twenty organizations joining in, including, of course, the NUTG, who played a very active part. The National Union proposed that members, their husbands, children, and friends should keep their eyes well open for beauty spots defaced by litter, especially at weekends or after bank holidays, and for striking examples of carelessness in either town or countryside. The members were asked to watch out for the littered pavements outside cinemas or at bus stops where people are apt to drop paper wrappings, cigarette packets, cartons, bus tickets, etc—but also to note well-used and adequate litter containers and good anti-litter slogans. It was hoped that members would photograph all these examples of good and bad and send snapshots both to the NUTG and to their local newspapers. Suggestions for combating litter were invited but only one good idea was reported—from Driffield's president, who suggested that every family going on a picnic should appoint a 'litter lad or lass, aged from $5\frac{1}{2}$ to 12, to be responsible for all the family's rubbish, and have a special sack or bag for it'.

At this time, reported Mrs K. Taylor, the Townswomen's representative on the Keep Britain Tidy Campaign, there was no law that could be enforced on litter. By Section 13 of the Public Health Act of 1925, local authorities could make and enforce by-laws about litter, but of course action was far from uniform about the country. So Mrs Taylor made the suggestion, entirely in line with the Townswomen's usual way of going about things, that Guilds should find out what their own local authorities were doing about the litter menace. Meanwhile the national group went on putting on pressure and at midnight on 6 August 1958, an Anti-Litter Act came into force. Everyone knew that it would be well-nigh impossible to enforce. The TG national general secretary commented 'The bitter truth is that indifference of the general public has earned for this country the reputation of being one of the dirtiest in the world. Local authorities are primarily responsible for the enforcement of the Act and on them also rests the responsibility for the irreducible minimum—the bottle that breaks, the banana that squashes, but the crumpled newspaper blowing across the park and the fringe of orange peel and apple cores ferreted out by the incoming tide and the cigarette carton thrown out of the

Scenes from *The Gift*
presented at the Scala
Theatre as part of the Guilds'
Silver Jubilee celebrations:
(*above*) the Nightmare scene
(*left*) 'Life's a Proper How
D'you Do'.

NUTG's first annual dinner, London, May 1938.

After many years at the Ried camp, this old couple were given their own flat in one of the new buildings.

car, the sweet wrappings scattered along the pavement, these are all individual responsibilities. Had their "owners" stopped to think, they would no doubt have curbed themselves, but they didn't— and their carelessness last year cost us £11m.'

After the 1956 National Council Meeting at Edinburgh, a Manchester delegate wrote to express her horror 'at the sight of so much litter on the lovely lawn at Lauriston Castle' (where the Townswomen had attended a reception). 'Cake papers, doyleys and empty packets strewed the grass. There was no one to blame but our delegates from all over Britain. I spent some time with several members of the South Manchester Federation clearing as much as possible of this litter, putting it in a large polythene bag. Did we leave Lauriston Castle grounds as we found them? I'm ashamed to say we did not.' But perhaps the 'Keep Britain Tidy' campaigners had really struck home with their propaganda. A Chislehurst Townswoman had a very different comment to make after the 1960 NCM at the Royal Albert Hall: 'Several thousand ladies picnicked around the Albert Memorial, and when they left the gardens there was not one piece of litter left to tell of meals eaten, not even an apple core. Which proves what can be done with a little thought and consideration.' And with a great deal of intensive propaganda?

It wasn't just chance that the TG in Sileby tracked down litter with such thoroughness and efficiency, nor that the thirteen TGs of South-west Herts surveyed public conveniences so carefully. The Townswomen had been trained from the word go in *practical* education. In 1943 the national secretary reminded members 'We are pioneers in the field of adult education for urban women. We have handed on the fruits of your and our experiments to others and all the time we are perfecting our experiments in democratic control.' The NUTG educational methods were original and effective, especially the 'reconnaissance'. This in-depth study of a chosen subject grew out of discussions between the 'civic groups' leaders at 2 Cromwell Place early in the war. One of the staff organizers, Mrs Presland, seems to have invented the method and in 1943 a 'reconnaissance' was staged in front of a number of Federation delegates and others who had come to London for a meeting of women set up by the Government.

Mrs Presland listened to the criticisms of her guinea-pig audience and revised her pattern. In the event, it was usual for an NUTG organizer to go to a Guild's planning meeting and divide the subject up for work by groups—investigation, 'for those who like to go about seeing things and places, talking to people, noting what they see and hear'; study groups 'for those who like reading and research'; discussion groups 'for those who can meet more often and like to learn from talking to one another'. 'An Action Group may visit a works, an institution, or a film. Illustration is by members who can collect, make and mount an exhibition, or demonstrate by examples of drama and music.'

The reconnaissance groups would meet for two or three months on their various projects, but occasionally together to 'experience the pleasure of working together and to ensure that their findings are really the result of team work'. When the groups were ready the staff organizer would pay another visit 'to act as stage manager', calling on each group to report its findings or to give its illustrations. Most of the results were original, ingenious, rather surprising and gratifying to the members themselves—and 'good entertainment'.

For a good many years this 'exploration' method was very popular among Guilds. Its great attraction was that it involved not just the social studies section, but practically all the membership, whatever their interests or their skills. Mrs Presland reported on the 'reconnaissance' method to the first Council meeting held since before the war, at Southport in March 1945. It was hard to describe, she said, and had to be seen to be believed. It was 'learning how to learn' and a method of study specially adapted to suit the needs of Guilds. Each Guild chose its subject from a list suggested by the National Union.

Professor Robert Peers, of the Department of Adult Education, Nottingham University, was the main speaker at this conference and spoke about the purpose and methods of discussion, which he thought the essence of adult education for citizenship. As far as one could go back in history, he said, there was the practice of meeting together for discussion, though the method had been adapted to new purposes in our times—as was the custom of the British people. One of our most ancient institutions was the Guild, Professor Peers said—their members met once a month, just like the Townswomen, who had borrowed the name. He was interested in the TGs' experiments in the form of study groups and reconnaissance, for he felt strongly that discussion in the Guilds or any other group, however informal, was only effective when there was a basis of real knowledge. (At this Southport conference, the chairman, Miss Joan Loring, apologized for Professor Peers' delayed arrival. Apparently no one then knew that this was, in fact, the first day of his honeymoon. His widow confided, many years later, that one reason he had accepted the NUTG invitation was that it would enable him to get petrol coupons so that he could take his bride on holiday!)

The list of reconnaissance subjects grew quite impressive: The Child Under Seven, The Adolescent, The Family in the Home, The Care of the Aged, The Land, A Country of the World, Local Government, Water Supply, Transport, Crime and Punishment, Holidays, Standards in Everyday Life, The Cinema, The Press, The English Language, A Survey of Party Politics, The History of Women, A Townswomen's Guild. The favourite subject probably was always 'Our Town' and a charming example of the way a reconnaissance worked comes from Clevedon, on this theme. The natural history group compiled a diary of rambles illustrated by drawings, paintings, photographs, pressed leaves and ferns. The historical group visited churches, manor houses and buildings of interest. Clergy and owners lent pictures and prints. The literary group discovered that Tennyson's friend Arthur Hallam is buried in Clevedon and that Thackeray used to visit the old manor house of Clevedon Court and wrote much of *Vanity Fair* and *Henry Esmond* there. The civic group compiled reports on all social services and local government and visited craft workers, including a cottage pottery, as well as industries —for example 'the third largest cake factory in the country' where 33,000 yards of Swiss roll were turned out weekly. The handicrafts group worked on an embroidered map of the district. After all this the TG had its week of making 'our own town' better known to its inhabitants, with talks, lectures, music and drama.

More forward looking and perhaps basically more useful was a reconnaissance undertaken as late as 1956 by forty to fifty members of St Austell TG, Cornwall, into 'Crime and Punishment'. They studied the history of penal laws, official attitudes to punishment in the past, and current trends and statistics. They were exceptionally fortunate in having the willing co-operation of the Dartmoor prison authorities and the Home Office seems to have taken note and to have telephoned the local WRVS organizer to say that 'the women's club making this survey' must be given every help.

St Austell's 'investigation group' concentrated on prisons, remand homes, and other places of detention, past and present, gathering information from books and visits. The study group, led by the wife of a local grammar school headmaster, presented four papers on criminal law, surveying its application from Saxon times onwards. They went to considerable trouble to see how the modern notion of re-education was successful. The discussion group had many lively sessions, and came to the conclusion that open stalls and counters were a serious temptation to people with a tendency to kleptomania. They favoured the retention of the death penalty but thought the public should be given a chance to express their views. Members paid visits to courts and commented afterwards on the conduct of magistrates' courts and on inequalities in the law. The 'exhibition group' produced pictures, posters, graphs, and models of pillories, ducking stools etc. Material was provided by the Chief Constable of Cornwall and prison officials.

Reconnaissances were thoroughly enjoyable, and an excellent exercise in the fact-finding on which the NUTG laid so much emphasis, but as time went on they gave place gradually to another pattern of self-education—the 'social studies' theme launched at a national level, probably at a delegate conference, and carried through in stages at residential or one-day schools, sometimes national, sometimes regional, usually supported by a 'study theme' booklet which outlined the potentialities of the subject and gave advice on how to pursue various aspects of it. In 1955 the study theme 'Citizens in the Making' was prepared by the Social Studies adviser, Lucile Spalding, and within six months 800 copies of the booklet had been sold, far more than any previous study plan. Miss Spalding commented briskly at the time 'A difficulty in the way of several Guilds was that lecturers and tutors had no lecture course ready which really filled the bill and tended to offer lectures on "child psychology" or "the influence of home training" which tended to deal with that abstract animal "The Child",

the very thing the study plan tries to avoid. So here is a useful
warning. Guilds, Federations and the National Union should all
try to make future plans of study known to local authorities before
they are actually issued.'

She added, 'I have been surprised to read of quite a number of
Guilds concentrating on "delinquency"—surprised because I
had already been told by many, many Guild members that they
had already studied delinquency at some length and so hoped the
new Plan would stress the positive side of young citizens—which
it does. One Federation suggests that as nearly every mother thinks
she has made a good job of bringing up her own children she feels
it is the other mothers who need guidance, and resents any
suggestion that she herself may have something to learn. I have
myself occasionally felt that sooner than bring it too near home,
some members prefer to look in the direction of "bad" families.
Yet in cooking, sewing, singing and so on, women want to improve
their techniques, however skilled they may be. Why not in mother-
ing?' These were the comments of a childless woman, but Miss
Spalding undoubtedly put her finger on a sensitive place.

The first major post-war study plan, prepared by Miss C. L. H.
Cowper, had been on 'Women in a Changing World' and according
to the chairman at the time, Mrs Mary Courtney, its impact
lasted for years. It was divided into three parts, the Home-maker,
the Woman Worker, and the Woman Citizen, and one of the
speakers at the first conference was that remarkable pioneer,
Dame Caroline Haslett, founder of the Women's Engineering
Society and of the Electrical Association for Women. When the
Townswomen came together in conference to discuss 'Women at
Work' a personnel management adviser at the Ministry of Labour
commented that in 1851 only domestic work was really open to
women. In 1951 the number of domestic servants had greatly
decreased—and a third of the whole working force was then
women. A leading probation officer put the view that was held very
generally in the early 1950s by social workers, magistrates, and
many members of women's organizations, that delinquency among
children and young people was clearly linked with the increasing
number of mothers going out to work, who 'could not attend
properly to the upbringing of their children as well'. The debate
continued over the years. In 1963 Mrs Corbett Ashby wrote to

The Townswoman saying that according to the latest Ministry of Labour figures, one worker in six was then a married woman— i.e. 3,683,000, half of all women workers. 'Would it not be sensible,' she asked, 'to remove the controversy from whether married women should or should not work and discuss what social changes are needed to allow the married woman [by then obviously an indispensable part of the labour force] to contribute to the national economy and to her own family's well-being with the least strain to herself and her family?'

Towards the end of the next decade, more than 50 per cent of all married women had a job outside the home and in the London area 42 per cent of *women with children under five* had a job. Social studies conferences, 'disturbing figures by experts' and heated discussions in Guilds by predominantly stay-at-home wives were powerless, it seems, to stop the march of women out of the four walls of home, whether for good or ill.

When the Townswomen got on to the third phase of this study plan, 'The Woman Citizen' they had some trenchant thoughts from Miss Margery Fry, who started with a rousing history of the struggle for emancipation and of the women's movement generally, from Mary Wollstonecraft to Eleanor Rathbone, pioneer of family endowment and the first friend of the NUTG. Of public service, Miss Fry said, 'One may say that what appeared in the 1870s to be merely the sphere of sporadic and unorganized private charity is now universally recognized as a public duty. I remember a wealthy and wheezy lady at a "ladies debating group" early in this century who when things that are now taken for granted as matters of administration came under discussion said "But if things were like that, what would become of people like me and Lady Brown, who spend all our time in charity?"' Miss Fry declared firmly 'The spirit which inspired the women's movement is still needed, and its results can never be final.'

Both Mrs Courtney and the national general secretary who followed Miss Cowper, Lillias Norman, were convinced internationalists, and as is related in the following chapter they persuaded Townswomen in great numbers to study 'Paths to Peace' and the work of the Parliamentary Group for World Government, beginning with a two-day conference in London in 1958; but at least as influential and memorable a study theme launched in the same year was 'Loneliness in Towns'. Of this study booklet 1,200 copies were sold, which may have been a record. Though it is recorded that 'members of a Guild in Croydon Federation left the section because they found it too depressing' for most Guilds it was just the thing to involve their kindhearted and energetic members to the fullest extent. The National Council of Social Service produced a very informative and stimulating handbook and the Women's Group on Public Welfare was the spearhead in attempts to get action moving 'to dispel some of the frustration, unhappiness and even anguish which loneliness causes to un-counted thousands of people of all ages in our cities and towns'.

The Social Studies adviser wrote: 'The immensity of the problem and its complexity are not always realized. It is no use saying of a lonely woman living in our town "She has only herself to blame; keeps herself to herself and hardly answers if you try to be friendly. Why doesn't she join the Townswomen's Guild or some other organization?" This is to overlook the psychological and human problems which often make people over-sensitive and difficult to help. It is as senseless as telling someone suffering from indiges-tion "The doctor says it is only nerves." The disorder of a nervous complaint calls for every bit as much sympathy and understanding as an organic disorder.'

True though this is, many local Guilds found that people just needed to be asked. An admirable, and by no means untypical, form of direct approach was recounted by Mrs W. Wilson, of Anlaby Park, Hull: 'Our local newspaper had articles and reports on loneliness in several issues. I wrote to the reporter and offered to invite relays of 12 lonely women to tea and a chat and to in-troduce them all to others in their own districts. The response was overwhelming, so the reporter and I got a room for a meeting. We had to turn away 80 women—some had travelled miles to attend. We opened up two other rooms, and the hall and stairs were crowded. After eight meetings and innumerable tea parties we can say friendships and happiness abound. Although it is a Her-culean task it is already proving worthwhile and should be nationwide.

'Some of the women are too repressed and frustrated to go out alone, but knowing that all women at our first meeting would be similarly placed they ventured to it. We hope to get them to join a Townswomen's Guild when they have found friends. Seventy-two have already been in relays to my house and all are given a "friendship plant" to cherish, grow or pass on. It shoud be borne in mind that some of the lonely ones, through sheer loneliness, have become bitter, queer or arrogant. None dare come forward to help and may have to be guided into doing jobs. We cannot have a real committee as all are strangers— or were. I am chairman, secretary, minute and press secretary and hostess. Money is the stumbling block, for a room with warmth and light, refreshments, games etc all have to be provided and many cannot afford even a small weekly sum in addition to bus fares. But dozens of obstacles and teething troubles have been overcome. I could scarcely believe that there is as much loneliness in all of England as there is in every town.'

Lucile Spalding warned the Townswomen that the loneliness study plan needed 'intensive field work' and she set out a detailed work scheme for them. 'Approach your public library for the loan of a study box of recommended books. Get a member to look up in the public library useful books on public health, social medicine, health visiting etc. Talk with Town Hall officials, local journalists, clergy, voluntary welfare workers like Citizens Advice Bureaux and the WRVS. List for information Assistance Board officers, district visitors, Labour Exchange officials, landlords, rent collectors, gas and electricity meter readers, cafe owners etc. The study involves going out and finding out for yourselves, in small groups, and keeping careful records. It is NOT a busybody, nose-poking exercise and knocking on doors asking if people are lonely.'

A conference on the theme in Leeds had an unexpected bonus. Members continued to discuss the subject on the bus going home. A stranger leaned over and spoke to them, saying she was herself a lonely person and would like to know the name of the organization to which they belonged, for she thought it would suit her own need.

An interesting facet of the public work of the National Union of Townswomen's Guilds is that though there has been quite a strong and a continuing interest in the status of women it has never been a campaigning feminist organization. The 1962 study theme 'Everywoman' brought a thousand women to the opening London conference whose purpose was to survey the status of women in different parts of the world, to consider a few of the more

urgent needs of people at home and abroad, and to examine some of
the opportunities of service. There were also 14 short residential
courses on the 'Everywoman' theme, attended by 540 members
from 58 of the Federations. But neither that year, nor any year up
to 1968 was there a resolution at the National Council Meeting
urging any kind of action, or even expressing any opinion, on the
status of British women. (But in 1968, the jubilee of the granting
of the franchise to women, the NUTG was very early off the ground
among the big national women's organizations, supporting Mrs
Joyce Butler's first Private Member's Bill to outlaw sex discrimination.) A rousing call to the Townswomen came from Mrs Charlotte
McKnee, a lecturer in history and international affairs at Edinburgh University, at the opening 'Everywoman' conference. 'We
must discover how to be partners with men but not copy them,
or necessarily follow man-made paths. We must, with great
intelligence and compassion and with a firm grasp of the facts,
decide what our role is to be.'

Lillias Norman, national general secretary, added her own
encouragement to thinking about the status of women: 'The franchise is just a milestone on the path of true emancipation and it is
worth asking ourselves whether we take enough interest in the next
steps. Many of us, for instance, are ignorant about the anomalies in
the income tax laws, the inheritance laws, the signing of contracts
in our daily lives. The law must of necessity be behind the times
but need it be so far behind? . . . It will only change if the public
attitude demands it.'

The attitude of home-making women, such as the majority of the
members of the Townswomen's Guilds were, and probably still
are, was not likely to move rapidly towards equal rights, equal pay,
equal opportunities, even equal education, so long as they were
largely dependent on their husbands. It was only when they began
to come up against the irritations of husbands being required to
sign their income tax returns, or to be solely acceptable for mortgages
or even hire purchase agreements that they began to take a more
'feminist' view. Alice Franklin, the founder secretary, must have
been a convinced feminist herself, but she perfectly understood that
her members were not all of the same opinion, and she always put
the Townswomen's Guild and its common meeting ground before
any private conviction of her own. She wrote, for instance, way

back during the war years, 'It is difficult to tell the proportion of feminists and anti-feminists in the Guild world—probably fifty-fifty, and the reformers are more likely to be more vocal than some of the "antis" who may be apathetic or inarticulate.'

The NUTG's staff officers, from Alice Franklin and Gertrude Horton through to Lillias Norman and Marjorie Erskine-Wyse, were undoubtedly women of independent mind, who could hardly avoid taking a feminist line, and so were some of the national chairmen, but as a whole the Townswomen were more easily involved in more general, and especially more domestic, topics. Government departments and other representative bodies have long regarded the Townswomen's Guilds as ideally representing the 'ordinary' housewife and have sought their opinions on all kinds of subjects. In 1951 the British Furniture Manufacturers entertained members of the executive to lunch to show the new examples of furniture; in 1959 the NUTG took part in a question-naire on bedding and the manufacturers did, in fact, act on their views; in 1963 the Home Office sought the Townswomen's views on jury service and the Ministry of Housing on sewage and British Rail asked their opinion (in 1952) on restricted passenger services. Members participated, too, in a detailed questionnaire on the working of the National Health Service and the report on their answers said 'There is no doubt that the majority of members consider that the freedom from financial worry on account of present or possible future illness is the greatest benefit of the NHS. Guilds spoke of the benefit to the aged and housewives "who no longer neglect themselves for fear of incurring expense, and feel free to visit doctor, dentist or optician". The fear of not being able to obtain specialist or long-continued treatment had been removed and people were ready now to seek early examination and diagnosis, knowing that x-ray examination and, if need be, expensive drugs were freely available to all. Guilds did, of course, have their com-plaints of the NHS, notably the overcrowding of doctors' surgeries, but it is good to be reminded of what a sense of relief the NHS brought to older people and to non-earning mothers.'

Mrs Mary Sobey, when national chairman, stressed how often the NUTG was asked at very short notice to answer enquiries from Government departments, other organizations and the press, asking for Townswomen's views on the latest innovation or reform.

'It is difficult', said Mrs Sobey, 'to give an on-the-spot reply but as the second largest women's organization we cannot remain silent on these matters. We are invited to send representatives to important bodies such as the Status of Women Committee and the Women's Consultative Council set up by the Prime Minister [now the Women's National Commission]. So we have drawn up another scheme for a network of correspondents, members whom we know to be interested in Public Questions and ready to study pamphlets as they are published. The invited correspondents have accepted this challenge with enthusiasm and we hope that in this way we can be a little more informed on the reaction of Townswomen to new issues and proposals.'

All Organization Women with long experience in their various associations know that some kind of consultative group is desirable, especially in these days of an expectation of instant reaction by the media, because the decision-making body, the annual debate conference, which is the only real authority for a public pronouncement on policy, meets only once a year; yet it does not seem easy to establish or maintain. Probably a good understanding between the chief executive, who after all is normally in her office and available for comment, and the national chairman or working president, and harmonious relations with the executive committee work as well as anything. Delegates' meetings, in fact, are not just for the purpose of deciding questions of public policy. They must look inwards as well as outwards, recharge the organization's batteries as well as reiterate its significance to the outside world.

When one disenchanted Guild member called the National Council Meeting 'a ghastly and expensive farce' the then chairman of the Public Questions sub-committee, Mrs M. E. Rice, answered her in words that could scarcely be bettered and which can apply to every organization that holds annual conferences: 'A national organization must be seen to be national. If we never came together at a fully representative national meeting we should cease to be national. There is logic in this situation and it makes anthropological sense. I don't know if the critic equates farce with ritual. Ritual enforces the structure of the meeting; it helps to sustain the purpose of the meeting; it underlines the continuity and enduring solidarity of the movement.'

So if the newspaper press comments lightheartedly each year on the May meetings in the Royal Albert Hall of the Townswomen, and of the WIs too, stressing the colourful hats and recording discussions only on topical issues (preferably dealing with sex or violence or both) it need not undermine the importance of the gathering, especially not in the minds of the members themselves. The Royal Albert Hall is itself such a remarkable building that it sets a scene as impressive in its way as a great cathedral. The shape and decor of the interior are reminiscent of one of Queen Victoria's crinolines, for it is a vast circle, and almost all the way round the perimeter run four tiers of boxes—flounces, as it were, round the skirt—backed by scarlet curtains. There are cream curtains, plum-coloured plush and much gilt along the edges of the boxes and balconies. And the Albert Hall holds at least 5,000 people. Imagine every seat filled by a woman in her ritual new spring outfit, shiny hair-do and piquant spring hat, and a steward at the end of every row with a scarlet sash over her shoulder. Dazzling. Breath-taking. And really quite extraordinary, for these women are delegates (3,000) and friends and observers (2,000) from 2,700 Guilds and 115 Federations from the north of Scotland to Cornwall, from the Isle of Man to the Isle of Wight, from Northern Ireland to the westernmost tip of Wales.

Twenty years ago this annual gathering was held in Edinburgh at the time of a rail strike. The national general secretary, Lillias Norman, recalled the alphabetical roll call of Federations as one of the most vivid memories of her term of office. 'As the delegates from within each Federation stood in response, it became clear with a mounting sense of excitement that no token representation was gathered here but that almost a full complement had overcome the hazards and difficulties of a railway strike to be present and share in the essential business of the TGs. When it was finally evident that every Federation was represented a feeling of pride and satisfaction permeated the meeting.' (It was indeed a remarkable feat, for in 1955 comparatively few Townswomen had cars or could drive.)

So the National Council Meeting is more than a meeting; it is a symbol of the importance of the movement, as Marjorie Rice said. It is a reminder, too, that the women's organizations are a remarkable fragment of British social history. In this book, one such assembly must represent the forty or so that have taken place since the formation of the first Guilds in 1929 . . . the NCM of 1976, at which Dame Margery Corbett Ashby, a small, alert figure in elegant black and white, was still keenly watching from the Royal Box what the daughters and granddaughters of her co-founders were up to. From the intimidating height of the top gallery it would have needed strong opera glasses to pick out the chairman who was controlling this vast meeting with serene efficiency. No stranger could have guessed that Mrs Eileen Coram, a small woman in a shiny yellow straw hat and neat cream suit, was making her début in the chair at this annual delegate meeting. She would stand as the perfect example of a typical Townswoman, for she joined the Ealing Guild as a young mother in 1945—this was because she had been asked to help with the teas at her son's school VE Day celebrations, where it was so clear that she was a born organizer that she was urged to join the TG, where she would find plenty of scope. Indeed she did. In the Ealing Guild she served as treasurer, drama sub-committee chairman, Guild vice-chairman, and chairman—and so on up through the chain of Federation and Central Council delegate.

Her competence in money matters was probably exceptional due in part to her having been a retail trade buyer and a director of two property companies, and she served efficiently as national treasurer before being elected to the chair.

Mrs Coram said afterwards that yes, of course she had been nervous at first, faced with that intimidating array of faces in the Royal Albert Hall, but it very quickly wore off once the proceedings began, even though she had not the chairman's usual 'prop and stay', the national general secretary, for Mrs Erskine-Wyse was then already too ill to appear; and even though she had to welcome a royal visitor, the young Duchess of Gloucester. It all went swimmingly, and dead on time, though the Duchess's arrival slightly altered the schedule. Guild internal affairs had to be given adequate time, including the committee chairmen's reports, the acceptance of the 1977 budget of £100,000, and the 1975 annual report.

Five 'public question' motions were already on the agenda and two 'urgency motions' were accepted for discussion. People who have huddled together in a corner at a conference with a blunt pencil or scratchy ballpoint pen to draft a resolution on a scrap of paper in response to some wave of feeling among their friends and fellow delegates would be startled at the process by which Townswomen get their motions discussed—it takes more like six months than six minutes and all has to be done scrupulously in accordance with the guidance laid down in the NUTG's Public Question leaflet—Guilds are told they should not send forward a motion unless it has been considered by a study group or working party, and when approved it must then be taken to the local Federation for their endorsement, for a Guild must have a Federation seconder for its motion at the NCM. The motion must, all along the line, be accompanied by factual information on any relevant existing legislation or on the relevant sections of Government reports.

Then, 'having got past the Federation hurdle, your motion together with all the supporting evidence is sent on the appropriate NU form by the Federation secretary to the National Union, for scrutiny by the Public Questions sub-committee'. The number of motions submitted each year varies considerably. It has been as many as 104 and as few as eleven, but nowadays runs around twenty. These motions are parcelled out between the PQ committee members who vet them to see if they are competently drafted and all in order. By the January meeting of this committee the members have been told how many motions the conference agenda can take —usually four, with the possibility of two urgencies—and they make their choice, on debatability as well as usefulness. As a rule 'controversial' motions are preferred to what the Handbook calls 'pious expressions on matters of opinion' about which nothing can be done—which seems to carry the risk that the NUTG misses the one opportunity it has of stating its commitment on matters of major social importance. A declaration of faith can sometimes be inspiring; it is also a reference point when the organization's policy is questioned.

For some unexplained reason the NUTG has always been sternly warned about 'emotionalism' in the matter of resolutions. The Handbook opens: 'Women tend to think with their emotions; men state principles; women evaluate a problem by studying the effect on the individual. This personalization of a problem has its dangers. Therefore when we are faced at a Guild or Federation meeting with stories of suffering and hardship and wrongs to be righted, the first essential is to get to know the facts.' Mrs Rice, a clear-thinking, rational person herself, went further. 'It is essential that nationally 200,000 women arrive at decisions that are based on facts and not on feelings, on truth insofar as it can be known, and not on prejudice. This is a difficult problem for women, who tend to personalize a problem. Soft-hearted and with sympathies readily aroused, we are apt to allow ourselves to be swayed by outraged feelings that in some cases verge on hysteria, blinding us to the hard facts. The weapons we need to use are flexibility of mind and intellectual scepticism. Let us discard our blinkers so that we get the question into perspective.'

Having done all this preparation for voting on motions at the annual conference, TG delegates are given a freedom of judgment which is very rare. The NUTG tradition is entirely against mandating their delegates on how to vote. If the delegate is not to be allowed to make up her own mind when she has heard fresh evidence, and convincing new arguments, she might as well stay at home and send her vote by post; the accepted opinion holds. This is indeed a high form of democratic responsibility, practised by very few organizations, one suspects.

If at the 1976 NCM any delegate voted against the consensus of opinion in her local Guild, only she and they would know, but the pros and cons were certainly skilfully put. There was, for instance, a notable maturity and lack of sentimentality in the debate on the motion to recommend an increase in the dog licence fee, which has remained at the same figure, 7s 6d (37½p) ever since it was introduced, before the turn of the century, so that it is now ludicrously out of keeping with the increased incomes of dog-owners and the current value of money. The RSPCA is itself in favour of an increase, and urges that no dog should change hands without a dog licence being produced. Some of the facts the proposer brought out were: The United Kingdom has the lowest licence fee for dogs—in West Germany it costs £20. The Isle of Man's fee is only 50p but with the purchase of the licence goes a small tag to fix to the dog's collar, so that the animal can be traced. The Department of the Environment estimates that the dog population is 5,800,000 and that approximately half are un-licensed. If there is one subject on which the British, whether male or female, are thought to be sentimental and irrational, it is dogs. But what did the Townswomen decide? They agreed to ask for legislation to make the dog licence £2 for a dog at twelve weeks, or £5 for unspayed bitches; they turned down amend-ments to increase the licence to £10 and also to leave the fee as at present for old age pensioners. No wave of sentiment there, for the majority against soft-heartedness towards pensioners was overwhelming.

The resolutions on this agenda certainly filled the aim to be well-varied and controversial. They were also rather surprisingly 'contemporary' in their subject matter . . . that is to say that the motion on log-books of written-off motor vehicles recognized how many members of Townswomen's Guilds are now car drivers, and so personally concerned; the Executive Committee's motion on the admission to licensed premises of children under fourteen in the com-pany of an adult produced, of course, the argument 'for', as people accustomed to taking holidays abroad with their children found it very disconcerting that when out with the family at home they could drink outside a pub if it was fine, but not inside if it was wet. In the early days of the NUTG very few members would have gone with their husbands to a public house let alone with their children.

But the opponents were not only the predictable older people who thought it quite wrong to expose children to the smoky beery atmosphere of the bar, and to hearing bar 'basic English', but young women, one of whom pleaded quite passionately that the image of the pub should not be changed by having children running around. She wanted this one place to remain where she could escape from 'family life'!

Two other resolutions, more predictable on the agenda of a women's conference, were on the sterilization of girls and parental responsibility for juvenile offenders, and the imposition of 'more realistic fines'. Of the two urgency motions one, a request for a cheaper Christmas postal rate, brought out some sardonic mirth —'what a hope', the delegates were obviously saying to one another—while the other brought out an expression of deep concern about the processing of nuclear waste at the Windscale plant. A similar motion was carried the week before at the annual congress of the Women's Co-operative Guild—which raises intriguing questions. Do the women's organizations on the whole speak with one mind? And if they do, are they influential in shaping legislation? Are their annual expressions of opinion, pious or not, really much good or might the delegates just as well save their breath?

Women's Forum (formerly the Women's Group on Public Welfare) has kept an index of resolutions passed by forty women's organizations (or organizations with a predominantly female membership) since 1962. It would be impossible to compare the content of these resolutions in detail without access to the agendas of all the separate organizations, but there are some noteworthy points to make. There has been an overwhelming preoccupation with education, at all levels. Some of the resolutions might be, as with the Townswomen, about students in revolt or legislation to provide that recipients of state grants for education be obliged to take jobs in the UK for not less than two years; or, as again with the NUTG, about increased training facilities for women in middle life; or, as with the National Federation of Women's Institutes, about primary education in villages or education in parenthood; or, as with the National Council of Women, about reading standards in schools; but the resolutions listed in the Women's Forum index add up to nearly fifty educational topics, and the actual resolutions passed to nearly 200 by practically every one of the listed organizations, which adds up to a pretty impressive level of concern.

Is this kind of concern *effective*? In one or two instances it undoubtedly was, as for instance in the improvement in widows' pensions—even before the NUTG existed the Women's Institutes had called on the Government in 1924 'to introduce legislation giving pensions to civilian widows with dependent children, free from the taint of Poor Law relief' and one of the first subjects of a 'Public Question' motion on the Townswomen's agenda in 1957 was an attack on the notorious 'earnings rule'. This urged that when a widow's earnings exceeded £2. 10s (£2.50), she should not forfeit so large a proportion of her pension as at that time. This campaign against the earnings rule brought many of the major women's organizations into battle and they were in fact completely successful, for widows' pensions are now free of any deduction on account of their earnings. (The battle front has now moved to the taxing of widows' pensions, and also to the removal of the earnings rule from the pensions of all 'senior citizens'.)

Practically all women's organizations have been concerned about cancer detection, many about family planning, road safety, family allowances and public transport, including concessionary fares. There is an increasing number of resolutions about consumer protection, different forms of pollution, pest control, chemical additives, and, as would be expected, concern is strong over the provision of refuges for 'battered wives'. Is it true, as many commentators seem to think, that the women's organizations' expressions of opinion tend to be conservative, moralistic, repressive, condemnatory? The Woman's Forum index doesn't give much support to the allegation. 'Moral standards' were certainly of concern. The Townswomen protested in 1964 at the 'casual treatment' by the BBC and ITA of moral standards and sadistic displays of violence; they urged the Government in 1966 to retain capital punishment 'until a national plebiscite is taken'; and in 1972 asked for the death penalty to be restored for the murder of prison officers and police; and in 1971 again called on the BBC and ITV companies to 'curb the portrayal of immoral behaviour and violence, except for news items, and the use of bad language on television and radio'. But it would be misleading and unfair to over-emphasize these aspects of the women's organizations' concern for the quality of life. They must be offset by motions such as the Townswomen's NCM accepted in 1971:

'The NUTG view with disquiet developments in science and technology which if uncontrolled are likely to have major effects on human life and environment. They therefore welcome the formation of the British Society for Social Responsibility in Science.'

'The NUTG are deeply concerned with the menace to civilization of chemical and biological weapons and urge the Government to make every effort to achieve an early conclusion for the prohibition of chemical and biological warfare to supplement the 1925 General Protocol.'

It is in attitudes like these that many of us feel the women's organizations can exert their best and most significant influence.

7

Wider Still and Wider

The founding mothers of the National Union of Townswomen's Guilds were all internationalists especially the president, Margery Corbett Ashby, who was, at the time of its launching, the president of the International Alliance of Women, and had, in fact, been present at *its* launching, in 1904 in Berlin and at the silver jubilee in the same city in 1929, the year of the formation of the first Townswomen's Guilds.

There is a case for saying that all women's organizations tend to forge international links, perhaps more readily than men's, because they have more intimate common interests, and are more conscious of their common bonds. A woman may, like a man, think of herself as a teacher, a lawyer, a doctor, but she also is apt to think of herself as a mother and homemaker in an immediate and fundamental kind of way in which a man is not likely to think of himself as a father and home-owner. Women have *always* compulsive subjects to discuss together—home-making, rearing and education of children and, increasingly in this last quarter of the twentieth century, the self-determination of the female sex, their right to work, to equal status in society, to control their own fertility.

With such a lively leader as Dame Margery there was bound to be a spin-off in interest in international affairs among the new Guilds, and the thirties, when the NUTG was growing apace, were a time when peace movements had a very strong appeal for thinking citizens. When Mrs Corbett Ashby set off from Southampton on the liner *Olympic* in February 1938 to take part in round table talks on disarmament in the United States, a party of thirty Guild members saw her off. The Atlantic crossing was rough, the ship was delayed and Mrs Corbett Ashby had to go straight from the ship to the railway station, change into evening dress on the train, and appear immediately at a vast banquet in Washington where the veteran feminist Carrie Chapman Catt and Eleanor Roosevelt were both speakers. In 1934 the annual council meeting of the TG urged that Guilds should make a study of world peace part of their next year's programme, and on the motion of the Eccles Guild this was reaffirmed the following year.

But it was always on a person-to-person basis that Townswomen felt most involved in international co-operation. During Mrs Mary Courtney's chairmanship a determined effort was made to involve the Townswomen in the work of the Parliamentary Group for World Government. Mrs Lillias Norman, the national general secretary, was also a convinced internationalist who had previously worked with UNRRA, and strongly in support. The Executive Committee agreed to a series of articles in *The Townswoman* on the work of this all-party group and urged delegates to the forthcoming National Council Meeting to study 'The Parliamentary Path to Peace' so that they should be well-informed and able to ask questions when Lord Beveridge spoke to them on behalf of the Parliamentary Group. During November and December 1956, well over a thousand Townswomen attended meetings in the House of Commons organized by the Group. But one questions whether this formal approach to international co-operation had anything like the impact of the visits and exchanges made by Townswomen through their own Guilds.

In personal contact with our 'ex-enemies', the Germans, the NUTG was very early off the mark. The first contacts came through a former NUTG organizer, Mrs Betty Norris, who was sent to Germany by the Women's Group on Public Welfare at the request of the Control Commission. The Nazis had closed down all German branches of international organizations, and now there was a yearning to resume links with the democratic organizations of the western world. The Control Commission had approved the 'adoption' of German women's organizations by British organizations. The idea was that magazines and periodicals should be passed on and that this might lead to pen friendships. In the

1970s it is difficult to appreciate the atmosphere of shock, apathy and frustration that the Women's Group on Public Welfare visitors found among the German women. They wrote: 'While realizing sympathetically the great difficulties of the Control Commission and the apathetic attitude of the majority of German women, who with very little remaining energy are almost wholly preoccupied with the questions of food, shelter and clothing, we consider that there should be experiments on a broad scale in education in democracy among the women of Germany by outstanding English women with wide experience of informal education, a good command of the language and, not least, human sympathy.' Miss Norris and her colleague hoped that a party of German women could shortly come to England to learn the ways of British women's organizations.

They did. In June 1947, only two years after the end of the war in Europe, a party of six arrived from various German organizations. They all spent an hour in the NUTG's Cromwell Place headquarters learning about the range of the work, but one, Fraulein Richter from Kiel, concentrated on the Townswomen's methods. She saw Guilds being formed, from the first public meeting to the programme-planning round-table conference. She went to a Guild meeting in Hawick, Teviotdale and a conference on 'delegates and delegation'. When she got home she wrote, as chairman of the Schleswig-Holstein Deutsche Frauenbund, saying that she would like to suggest to her members 'Make Do and Mend' afternoons, and wondering if Townswomen's Guilds would 'send from time to time little parcels of sewing needles, thread, mending cottons for darning stockings, sewing silks, darning needles, pins and other materials. It needn't be very much, but perhaps one or two of your Guilds might be prepared to become the "godmother" of a group in Schleswig-Holstein. None of this material can be had here now, and will not be in the next few years.'

It wasn't much to ask, but it was very soon after the husbands and sons of these women had been dropping bombs on one another. Were the Townswomen and, indeed, were the Frauenbund members ready to hold out a sisterly hand to one another? This is not recorded; but undoubtedly the interchange was the beginning of a heartwarming breakthrough. In 1948 another party of German women arrived here, one pair going to Liverpool under the auspices of the TGs. In 1949 an ex-teacher of English in Eastern Germany, currently working with women's and youth organizations in Osnabruck in the British Zone, was entertained by Townswomen and attended various typical meetings, including a 'reconnaissance' into the NUTG's origins and development by one of the earliest Guilds, Burnt Oak.

By 1955 visits by parties of Townswomen to Germany were quite frequent. A notable one organized by the South-west Essex Federation took nineteen women to Cologne and Weilberg. The Townswomen stayed in the homes of the Deutsche Frauenring and the following Easter received twenty-one German women in their homes on a return visit. These women laid bunches of flowers on a memorial at Runnymede to 20,455 British airmen in unknown graves, little knowing then that one of the airmen commemorated was Sgt John Elwell of Coastal Command, killed on a U-boat hunting mission in 1943, whose mother, Mrs C. J. Elwell, was the social studies chairman of the hostess Federation. She was, in fact, one of the NUTG's most sincere and devoted workers for international understanding. Mrs Jessica Moore, the chairman of this Federation, a powerful driving force in international work as became plain later, stressed how much support she had from Mrs Elwell . . . and it was to Mrs Elwell that the Federation entrusted a historic resolution at the 1956 National Council meeting.

This read: 'In view of the increasing influence of Townswomen's Guilds in the sphere of home affairs, the time has arrived when the NU should seek closer relations with women's organizations in other countries which have objects consistent with the NUTG, in order to establish common understanding, greater co-operation and action to bring about and preserve world peace.' This step forward naturally encouraged exchange visits between British women and women with similar interests in Europe. The enterprising South-west Essex Federation was the first organization invited by the Union des Femmes Européennes (women's section of the EEC) to Paris in 1957. The climate of opinion was being created for one of the most remarkable achievements in the whole history of the NUTG . . . the clearing of the Ried Refugee Camp in Austria.

As a result of a British-sponsored resolution in the United Nations Assembly in December 1958, the year 1959 was designated World Refugee Year. For some years the NUTG had sent a representative to the British Council for Aid to Refugees, but the first 'appeal' to the membership came in an article in the June 1959 *Townswoman* which began: 'Would you be willing to give a penny a month for 12 months as a thank-offering for the home you live in? Would you be willing to give a penny a month for the freedom you have to move about when and where you will in your town and country? Would you be willing to give a penny a month as a thank-offering for the food you can buy in the shops of your town? If your answer is "yes", and you do in fact put three pennies in a box each month from now until the end of May 1960 you will have gone some way to solve the refugee problem of the world. That may sound ridiculously simple, but it is based on facts and figures given by responsible people who are organizing World Refugee Year.'

Though few people remember now, the aims of the UK Refugee Year committee included resettlement of European refugees from China, aid for Chinese refugees in Hongkong, and aid for the Palestinian refugees, but it was the resettlement of the 'displaced persons', the 600,000 men, women and children who were living in camps in Austria, France, Germany, Greece, Italy, and Turkey which caught the British imagination. It seemed from the start that adopting a refugee camp and concentrating every effort on finding permanent homes for its inmates was the sort of project that would most appeal to the warm-hearted Townswomen. And so it proved. Many letters of support for such an idea reached the NU during the summer and the National Executive discussed the idea thoroughly at its September meeting and committed the NUTG to a project to 'adopt a camp for clearance—one of the smallest official camps offered for financial assistance to the UK World Refugee Year Committee'. It was natural that the Executive should be cautious—they did not want the project to be a failure and could not possibly know what a wave of sympathy for the homeless refugees was sweeping the country.

Margaret Playle, the NUTG's press officer and editorial consultant, was undoubtedly a major factor in the success of the Townswomen's campaign. She determined to see the camp for herself, and reported through *The Townswoman*. 'It is difficult to bridge 600 miles . . . Let us clear our minds of all ideas of grandeur and officialdom that may be called up by such titles as "Refugee Secretariat", "Refugee Bureau", and so on. They really only refer to small rooms in wooden barracks which take a good deal of finding on the outskirts of the town. In them are a few people and many index papers—the life histories of the flotsam and jetsam of invaded lands. Here there are two pictures to bear in mind: The camp itself. The wooden barracks: each building divided into 20 to 25 living quarters, rooms with for the most part only the barest necessities, too hot in summer, too cold in winter. One lavatory and one washroom serving all the families. Every drop of water must be carried from the washroom to the living-room and heated there on the stove. No privacy, no comfort. But with only a very few exceptions the rooms were spotlessly clean, and this was quite early in the morning when there could be no idea that visitors would call. Here a man lay ill in bed. There a young girl, 15 years old, was looking after the two youngest of six children while her mother, a TB case, was out shopping and the father was at work.

'The thing that everyone seemed to have in common was a love of growing things . . . carefully tended plants in the rooms, carefully tended flowers and vegetables bordering the paths outside. Every few yards were raised flower beds surrounded by a wall about two feet high. The bricks were grey but someone with uncanny foresight had decorated them with large dots of red, green, and white paint, exactly as if they had been prepared for a TG rally or garden fete. When I came upon these "TG" beds I could not help thinking it was in some way preordained that Ried should be in our care.

'The second picture: A young Yugoslav girl, herself a refugee and now working with the refugee organization, came with me to a camp which was being cleared as quickly as possible. Blocks of flats had just been finished and stood in a group near the camp barracks—the white and bright orange-yellow of their outer walls in happy contrast to the black huts. The Counsellor was a middle-aged woman who would have fitted into any TG scene unremarked, and she took us into the flats to see what was going on. What a scene! Men, women and children were hurrying to and fro with

beaming or earnestly radiant faces. Two young boys were hauling
sacks into the basement, containing wood for communal use during
the winter. Men were unloading furniture—given to the refugees
by the Austrian State—and carrying it into the rooms. Women
were measuring, mostly by foot, the space in the rooms, planning
where the bed or beds would go, where the table would look best.
It was superfluous to ask if they were happy. How could they not be?
Each family had a well-fitted bathroom and lavatory. What must
it be like, I wondered, to have such privacy and comfort after
sharing a dismal closet with any number up to 20 families for 10,
12 or even 15 years? And what would be the rapture of seeing hot
water spout from a large boiler into a gleaming enamel bath after
having to carry cold water from a communal washroom, bucket
by bucket, heat it on a small stove and then wash as best one could
in a shared room?'

Miss Playle was a truly intelligent and compassionate link
between the Townswomen and the dwellers in the Ried camp.
She was also an excellent journalist. She passed on a comment
made to another visitor to the camp by a small child. 'We are going
to give you homes,' said the well-meaning visitor. 'We have got
a home,' said the child. 'We need a house to put it in.' Having
described a visit to the home of an elderly crippled Pole, a father
of six, Miss Playle related how she went with him and the camp
counsellor to a farm which with the TGs' help could be the
'house' to put this 'home' into. 'It must have been like a glimpse
of the promised land to this ex-farmer as he walked and then almost
leapt from place to place seeing a comfortable sitting-room,
well-equipped kitchen, bedrooms, the byre filled with fodder for
the winter, the cowstalls, the stretch of rich grass where the cows
grazed and the apple trees. His only comment, many times repeated,
was "big . . . beautiful".

'But when he was asked "Would you like it?" his first words were,
"Where is the school?" With such descriptions Miss Playle must
have touched the hearts of the Townswomen at home. She had to
say to the Ried refugees that she could only 'hope' that the means
would be forthcoming to help them, and at first the response to
the Refugee appeal did not seem to justify her 'hope'.

In January 1960 it was reported: 'Half-time. What is a little
mystifying is that the total received of just over £900 has come

from only 108 Guilds and four Federations. We have still to receive donations from more than 2,000 Guilds.' A 'Stop Press' announcement in the same issue said, however, that £2,000 had been received and in February Miss Playle was writing 'It is exciting to be at headquarters these days and see how the goodwill barometer is steadily rising towards the target of £8,000. There are still four months to go before the end of World Refugee Year—and we are still waiting to hear from over 600 Guilds.'

News was constantly passed on of Townswomen's efforts—and of how the money already raised was being allocated—towards rehousing the Pole's family in the farm he had been taken to see, for instance. Members of one Guild were each given a matchbox and asked to put a penny a day in it—which resulted in a cheque for £10. Many Guilds asked to 'adopt' a family and went on sending letters and gifts even though the refugees, who were Yugoslavs, Czechs, Poles, Hungarians, and Rumanians, were unable to write letters in reply.

The United Kingdom reached its £2m target in mid-February and decided to double it to £4m. The NUTG reached its £9,000 target by mid-March . . . and the money still rolled in. At the Annual Council Meeting on 25 May the amount handed to Christopher Chataway was £28,284, three times the target figure, and the final amount was the staggering sum of £48,280. In June 1960 it was reported 'World Refugee Year has come to a close. We have no further moral obligation, but there has been a wonderful response to the suggestion that Guilds might continue in friendship what was begun as a salving of the free world's conscience. It seems that not a single family or individual to be settled under the mandate from Ried camp will be without friendly contact with our movement in the future.'

The flow of gifts—some carried in their luggage by TG holiday-makers to Austria, to save the cost of postage—was as remarkable as the raising of money. When Miss Playle went back to Ried in the summer of 1960 she heard countless words of thanks for all sorts of gifts. 'A cheerful little woman bustled up to me one day and asked me to bring back her thanks for the beautiful warm blanket she had been sent. It was the familiar patchwork of knitted squares, carefully draped over her sofa. She brought it out to be photographed, draped over her arm. It seemed to me that every hut possessed one of these blankets, for decoration in summer and warmth in winter. Tea, coffee, soap and other presents taken by members on the music study tour to Linz via Oberammergau proved most acceptable and the Counsellor had been able to distribute lovely little garments for children and other clothing for adults. In one very bare hut I met a widow grieving for her husband—but she had a new dove-grey coat which really fitted her.'

A year later when Margaret Playle went to Ried, in 1961, the area where the refugee huts had stood was bare ground. 'Now a high building stood here, and as I went to the entrance I was greeted by an elderly widow. She and other UNRRA refugees had moved in just three weeks earlier. I wish you could have seen the pride with which I was shown each home, longed for during arid summers and dreary winters spent in communal barracks, and the tears of joy because they had not believed "there was so much kindness in the world". This was especially so in the case of the old people, ill and alone, who were in direct touch with Guilds. The letters, the Christmas cards, the birthday greetings and calendars were all brought out to show me.'

Describing one of the new flats, Miss Playle said that Herr and Frau K were having to make do with the bits and pieces of furniture they brought from the camp. 'Their beds are contraptions of pieced-together wood and the coverings are any more or less suitable pieces of material they have been able to get together, surmounted by knitted blankets provided by Guilds. Later they will get an allowance of necessary furniture but the requisition sent in by the camp counsellor is taking its appointed and official course. . . . They are in touch with members of a Guild who requested Herr K to send a life history, which is being read in monthly instalments at Guild meetings.'

In this new block there were sixteen flats, four on a storey; each group of four contained a one-room flatlet, always occupied by an elderly widow; a two-room flat for husband and wife or parent and child; and two family flats with three rooms and separate kitchen. The basement had a large well-equipped laundry, fuel storage and other cubicles and room for bicycles. This was the task the NUTG had set itself, but the extra money raised enabled two more buildings to be built, and fifty-six dwellings and twenty single-room apartments for 'non-mandate' refugees—that is to say for people who were not 'stateless' but who, though they had taken out Austrian citizenship, were too old or ill to work. These were the people who were most in need of supplementary help and kindness from Guild friends in Britain.

And so, in November 1962, Miss Playle and the then national treasurer, Mrs D. M. Railton, paid an official visit to the opening of the last two blocks of flats, were loaded with gifts of apples, onions and garlic, and received the thanks not only of the refugees but of the Austrian Secretary of State, the Mayor of Ried, and many other dignitaries. A bronze plaque commemorated the NUTG's achievement in one of the flat blocks. This was not, however, quite the end of the story. Early in 1963 it was obvious that heating was a grave problem for the older people, especially as some of the stoves handed out to the refugees were great eaters of fuel. Members of the NEC visited Ried and decided that more efficient stoves costing about £30 should be bought by the NU, to remain their property so that they could be passed on if need be. In 1964 an appeal for money for fuel was launched and again proved a success, and coal was provided as long as it was needed for the elderly. But Mrs Railton in her final report summed up by saying that 90 per cent of the families had become integrated into their community and required no further help. In fact they did not wish to be reminded that they had ever been refugees. 'The younger people', she wrote, 'are very proud. Only 5 per cent still require looking after a little longer and are certainly grateful to their "adopters" for occasional monetary help and for Christmas and birthday cards'—these were mostly the elderly people.

The first official NUTG study tour was organized in 1958 by the drama adviser, Alison Graham Campbell, to Salzburg. The idea came to her partly because her husband, Dr Sander, was a refugee and she had long wanted to visit Austria, his native country. The tour was a shining success and the forerunner of many organized by Miss Graham Campbell and others. There was a fantastic 16-day, 2,500-mile trip in 1960 by forty-one South-west Essex Federation women to Brussels, Bonn, Heidelberg, Munich, Merano, Venice, the Austrian Tyrol, Innsbruck and, finally, Oberammergau for the passion play. Later parties went to Greece, Russia, and the United States. A remarkable chairman of the international sub-committee,

Mrs Jessica Moore, organized many of these tours—and as professionally as if she had been trained over the years as a courier. She coped without flinching with all the problems a travel guide can experience—even on one occasion with a Guild member who suffered a detached retina on a Russian tour and urgently needed treatment, but refused to go into a Russian hospital. She had to be rushed home by plane—organized, of course, by Mrs Moore. There are times when the resourcefulness of the volunteer 'Organization Woman' is breath-taking.

An extract from some 'guidance notes' drafted by Mrs Moore indicates the thoroughness with which she prepared her ground. 'It is advisable to add to the fare an average of 10s [50p] for porters and to delegate one member to take full charge of luggage and porters. It is recommended that members should carry an overnight bag for use both ways on the journey in order that the main luggage can be left together. This facilitates porterage in the morning when time is limited to leave the boat. Another 10s can be added for the gifts for organizers—there are usually more than one—and for small gifts for mayors and other people representing organizations which give hospitality. For this purpose there is a very good, small and cheap book on London, which is always very acceptable. Linen is usually preferred for the organizers. It is a good idea to ask each member of the group to bring with her a small additional gift, soap, lavender water, notelets etc, in case an occasion presents itself when one needs to give someone a small acknowledgement and not necessarily officially. Cigarettes are not recommended for an official gift. In some countries such a gift could be almost an insult (although one's host is always glad to receive English cigarettes). A half bottle of whisky would be more than welcome, both officially and unofficially.'

Whether on 'study tours' or 'exchange visits' what a splendid time the Guild members had, what a marvellous enlargement of experience for women some of whom had never been abroad before and few of whom had ever visited the homes of people living in other countries. There are many memories still available, in local newspaper cuttings, in reports to Federations and Guilds, and in *The Townswoman*. One has to select just one or two to give an idea of what the members did and how they reacted to 'life abroad'. A Buckhurst Guild member who was one of a party of sixteen from the South-west Essex Federation on a tour arranged by Jessica Moore to Freiburg in the Black Forest was particularly lucky because she was able to renew contact with a young woman who had visited her from Vienna as a girl on an exchange visit. She married a German and moved to Freiburg where 'they both attend university and will eventually teach grammar school. They now have a daughter of two months and take it in turns to attend university and mind the baby. They are both champion fencers— this is how they met.'

Here are more typical extracts from an exceptionally vivid account: 'Frau Faulhaber [the hostess] says her husband and friend have gone hunting in the Kaiserstuhl and we will join them for a meal. So off we go, about 30km, a wet night, dark roads, whizzing along, and arrive at an old village where at a lovely old hotel we have a grand meal with lots of wine with the two hunters. Then back to Freiburg again to the friend's house, more wine, more music and we leave about midnight; lovely time.'

The next day the Mayor of Freiburg invited the party to attend a performance of *Il Seraglio* (Mozart) at the Civic Theatre. Their 'study' visits included two old people's homes, 'very modern, with single rooms for each inmate', a school, where 'two classes stood up and sang English songs', new blocks of flats, some of which had been built for the French occupying forces, and 'a settlement of old army huts where refugees, bad payers etc were housed until new accommodation could be found. After this we went to a permanent Gypsy encampment where there were old shacks made of odds and ends, lots of dogs and children roaming about. I was glad to get out of it.'

The following spring, a party from the Freiburg Frauenring paid a return visit and the Townswomen were able to lay on an 'international evening' of exceptional interest at which women from Egypt, Scandinavia, Czechoslovakia, Malta and the United States gave greetings. Other parties of Townswomen went to France, and entertained visitors from Holland and Denmark. Mrs Moore was indefatigable in putting Guilds in touch with contacts who would help them to arrange visits or exchanges.

The second tour to the USSR had been arranged when the news of the invasion of Czechoslovakia shocked the western world, and there were, of course, suggestions that it should be cancelled.

The National Executive decided to go ahead, and Mrs Moore later reported: 'Most of our members told me in private conversation how glad they were that the tour had been proceeded with. The general feeling was that the ordinary people longed for some contact with the Western world and this was borne out by the patient waiting at the airport for our arrival and at the hotel, to be available for the wishes of our members. They shared impromptu tea parties with long discussions and several invited members to their homes. They came every evening and were a great help to us. A young married teacher of English with children was a particular friend to us. This girl accompanied us to the theatre. On her way back she met some of our members and stayed with them, shopping and sight-seeing, until it was time to return to the theatre to see that we arrived back safely at the hotel. She seems to thirst for outside contacts, and she is only one example.

'I had been advised to raise the question of Czechoslovakia wherever I went and I did this. In only one case was an attempt made to justify the Soviet action. To this woman the reason was quite clear. I answered that in every crisis the first casualty was truth, and there I left the discussion. The others begged me, and not only me, not to judge them by their leaders. One elderly lady cried as she told me that for the first two days she had sat glued with horror to her radio.'

Mrs Moore summed up her philosophy as an internationalist in this report: 'As a women's organization our mission is in particular with the women of all nations and not with governments. I feel we should be failing in our international undertaking if we broke off association with the Soviet women. We were all glad to hear that after discussion Manchester had decided to continue their "twinning" association with Leningrad. My own feeling is that we must continue to have cultural and educational exchanges with women everywhere. We have now close contacts with Germany, Italy and Japan. How far should we take an abhorrence of what governments do, and when do we stop taking action, especially when the governments remain the same politically?'

Since most of these emissaries from the West were mothers, it seems right to quote a reminiscence by Mrs Duckworth, South Staffordshire, who was on the first Soviet tour. She made the acquaintance at the Palace of Babies in Leningrad of Igor, 'a white parcel of blankets tied around the middle with a bow of ribbon'. At the brief registration ceremony the interpreter explained the British custom of giving a baby a present of silver and amid solemn handshakes and thanks from father, Igor's little arms were filled with halfcrowns.

From 1965 onwards many Townswomen enjoyed study holidays at an Anglo-Swiss centre at Duerrenaesch, just over an hour's coach ride from Basle, Zurich and Lucerne. Mrs H. M. Wykes, the then national chairman, Mrs Moore, and a member of the NFWI visited this centre, looked it over and reported 'Several houses in the village have been purchased to give reasonably priced holidays to Swiss "exiles" and it is now proposed to set up a British Centre there. We are taking a pilot group in the spring when we will study Swiss customs, visit factories, art museums and explore the beautiful regions of Lucerne and Interlaken.' The deputation's hope that Guilds and Federations would make up parties of about thirty members was realized, and later two similar centres were established at Les Diablerets and Lugano. Discussions of Swiss neutrality and Swiss culture were interspersed with such jollities as 'an evening with Franz Hug and his Merry Swiss Alpine Yodelers'. In the year 1966, for example, no fewer than sixteen TG parties stayed at Duerrenaesch.

Informal contacts with the women of other countries may in the long run prove to be the most important aspect of the Townswomen's international work, for friendships begun and fostered in people's homes usually endure, and can be resumed after a gap of many years. But of course, official links with women's organizations in other countries are also of great importance. These developed greatly in the sixties and seventies and are still in being. From 1961 the NUTG had an international sub-committee, set up originally rather more as a think tank than as a planning body, for no money was budgeted for it, but the influence of this committee was soon manifest. In 1962 the decision was made to affiliate to the International Alliance of Women, its veteran honorary president, Mrs Corbett Ashby, having assured the committee that it was not party political and that there was complete liberty of movement for each affiliated society. The NUTG was represented on the Alliance's five commissions, concerned with equal moral standards, civil, political, economic, and educational rights and with international understanding.

When the Townswomen sent a delegation to the International Alliance of Women's diamond jubilee conference in 1964, Mrs Jessica Moore moved a resolution on world population expansion which had been passed at the Edinburgh National Council Meeting the previous year and was supported by all the British affiliates of the IAW. It was passed with only one delegate voting against— thirty-three countries were represented, under the chairmanship of Mrs Ezlynn Deraniyagala. In a moving little ceremony she took a ring from her finger and put it on a finger of her successor, the Begum Anwar Ahmed, wife of the then Pakistani ambassador to Washington. The Townswomen's resolution undoubtedly had a powerful impact. Moving it Mrs Moore said how difficult it had been to get 'some influential governments' to recognize that there was any connection between population growth and the health and well-being of a nation. At last, however, a motion had been placed on the agenda and passed by the Economic Committee of the UN in December 1962. In the General Assembly it was supported by Ceylon, Denmark, Ghana, Greece, Nepal, Norway, Pakistan, Tunisia, Turkey, the United Arab Republic, and others, but 'there proved to be a bone of contention in the clause that the United Nations should give technical assistance as requested by governments with national projects dealing with population problems. France, supported by Peru and the Argentine, asked for the deletion of the phrase and as the voting was 34 for and 34 against, with 32 delegates abstaining, the phrase was deleted and the whole motion emasculated.'

Mrs Moore explained that had the motion been passed the World Health Organization could have helped the lesser developed countries in planning adequate maternal and child welfare facilities in which education and services in family planning methods would have been an integral part, methods designed to be socially acceptable in that particular country. It was vitally important that this service should be recognized as coming under the United Nations, for World Health Organization help would be much more acceptable than any coming from individual countries regarded as 'imperialistic'.

Mrs Moore's speech moved many delegates deeply. 'What

woman who sees hope for five children will want to bear ten to allow for casualties?' she asked. 'We want a world in which every birth is accompanied by a *birth right* and a dedicated effort to advance in the developing regions of the earth the essential conditions conducive to human dignity, freedom, justice and peace . . . It is self-evident that a society which practises *death* control by the use of modern drugs must at the same time practise *birth* control, otherwise we have more and more people to share less and less. Probably never in history has so obvious and significant a fact been so widely evaded and minimized. Should we not now use all the resources of science to avert the reproach that we have freed men from disease only to let them die from hunger?'

Population control was a subject in which many Townswomen had taken an interest for many years. When it came to deciding on a project to support as a contribution to International Women's Year, 1975, an educational project concerned with women in Lesotho was adopted by the Central Council partly because it was recommended to them by the Population Countdown campaign and included a scheme to integrate family planning with rural development in the Thaba Bosiu area.

This project ran into trouble partly because the Population Countdown campaign was brought to an end and its work handed over to the International Planned Parenthood Federation, but also because the Lesotho government, having approved the plan, later raised objections to its family planning aspect.

Mrs Marjorie Rice, then the national chairman, had called the Lesotho scheme 'a landmark in our history' because it was a proof that the NUTG was 'a caring community' willing to take up the challenge of the problems of the developing world and to accept their responsibility as parishioners of this 'tight little inter-dependent world of ours'. The acceptable substitute for Lesotho and the £10,000 raised by the 'caring' Townswomen proved to be a Save the Children Fund project in Nepal, described for them by Michael Prosser, Save the Children Fund field director. The children's clinic at Surkhet, Nepal, he said, was functioning temporarily in a small thatched hut in the market place (previously used by the Nepal Children's Organization as a pre-school feeding centre). 'It is only too clear,' he urged, 'that the clinic

is long overdue and that without the TG gift of £10,000 it might
have been impossible.'

The thatched hut was very much a make-shift and not designed
as a clinic, 'but with luck the foundations for the new stone building should have been finished before the rains begin again'.
Supplies of roofing slate had to be carried from Dailekh, two days'
journey to the north. Sukhet is the centre of a population of about
104,000 with at least 30,000 children. It had one hospital of fifteen
beds and a good local doctor, but no X-ray facilities or other
basics until the Save the Children Fund moved in. 'There is still
no motor road to Surkhet so apart from twice-a-week scheduled
flights, which often don't take off in the rainy season, the only
link with the outside world is by trail (not train!) to Nepalgani
on the Indian border.'

Mrs Rice's successor as national chairman, Mrs Eileen Coram,
also had a heart-warming letter from an Andover doctor, the father
of the doctor running the Surkhet clinic. Dr and Mrs James
Arthur went to Surkhet to visit their son, his wife and their
baby son born in Katmandu in April 1976. 'The Nepali people
are delightful,' wrote Dr Arthur. 'So patient and good and full of
fun and joie-de-vivre, even in the very basic circumstances in
which most of them live. I was full of admiration for the efforts
of the whole team and felt your money could hardly have been
better spent, given that it was earmarked for a medical charity.
I felt I must write and say how rewarding it was to see generosity
so wisely directed. "NAMASTE" as they say in Nepal—I salute
all the divine qualities in you.'

The young Duchess of Gloucester, too, was able to tell the
delegates to the 1976 National Council Meeting how much their
generosity was needed and deserved in Nepal, which she had
visited and greatly admired. But the scene was set most vividly
by an account in *The Townswoman* by a missionary nurse, Rona
Nichols, who had worked for four years in what was known as
'The Shining Hospital' at Nautanwa in Nepal. It must have
convinced every Townswoman, even those most disappointed over
the failure of the Lesotho project, that their money was being
worthily spent. 'Nurses in Nepal', wrote Rona Nichols, 'do many
things which only doctors do in England. There was always a
baby or a small child with an abcess which needed incising, often

under a general anaesthetic, or a girl or a woman with a broken
arm. It's the women and girls who have to climb trees or hang
over dangerous precipices to cut leaves for the buffalo. Inevitably
accidents happen.

'Working in the wards gave us plenty of exercise in the art of
adaptation. No shining trolleys to push around. No familiar rows
of white-sheeted, tidy beds. "Shining Hospital" sheets were made
of cheap greyish cotton from the bazaar, with blankets of brightly
coloured knitted patchwork sent out from England and Germany.
Patients slept in their everyday clothes because they refused to
take them off. Shortage of water, lack of sanitation and no electricity were minor problems compared with the difficulties we had
in persuading patients to eat foods vital to their recovery after
illness or operation. We always had five or six cases in the wards
of severely burnt children, but if they were high-caste Hindus their
faith forbade them to eat eggs and meat. Without the right high-
protein diet many did not recover . . .

'A fly swat would scarcely be considered an essential piece of
equipment in a hospital theatre in England. In Pokhara it was
indispensable. Without any proper windows flies were liable to
settle on a patient's wound or on the surgeon's hand. It was the
duty of one nurse to keep them at bay. Another stood as close as
possible to the patient, directing the beam of a torch into the
wound.'

One can appreciate why Mrs Rice described the International
Women's Year fund-raising exercise for overseas aid 'a landmark'.
Townswomen had been delighted to participate in visits abroad
and exchanges. They had not been quite so ready to accept all
the implications of internationalism. A motion put forward at the
1962 National Council Meeting declaring that 'the cultivation of
an international outlook should begin in the primary school and
include the study of one European language' was narrowly lost on
a card vote. Two years later a similar resolution *was* accepted by
an overwhelming majority and the national general secretary,
Mrs Norman, rejoiced in the swing in opinion. 'During these
two years', she wrote, 'we have grown more conscious of how
Britain has grown closer to the other countries of Europe and,
indeed, of how the interdependence of all countries has increased.
It is therefore only natural that we should want our children still

at school to find their way easily about this shrinking world and to speak without inhibitions to others in their own language.'

While rank and file Guild members were going off to Duerrenaesch or Les Diablerets, executive members were extending the NUTG's official contacts with women's organizations abroad. In 1965, Mrs Moore, as chairman of the international sub-committee, attended the annual congress of the Union Féminine Civique et Sociale when it was celebrating its fortieth anniversary.

The following year was a bumper one for European contacts. Mrs D. M. Railton, as national chairman, with Mrs H. M. Wykes visited Poland, at the invitation of the League of Polish Women, members of which had previously visited the Townswomen's national headquarters. (To the grief and shock of Townswomen, Mrs Railton died suddenly only a few weeks after her return home.) Other conferences attended included the Women's Commission of the European Movement on 'The Use of Leisure' in Cologne (Mrs J. Moore); the Union Féminine Civique et Sociale on 'The Woman's Role' in Angers (Mrs P. G. McConachey, international sub-committee); the International Federation of Women Councillors in Paris (Councillor Mrs I. Lea).

As soon as the Townswomen's international sub-committee started to lay plans, it decided to set up national conferences on international themes—in accord with the movement's educational pattern. The first of these on 'The International Outlook' was a stimulating start, in 1965, for the opening speech by Miss Edith Davies, education officer of the British Council's main centre at Cologne, was followed by contributions from other organizations with international committees, the Business and Professional Women, the National Council of Women, the National Federation of Women's Institutes and the Soroptimists. Mrs Corbett Ashby was greeted with affectionate enthusiasm and talked about the International Alliance of Women. She was followed by Frank Judd, chairman of the UK Committee for International Co-operation Year, and by Dr Elizabeth Monkhouse, of London University, a very faithful and valued friend of the NUTG who spoke on 'The Promotion of a World Outlook'. Dr Monkhouse spoke again at the next international conference, at Caxton Hall in 1968. This time 'Human Rights' was the theme, and Dame Joan Vickers (now Lady Vickers) spoke on discrimination against women and Philip Mason spoke on racial discrimination. In this same year chairmen of no fewer than fifteen British women's organizations visited Germany as guests of the Townswomen's old friends, the Deutsche Frauenring. In 1972 Mrs Eunice Hazlewood, new chairman of a new NUTG committee, the International Standing Committee, went with Mrs Brenda Pope to a Deutsche Frauenbund conference in Cologne on 'What is the State and Society doing to help woman fulfil her manifold role?' and 'How long does the child need the care of the mother?'. To these debates delegates from fourteen countries contributed papers in the situation on their own country.

The Foreign and Commonwealth Office had now set up a European Committee based on the Women's Group on Public Welfare and the National Council of Women to administer a grant for the promotion of closer links with Europe. To this committee the Townswomen suggested two proposals, both of which were accepted. The first was to send two delegates to a European Colloquy in Paris—Mrs Hazlewood, who had the advantage of being a fluent French speaker, and Mrs Robinson attended this conference, which had been arranged by the International Committee for the Liaison of Women's Organizations in Paris and the French group of the European Movement. The other NUTG suggestion was for ten members of the Deutsche Hausfrauen Bund to stay in London. They visited a day nursery, a primary school and an adult training centre as well as the Law Courts and Houses of Parliament and it was reported that they were especially enthusiastic about our 'self-help' pre-school playgroups.

Partly through the influence of their national general secretary Lillias Norman, the Townswomen had been encouraged to take an interest in the Common Market from the early sixties and it had been a subject of discussion in social studies sections in many areas. In 1963 William Deeds, then Minister Without Portfolio in a Conservative Government and now editor of the *Daily Telegraph*, called together representatives of all the major organizations so as to set up a woman's consultative council. This was intended to meet monthly to discuss questions submitted in writing. Mrs Norman and the national chairman attended this body's first meeting and the first question they heard discussed was their own, about the effect of joining the Common Market on the

National Health Service. 'We were then introduced', wrote Mrs
Norman, 'to a new word which I think we had better get used to,
"harmonization"—intended to convey the intention to bring the
social systems of the different countries into line with each other
without imposing uniformity.'

There are members of the NUTG who fear that commitment to
international, especially European, co-operation does not per-
colate very far down the line from the national leadership. It
may be so, but there have always been heartening signs of commitment at grass roots level. In 1971 following a London Region
education conference on the Common Market attended by no
fewer than 900 members the Alexandra Park Guild, North London,
held a discussion meeting at which it became clear that 'no one
knew enough about the subject of the Common Market to reach
an informed decision'. So one enterprising member, Sonia Marsh,
suggested writing to women in the EEC countries to find out
what *they* thought. What was their own experience? Did they think
they had benefited? Did they think Britain should join, and if
they did, would *we* benefit? The National Union supplied names
of a dozen or so women's organizations in the Common Market
countries and Alexandra Park Guild hopefully sent off their letters
of enquiry. Not all replied, but all who did, apart from one German
organization, replied in English, carefully and informatively.

Sonia Marsh reported to *The Townswoman*: On the whole the
replies were more reassuring than alarming. The president of the
Amicale Internationale des Elues Municipales (who was, in fact,
the mother of the French Foreign Secretary) said that the EEC had
'woken up' the French people, who had lost *l'esprit de competition*,
and had made them feel closer to the other nations, which was a
good thing for peace in Europe. She felt that 'Britain joining
Europe would be better for us all', but inferred that there might be
an initial painful period before any benefits were felt. The vice-
president of the Deutsch Hausfrauenbund warned of an immediate rise in food prices—inevitable in Britain, she thought—
but said there were undoubted advantages in the wider markets
the EEC brought, and that in Germany many household goods
had actually become cheaper.

Reassurance about national identity came from another French
women's leader: 'France's identity is still very much intact,'

she wrote. 'The other five [Common Market countries] have not merged into each other: their fundamental characteristics remain unaltered.' This French leader, Mme Larretgère, also stressed the EEC's political importance, 'due to increased numbers and of not wanting to be "smothered" between two blocs. We women do not want to become either Soviets or Americans, but we do want to transmit to our children the European inheritance and moral values of our ancestors.' The Dutch correspondents took a similar line: joining the Common Market had meant some sacrifice—milk and butter prices rose; Italian apples undercut the Dutch crop; the Dutch housewife had been affected by price rises, but earnings were rising. Yet 'Without England the Common Market is not complete; without England there is no Europe.' It was this Dutch housewife who assured the Townswomen of the North London Guild that 'for many months the women's organizations here have been a great influence on the Consumers' Department of the Common Market and it is regarded as important for British women's organizations to let their voices be heard too'.

This admirable Townswoman from Alexandra Park who summarized all the opinions and evidence she had so carefully collected commented modestly, 'To be privileged to have seen other points of view in these letters has opened my eyes as well as my mind; as a result of which I have experienced a complete turnabout of feeling.'

The opinion that the public in general was not able to understand fully 'the complicated financial and strategic effects of British terms of entry into the EEC' remained so strong, however, that in 1974 the National Council Meeting passed a resolution to the effect that the electorate should not be asked to vote upon this issue and that the Government should abandon the proposed National Referendum. The national chairman commented that the Government didn't take a pennyworth of notice of that resolution, but at least the Townswomen had done their very best to inform themselves. The NUTG was the very first British organization to send an official delegation to Brussels to study the institutions and decision-making machinery of the Commission of European Communities in April 1974. The delegates to the 1975 National Council Meeting were told, 'We had three days of hard concentration, listening to and arguing with French, Germans, Italians,

Dutch, Luxembourgers, Belgians, Danes, and British, all of them
dedicated to the task of building a united Europe in the hope that
never again will there be war among the European nations.' These
eight representatives, who included the national chairman,
national secretary, and chairman of the international sub-committee, were invited to so many Guilds and Federations to explain
to the members how the Commission works that they were 'just
about camping out in inter-city trains', said Mrs Rice later.

This strong desire to know more about what commitment to
Europe meant did not lessen willingness to hold out a hand to the
developing world. In September 1974 with the assistance of
Oxfam the international sub-committee set up a seminar on
Botswana, and representatives of 107 of the 115 Federations made
the journey to London for it. A questionnaire revealed that eighty-
one Federations had organized or encouraged Guilds to organize
some World Development activity. There had been nineteen
conferences, twenty-four one-day schools, fifty-seven talks to
Guilds and twenty-two studies of the theme, 'World Development
—the Next Ten Years'.

As ever, grass-roots interest was strong in personal relationships,
and it was fully realized that women from 'the developing world'
were, in increasing numbers, trying to adjust to life in the United
Kingdom. As far back as the early sixties, letters to *The Townswoman* had described the warm-hearted but largely unsuccessful
efforts of Guilds to draw immigrants into their fellowship. For
instance, Aylesbury Vale decided in 1959 to try to get into touch
with some of the coloured girls living in the district in the hope that
some might become members. 'We contacted a local organization
whose aim is to foster friendship between white and coloured
people locally. We discovered that they had met some limited
success with coloured men, but in spite of much effort had not
succeeded in enrolling any coloured girls.

'As many of these girls are employed as students in the three
local hospitals we wrote to the matrons, outlining the aims and
activities of the TG movement and asking for their co-operation
in offering friendship to the coloured girls on the staff. We had no
response at all. When discussing the matter with a senior member
of the staff of one of the hospitals she gave three reasons for our
failure. The first was lack of spare time. The girls not only have

to complete the standard course of studies but most of them have a limited command of English, which increases the time needed for study. The second reason is that in their own countries it is not the custom for women to belong to societies and groups and therefore they feel it is not right for them to do so when they are living here. The last reason, the most tragic, is that the girls are far more conscious of their colour than the menfolk and tend to suspect patronage in offers of friendship from white people.' Despite this, the Guilds went on trying but no one reported any black members, much less any black delegate to a Federation or Central Council meeting.

By 1976, holding out a hand of friendship to coloured neighbours was a very different proposition. A controlled but steady flow of immigrants from the Commonwealth had increased the coloured population to 1,175,000, or 3.2 per cent of the total population by 1974, and of these 40 per cent had been born in this country. The members of the Guilds who in the early sixties had wanted to invite the coloured nurses to their meetings no doubt still did, but what the NUTG wanted to find out was whether the women in the overcrowded areas where there might be as many as two black people to every eight whites, were so enthusiastic. An excellent new feature in *The Townswoman*, labelled 'Opinion' gave some factual answers to the distortions of prejudice . . . such as this, for instance, on the slander that 'blacks come here and sponge on our social services'. 'As a group black men tend to be younger than the whites in the community. Ninety-six per cent of black men were working compared with 77 per cent of white men and therefore were paying income tax and national insurance. Since there are fewer older people in the black community they actually take much less from the state at present than the white population—but of course, they have paid less into it.' (1976 figures from 'Facts of Racial Disadvantage.')

When the National Executive had their programme planning meeting towards the end of 1976 they agreed on a study theme that did great credit to their long history of concern to be good citizens and they moved into their Golden Jubilee Year, 1978–79, discussing 'The Challenge of a Multi-Racial Society'. Residential schools were organized on three aspects of the problems, education, health and housing, and employment. The chairman of the Public

Question and Current Affairs sub-committee, Mrs Ruth Jewell, and her Head Office administrative officer, Lady Henniker Heaton, started planning the series way back in 1976. Their great hope was to secure the company of representatives of the immigrant communities staying in the halls of residence for these schools, side by side with their white sisters. If this hope failed, it would not be for want of steadfast effort.

8

Things to Come

For three-quarters of a century women's organizations have been
an important strand in our social fabric. From 1928 the Townswomen's Guilds have been a valuable thread in that pattern.
No one can deny that the pattern is now changing. What is the
future for the women's organizations? Will the National Union
of Townswomen's Guilds as we know it now survive until the
turn of the century? One can only guess at answers; and hope that
what has so much enriched our national life will not now dismally
decline.

For their first forty years the Townswomen's Guilds expanded
steadily in membership, in the number of local Guilds and in
interests. In National Union planning and budgeting, being able
to meet the demand for new Guilds was paramount and success
came to be almost synonymous with 'formations'. So it was the
slowing down of the growth rate, even before this caused an
inevitable slight decline in membership, that first rang an alarm
bell for the leadership, and caused anxious self-questioning as to
how the movement could be given fresh life and energy. The
result was a remarkably enterprising decision to commission a
small-scale study of the movement which might 'highlight and
sharpen some of the critical issues facing the movement'. This
decision, taken by the National Executive but endorsed by the
Central Council, showed high courage, for it was made plain that
the researchers, Dr Eric J. Miller and Miss Geraldine V. Gwynne,
of the Centre for Applied Social Research, Tavistock Institute
of Human Relations, were not going to dodge any sensitive or

even painful issues. No comparable voluntary organization has commissioned a research team to hold up a mirror to its private as well as its public face in this way, and to report on the blemishes that mirror might reveal.

Almost all voluntary workers are acutely sensitive about their image. To be *criticized*, after all the effort they have put, unpaid, into work for the common good is very hard to bear. Most organizations indulging in self-questioning about their declining membership or lack of public impact, resort to platitudes about the need for change of one kind or another. The Townswomen had to take some quite hard knocks when the researchers reported in their 'Working Note'. Basically the Tavistock Study queried whether the 'all-purpose' large-scale organization of women can meet the needs of today's women, and this doubt applies, surely, to *all* similar organizations.

The Tavistock Study identified the purposes of the Townswomen's Guilds as:

1. to provide social and recreational activities for women;
2. to provide educational facilities for women;
3. to mobilize and present women's views on issues of local, national and international importance.

The question has to be asked not only in relation to the NUTG but to all the traditionally organized women's associations—*can* one form of organization perform all three functions effectively?

Probably the majority of women who join a Townswomen's Guild, or who remain members, do so for the company of like-minded women, whom they will meet regularly and with whom they will become involved in various activities so that some at least will become valued friends. Such women may be restless if sociability is reduced by pressure to take part in less enjoyable activities. What they really want is some version of a 'club', said the Tavistock Study, run by and for its members, almost certainly a local institution and quite autonomous. 'There would have to be an attractive pay-off to make it willing to pay a fee for affiliation to a national body.'

Is this sort of club atmosphere what a majority of Townswomen really want? Letters to *The Townswoman* seem increasingly to suggest that the rank and file members are getting impatient with the readings of minutes (really only a rather boring recital of what the members already know happened at the last meeting!), reports of delegates, financial statements and complicated election procedures. They seem less ready to consult the rule book at every turn, or to 'take instruction' from Federation or National Union officers, as once they would meekly have done from area organizers or National Advisers. These straws in the wind have caused many leading Townswomen to fear that the NUTG may gradually become a collection of more or less independent local units ('clubs') with very few, if any, national links. (The late Marjorie Erskine-Wyse was one of these.)

The second of the basic tasks, 'education', has always been regarded by the NUTG leadership as the cornerstone of the organization. It was to educate women to fulfil their potential as human beings and as citizens that the movement was founded. But has it not ceased to be a really important purveyor of 'further education' or a pioneer in informal methods as it was in the days of the 'reconnaissances' initiated by Mrs Presland, or the schools set up by the arts and crafts, social studies, music and drama advisers? Local education authorities, Workers' Educational Associations, University Extra Mural Departments and, today, the Open University and Radio Three study programmes provide an inexhaustible wealth of educational opportunity. The Townswomen have only to ask, and their need is met.

The Tavistock Study explored the possibility of some form of organization to publicize courses in local areas suitable for women's needs and to stimulate courses in subjects not already covered. There is even the suggestion of a national association of committees for the education of women. But surely nowadays the majority of women are happy to study alongside men, and men alongside women? The number of subjects in which only women are interested decreases as the number in which both are interested steadily grows (e.g. car maintenance, woodwork, family finance, among women; advanced cookery and wine-making, among men). It is by no means uncommon for a couple to go along together to a local evening institute—he may join a fencing class, she a pottery class, and they most likely enjoy a cup of tea or coffee together with the friends they both have made.

When a summary of the Tavistock Study had been published in *The Townswoman* Guilds were invited by the National Chairman to send in their comments, criticisms, opinions, and suggestions for the future of the movement. Is it significant that only 510 Guilds, less than 20 per cent of the total, and fifty-nine individual members, responded by putting pen to paper? Half the Federations sent in their views, but the members of Federation Committees were almost by definition the more committed members. All these submissions were analysed carefully and lucidly by the NUTG's administrative secretary, Lady Henniker Heaton, and what was revealed was that the people who were concerned to express their views were overwhelmingly hostile to the idea of the movement's functions being separated, or to being a member just of 'a women's club'. The majority, though, was silent and it was not possible to discover its reaction.

As to what the NUTG ought to be doing about educational policy, there was such a diversity of opinion that quotations from Lady Henniker Heaton's digest are necessary: 'Some members think that the movement should no longer regard education as a priority; some do not wish to pursue education in depth; some are opposed to the word itself; others are not interested in education of any kind; others actively resist what they call the "plugging of education by the National Union". (The Tavistock Study quotes a member as saying 'I think we put on a pose as an educational organization.')

'On the other hand there is the Guild which would make "education" the movement's first priority; the member who thinks a better approach to education would go a long way to attract younger women; and the member who cries passionately "Let us stop thinking of 'education' as a dirty word".

'Older members are not very interested in education and on the whole are less interested in public questions then younger women. They are however to some extent concerned with local issues and there is some support for the idea that the movement should encourage members to take a wider interest in current affairs.'

Forty per cent of the Guilds commenting on the Tavistock Study made no reference to education at all and 60 per cent had no comment on the regional educational conferences which the NU thought so important.

Unsurprisingly, some of the comments on the Tavistock Study

urged the setting up of a residential educational centre. Without any shadow of doubt, the National Federation of Women's Institutes' adult education centre, Denman College, has been a godsend to that movement and has been deeply and lastingly envied by the Townswomen's Guilds which have never been able to raise enough money to contemplate such a venture. Residential schools are undoubtedly one of the most enjoyable 'breaks' for fairly serious-minded people of both sexes. Those arranged by the NUTG in various halls of residence around the country are always popular—not only for their educational content, whatever the study theme may be, but for the company of like-minded women, and the feeling they give of belonging to a worth-while movement. It is probable that women will continue to enjoy 'schools' of this kind for many years to come, though of course some may be drawn to mixed groups, and all special interest schools for music, drama or social studies.

As for the NUTG's third basic purpose—to mobilize and present women's views on issues of local, national, and international purpose—the Tavistock Study floated the rather surprising notion that a 'National Union of Women' might be a possibility to exercise power to affect legislation and administrative action. This was, of course, a non-starter. Even the researchers scarcely made it as a serious proposition, knowing, doubtless, that no 'Women's Party' had ever begun to be viable in terms of the British political system. (Even in 1974, a Woman's Rights Campaign General Election candidate got a pitiful number of votes, though she campaigned on a broad social programme, and though interest in anti-discrimination legislation was probably then at its peak.)

The Tavistock Study admitted 'An effective political body requires a clear common cause. Where its members find such a cause around a felt deprivation—as for instance in the case of the Black Power movement or the Disablement Incomes Group— membership itself gives them an added feeling of personal worth. The doubt about a "National Union of Women" is whether, fortunately or unfortunately, there remain enough issues around which women might rally in large numbers. Some feminists will be roused by any evidence of sexual discrimination; some will be more concerned with equal opportunities for higher education;

but the recipients of widows' pensions and the wives of surtax payers may have quite divergent "political" objectives.'

The truth, probably unwelcome to a number of NUTG leaders, but quite plain to Alice Franklin, is that Townswomen are *not* instinctively feminist. They are almost by definition homemakers who put the interest of the family, including the bread-winning father, first and foremost and are not easily roused to feminist protest even when it is a question of limitation of educational or job opportunity for their daughters. There has never been an NCM resolution of protest about the discriminatory attitudes towards women of the Inland Revenue, the Building Societies or the hire purchase companies. The support the Townswomen gave to Joyce Butler's first Anti-Discrimination Bill in 1968 and to the Women in Media Rally in support of Willie Hamilton's Bill in 1973 (when Dame Margery Corbett Ashby, then aged over ninety, was one of the demonstrators who in twos and threes walked from Central Hall, Westminster, to deliver letters of protest to the Prime Minister, Edward Heath) was of the head rather than the heart. And without question, the majority of Townswomen are much less sympathetic to the new wave of the women's movement than they were to the old, out of which their own organization grew. The derogatory description 'women's lib' is enough to put an end to the mere possibility of co-operation, in many traditional Guilds.

The issues about which women are concerned are by no means all feminist. Of course many members would very much like the NUTG to act as a pressure group in various fields. The difficulty, as the Tavistock Study pointed out, is to find sufficient issues on which sufficient members feel really passionately. There are few who are sufficiently concerned about *any* issue to lobby assiduously at the House of Commons or to circulate petitions door-to-door, much less to organize 'demos' or marches. The sort of Public Questions motions that are debated yearly at the National Council Meeting may raise interesting controversy—the parents' rights when the sterilization of girls is under discussion, the price of a dog licence, the admission of children with their parents to licensed premises—but they are certainly not calculated to make members carry banners, let alone lie down in the road, as did the Committee of 100 in their passionate concern to preserve us from nuclear warfare.

It is true that when the women's organizations stand shoulder to shoulder on an issue—as they did on the payment of child benefit to the mother—they make the Government of the day listen and take avoiding action. But the sort of pressure applied then was very discreet compared, for instance, with the lobbying of MPs during the 1974 General Election by the National Association of Widows—a letter went to *every* candidate of the two main parties— or the packed-out rally of widows in the Central Hall, Westminster early in 1977, when the Government spokesman was submitted to a barrage of heckling about income tax on pensions almost as vehement as that of students aiming to silence Enoch Powell. Quite a high proportion of NUTG members must be widows, but it has never taken direct action about their grievances since an NCM resolution of 1964.

The pronouncement in the Tavistock Study which caused the greatest sensation, not to say 'huff', was that the National Union of Townswomen's Guilds was 'a culture of dependency and conformity'. Yet it was not challenged seriously by many TG leaders. They knew that it was unquestionably true that throughout the movement the rank-and-file members expected and counted on a decision, based on the rules and constitution, on every problem, however trivial, and that this reference to higher authority went on right up to the national chairman and the national secretary.

To cite an example of the sort of instance that still happens: a Guild might have a long-serving, much admired and faithful elderly member, rather badly off, whom they would like to honour. As there is no provision about 'life member' in the Rules and Constitution, the committee would raise the question with their Federation or even National Executive. 'Are we entitled to make Mrs X a life member, excusing her subscription?' The answer 'Please yourselves' would *not* please them, but make them acutely uncomfortable. The thought that it is ridiculous for grown women not to be able to make up their minds on a course of action which would give pleasure and harm no one seems to have been submerged in years of subservience to the rule book. It takes quite a brave and independent-minded member and to break that pattern, she might well find herself labelled as 'not quite reliable', or 'a bit irresponsible'.

Of course it is not only in the NUTG that conformity to rules has high priority. If we are honest we shall admit that for many people there is quite a lot of satisfaction in running a meeting or a conference 'properly'—everything moved, seconded, spoken to, voted on according to the book; standing orders adhered to scrupulously, votes of thanks moved, seconded and minuted by name. Discussing this (in 1977) Helen Anderson, retiring warden of Denman College, the Women's Institutes' educational centre, who was formerly music adviser to the Townswomen, said 'Rules are a great hazard for women. When they get together the easiest thing to do is to put themselves into running a meeting and carry out all the procedures, which you can easily understand. You think you are being awfully good, but you have ended up with a meeting with no content.' Miss Anderson saw this danger just as much in the Women's Institutes as in the Townswomen's Guilds, and she might quite likely have seen it also in Business and Professional Women's Clubs with their ceremonial gavels and presidential chains.

'Any chairman or president whose vision is limited finds "procedure" quite a stimulus,' said Miss Anderson. 'She is running a meeting in an orderly way, and the time goes and the actual content of the meeting becomes quite secondary. You can see how deep this commitment to procedure and internal organization goes when something like an increase in the subscription comes up.'

Another sensitive area the Tavistock Study mentioned was 'the respectable escape from the home'. Guild members very often used phrases like 'To get away', 'To get out' to describe why they went to Guild meetings, and this was with particular reference to the brief 'escape' from husband and children. Some young mothers were fed up with the endless round of dirty nappies; some wanted to get away from the whole business of housekeeping and family relationships. Older women whose children were past adolescence tended to hint that they wanted to run away from 'painful feelings of becoming redundant in what had been central areas of the role of wife and mother'. The key to membership of a Townswomen's Guild or similar organization is that as an escape it is entirely respectable. To get out to a cinema, theatre or to ten pin bowling or bingo might be much less acceptable to husband and family than 'going to a meeting' (though probably not if the 'meeting' were of a political party or a trade union). This would especially apply in conventional old-fashioned households where Mother needs a watertight excuse for leaving a cold supper on the table for husband and family. Not all husbands have always approved of Townswomen's Guild membership. Some have resented the time it can take up, if a woman becomes heavily involved in special study groups or in committee or Federation business, and some have even resented the independence of mind that membership tends to breed in hitherto meek and subordinate womenfolk; but for every one like this there are probably scores who are very pleased their wives have an independent interest. It was quite commonly said to the Tavistock researchers, 'They are glad to see us go.' The TG was practically never seen as a threat to the marital relationship except by the few men who wanted to control their wives' minds and activities.

The Tavistock Study was ahead of the Townswomen's thinking when it touched on the deeper psychological aspects of Guild membership. Even a hint that 'some detractors' allege that members of all-female associations have latent lesbian tendencies caused hackles to rise. It was a predictable comment and should not have been taken seriously by women who were long and happily married. More interesting was the strong anti-reaction to the suggestion that in the 'refuges of the Townswomen's Guild members might find support in marital and family difficulties'. The Tavistock researchers said 'Although it is almost certainly a function of the TG to provide a refuge from boredom or stress it is important to present oneself to fellow-members as conventionally happily married.' 'We don't know one another well enough to tell people we have problems', and 'You certainly wouldn't discuss your personal problems there' were the kind of responses they met, and among 112 members who completed questionnaires not one admitted to being separated or divorced. The overall impression was that there was a dearth of divorced and separated women in the Guilds which in view of the quite high proportion of broken marriages in the population as a whole made questions inevitable. Would divorced and separated women avoid seeking membership of an organization practically labelling itself as an association of married women? Or would such women be tacitly discouraged from joining or not elected to office if they did join?

There seems to have been no follow-up discussion on these questions since the publication of the Tavistock Study, which is odd when one remembers that the number of broken marriages increases yearly and that even the Mothers' Union which exists partly to uphold the sanctity of Christian marriage now admits divorced women. It is curious that though the Guilds can discuss the need to make special efforts to integrate black and brown women into the Guilds, there has been no mention of an effort to lessen the problem of the bitterly lonely and humiliated deserted wife. There is ground for a suspicion that the 'respectability' of the Townswomen's Guild may be a retreat from reality into a self-protective grouping.

One can easily see how offensive some aspects of the Women's Liberation movement may be to older Townswomen—not just the pronounced feminist stance or the opposition to hierarchical structures but the 'consciousness raising' sessions which many groups regard as a crucial initiation. 'Consciousness raising' means exactly the sort of voicing and discussion of personal conflicts and problems, and the readiness to have them discussed in public, which would be anathema to the great body of Townswomen.

One of the most insistent claims to a valuable influence in the life of the ordinary woman which the TG makes is that it provides for personal development . . . through acquiring new skills and interests, through attaining greater social competence and poise and through acquiring confidence to go on to fill 'public' offices of various kinds. The Tavistock Study rather pooh-poohed this claim. 'Cream rises,' the researchers said, 'on any jug.' It may be so, but one doubts if it rises except in a 'jug' which is fitted for this purpose. There are too many recorded instances of knee-knocking, almost paralytic shyness in new members for there to be any doubt that women do need the support of their fellows—and a bit of a well-intentioned prod in the back—to get on to their feet for the first time or two. This shyness may be quite absurd. No one is going to bite the raw recruit, or laugh at her, or even gently tease her. But paralytic shyness before an audience, before a micro-phone, before a television camera is a genuine phobia, and, in these days of 'instant communication', a disability which it is as well to try to conquer. So if the Townswomen's Guilds—and similar organizations—do provide this psychotherapy they are filling a very useful function.

Fewer women nowadays are 'born to blush unseen' than in the thirties when the Townswomen's Guilds started, but on the other hand politics has got tougher, and more experience and involvement at ward and constituency party level are needed for even a modest start on a political career. It is doubtful whether the 'politically minded' woman would now get her training in the Townswomen's Guild—or whether the woman trained only in the TG or a similar body would have a sufficient political ambition to make a career of it. It does seem a pity, though, that more women who have held office in Townswomen's Guilds, especially at Federation level, should not be appointed justices of the peace, or to hospital boards, or to industrial, pension or rent tribunals, and similar bodies. Vacancies in the ranks of school managers tend to be filled by nominees of the local political parties. This is a job which experienced Townswomen would do admirably.

Thinking about the future of the large-scale organizations like the National Union of Townswomen's Guilds one is bound to wonder whether the sort of hierarchical structure which the founders devised in the thirties is essential today. One can see that it would be practically impossible to throw it overboard in an organization as large and as old as the NUTG. Any serious proposition to destroy it and let individual Guilds go their own way would create panic—if it were taken seriously. The Tavistock Study actually threw out the suggestion that the dissolution of the National Union might be considered, but no one really took a scrap of notice. Yet the structure *is* being changed in various ways that are yet scarcely remarked upon.

A former Public Questions chairman remembers an educational conference in the Free Trade Hall, Manchester which was attended by at least a thousand delegates. This was regarded as an impressive achievement—but discussion, of course, was practically impossible. How could members make their voices heard from the floor of that great hall? Even if microphones were available they could not be whizzed round quickly enough to keep discussion freely flowing. To chair such a conference successfully must give the chairman an

exhilarating sense of pride, but the smaller, participatory conferences which the NUTG—and similar bodies—tend to prefer
nowadays, with delegates divided into workshops in which
the subject is tossed to and fro between not more than a score of
members, are obviously of much greater educational value.

One has to ask whether true 'Organization Woman' *creates*
and perpetuates the hierarchical type of set-up because it suits
her own, unacknowledged, appetite for status and power. Not
surprisingly, the Tavistock Study revealed that many TG officers
and committee women found the business part of the Guild
meetings the most interesting. It is the essential nature of Organization Women to enjoy making the wheels go round. It becomes
a way of life for them. The Tavistock researchers found that some
active committee women were faintly incredulous that rank and
file members should find the business boring and one put it well
when she said: 'It is only after you get time to assimilate all the steps
that you find it interesting and absorbing.' One of the questions
the Tavistock Study asked was 'Which aspects of Townswomen's
Guild membership do you value most highly? Predictably,
82 per cent of current officers said 'experience of committee work
and organizing', and only 10 per cent of the rank-and-file
members.

The Tavistock researchers were puzzled by the fact that the
TG members did not readily admit to enjoying the responsibility and status of being in office—but this is both a British and a
female convention. Women scarcely ever admit to enjoying power
and authority because the convention is that the exercise of power,
or desire to exercise power, makes them hard and unfeminine.
(Women might, though, admit to enjoying belonging to the
'in-group' and being at the heart of their organization's activities.
Some might even go so far as to admit to enjoying a bit of string-
pulling—but mostly they would limit themselves to asserting that
they like 'being busy'.)

Whatever the reasons, the satisfactions of making every aspect
of an organization tick over smoothly are great. Does this mean
that Organization Women will be tempted to thwart a loosening
of the structure they operate so successfully? The Tavistock
Study commented on the table on the platform which cuts the
officials off from the rank-and-file members on the floor, and

suggested that there was a risk that the officers might look down on the rank-and-file members in more senses than one—indeed claimed to have found 'a veiled contempt' for the ordinary member in the officers, and 'an overt respect which concealed real hostility' among the rank and file for the officials.

It is true that the exceptional energy and ability of 'Top Women' whether they work in salaried occupations or in voluntary service are apt to be as much resented as revered. Top Women tend to be admired rather than loved—because they seem to have the best of all possible worlds and to do with apparently very little effort what most of us spend a lot of our lives failing to achieve.

What seems to be less understood than it should be, and was not examined by the Tavistock Study, is that voluntary service has been a *career* for many Organization Women who did not wish or were not able to follow a career in paid employment. If you think of Organization Woman as a Career Woman many things are much easier to understand about her. It is obvious that sometimes her strong personality and her innate—though of course unacknow-ledged—ambition will lead to conflict. Until fairly recently voluntary service was the only way most married women could achieve real status and power and even become nationally known figures, and attend conferences abroad and 'glossy' functions like royal garden parties.

Certainly most 'leading ladies' of the voluntary organizations are animated by a deep-rooted sense of duty and desire to serve their fellows, but it would be strange if all of them, always, con-formed to one's ideal picture of the angelic mother figure who 'suffers long and is kind'. Some able women are by nature tough, dominant, aggressive . . . what one calls *femmes formidables*. Some, often those who excel on the public platform, have a pro-nounced theatrical streak which thrives on drama. Drama means conflict, and if this is missing, the 'leading ladies' tend to stir it up.

This kind of personality surfaces in almost all national organi-zations, and one should not be surprised or upset if career women, whether in paid or in voluntary employment, sometimes behave rather badly, any more than one is surprised or upset by that kind of behaviour in men. One comes too often upon the comment 'Women are funny, you know'—meaning that women do not always behave very amiably to one another, that they can be touchy, bitchy, secretive and devious. Interestingly, it is most often women who have worked only among women, and not been in a male-dominated world of business or profession, who accuse only women of being 'funny'!

These Top Ladies may not be universally loved, but they will certainly be missed if they take themselves out of voluntary organizations into *salaried* careers, as in the not too distant future they probably will. The voluntary services have been run for a century or more by the home-making women. Everyone knows it; everyone deplores the difficulty of getting volunteers for 'meals on wheels', for visiting the aged, taking the book trolley around the hospital wards, doing the flowers in church, because the women are out at work, earning money to pay the family mortgage, rates, and fuel bills. What is less often said is that the voluntary organizations are likely to run short of *leaders*. Many women at the top of big women's organizations spend almost as much time on their voluntary work as salaried women do in their offices. During Mrs Marjorie Erskine-Wyse's long illness, the national chairman of the NUTG, Mrs Eileen Coram, was at the headquarters office in Cromwell Place practically every weekday—doing not only the administrative jobs the national secretary would normally have done, but even filling mail sacks with outgoing mail and humping them into the entrance hall to be collected by the post office van.

Most problems concerning their future are common to all the older-type women's organizations. One or two have special relevance to the NUTG. For instance, is the Department of Education and Science annual grant so important to the movement that its activities should be tailored to be acceptable to the DES? In its early days the movement was absolutely delighted to be thought worthy of a Ministry of Education grant, and indeed the Ministry's first grant of £3,000 (and £350 from the Scottish Education Department) to help finance expansion of Guilds in the immediate post-war period was a vote of confidence in the NUTG's informal education methods that meant a great deal to the founders. One of the reasons the NUTG worked so hard to lift its craft and cultural standards was the belief that if they slumped the grant might be withdrawn. There is also the vexed question of fundraising for charity. It is believed that this is also a threat to the eligibility of the movement for a DES grant. But the question is occasionally asked and needs to be asked more insistently, 'On a Budget of just over £100,000, is a Ministry of Education grant of about £6,800 crucial?' An annual contribution of about £4 a Guild to head office would replace it—and would set the movement free to engage in whatever activities the members prefer. National officers reiterate that the job of the NUTG is not to raise money for charity, and they naturally deplore the fact that Guilds which raise large sums for charity are reluctant to help to finance their own national movement. But the fact is that this is exactly what a great many women's groups, by no means only Townswomen's Guilds, like best to do—whether the money is for local hospitals or a national charity like the Royal National Lifeboat Institution. The explanation is difficult to discover, but the fact is incontestable and when it is thwarted by a rule book or by pronouncements from the Top Brass, it undoubtedly results in rebellious feelings.

Another difficult area for the National Union of Townswomen's Guilds is the maintenance of educational charitable status . . . the advantage of this lies in being let off income tax (but not VAT on affiliation fees, which amounts to about two-thirds of the Department of Education's grant). The disadvantage is the risk of being virtually castrated politically. Ever since the Humanist Association lost its charitable status and immunity from income tax, voluntary organizations have been understandably nervous. The problem is this: if an organization is freed from income tax liability on account of being an educational charity, and not 'political', can it, in any meaningful sense, be a pressure group? There is a good deal of pressure on the NUTG from its most enterprising members to increase its 'pressure group' activities, but liability to income tax would be a serious financial blow. Yet without being able to apply 'pressure', isn't 'Public Questions' activity likely to be pretty pointless? This is a tightrope which all voluntary organizations have to tread with the greatest care, especially in times of national economic crisis. But the balance sheet which societies have to draw up ought always to give due weight to their aims and objects as well as to their income and expenditure.

For almost all women's organizations now, the greatest problem is that the membership is ageing and is not being buttressed by young incomers. This is very obviously so with the Townswomen's Guilds, for their great expansion came at the end of the war, and the women who were young mothers then are now in their sixties. Most have found their thirty or more years of membership of a Townswomen's Guild very rewarding and have no intention of giving it up; many of them are still energetic, physically and mentally, and probably account for a majority of committee members and office holders at both Guild and Federation level. But many of the sixty-year-olds are now a little reluctant to stand for office yet again. They have been the rounds, in Guild and in Federation. They would like to sit back a bit and let someone else do the donkey-work. But the volunteers are very few, in many Guilds. The most common reason for the closure of a long-established Guild is that it has proved impossible to find sufficient officers and committee members.

It is by no means always true that older people have a closed and rigid mind and resist all kinds of change. Some of the elderly members of the NUTG are the most forward-looking, the most 'political' and eager to propagate new ideas. But one cannot count on grandmothers to initiate revolution or to throw overboard the methods they have become used to over many years and which have served them well. To tell these old members, for example, that it is no longer really necessary to have a 'returning officer' in attendance at a Guild election is to cause alarm and insecurity. To say that new organizations like the National Housewives Register and hundreds of women's liberation workshops manage with a minimum of rules and constitution or none at all, causes a shudder. What satisfaction could there be in something so sloppily run? The young 'rebels' believe that the hierarchical structures are modelled on male 'secret societies' originally set up not just for 'bonding' but to instil fear and respect. The rituals such societies practised—which persist in a very modified form—are unsuitable for women as well as totally unnecessary, they say. It is a refreshing viewpoint which should be taken seriously, and not derided or mistrusted.

The generation gap does exist in the field of women's organizations, though it can, of course, be overcome. Townswomen's Guilds whose average age is sixty-plus are not likely to attract young women into their company, and if they do, they are not always willing to give place to them, listening to their ideas, electing them to office, or taking a back seat, especially if the young women have been inoculated with ideas of discussion of problems of personal relationships in the way the Tavistock Study suggested. It is the absolute reverse of the truth that the Townswomen's Guilds are complacent about their future. They worry obsessively about the failure to recruit young members. But it is a very disconcerting fact that nothing happened as a result of the analysis made by the Tavistock researchers. *Nothing.* After a flurry of discussion, everything has gone almost exactly as before.

One might deduce from this that the movement is ossifying and that within the foreseeable future it will have seized up as a national organization and will operate only in local units. But one can be too pessimistic. The British people tend to be gradualists and our institutions tend to change almost imperceptibly year by year. The NUTG is certainly more flexible than twenty years ago, and capable of further adaptation to current trends and needs—if the will is there.

But how long will there be the impetus and the will to keep alive single-sex societies? Those fine organizations listed in the first chapter of this book—where do they stand now? All have lost members in the last decade; almost all have financial worries. The postal rates and train fares are so high that communication with local branches—absolutely vital to maintaining a spirit of unity—has become difficult; for those which have London head-quarters, rates have become a frightening burden, and heating and lighting almost as big a worry. Almost all organizations report that their membership is ageing and is not being replaced by younger women.

There also is self-questioning about the *need* for single-sex organizations, or whether, indeed, they are actually desirable. Separate 'women's sections' for the political parties are worse than out-of-date—they are against the spirit if not the letter of the Sex Discrimination Act of 1975. Insofar as they limit women's activities to envelope-addressing, canvassing, fund-raising by jumble sales, bazaars, coffee mornings and the like and tea-making at party gatherings, they are deplorable, almost insulting. As for the 'professional' women's organizations, they were started in self-defence when women were few in most professions and came up against a good deal of hostility, ostracism, and discouragement. But do the Medical Women, the Engineers, or the Headmistresses still need separate organizations? Is there a real function now, as once there certainly was, for the British Federation of University Women? And how long will it be before feelers are put out to effect a marriage between the Rotarians and the Soroptimists, the Business and Professional Women's Clubs and the Round Table? There is absolutely no barrier to 'desegregated' organizations that can be defended in logic—especially since men's colleges have started accepting women students, and women's colleges admitting men. A few years ago the Women's Press Club of London accepted the invitation of the (men's) Press Club of London to open its membership to them. Since then the two institutions have run harmoniously as one, and women have played a useful role on committees and taken part in all social functions. They drink at the bar side by side with the men if they have a mind to, or sit at tables in the bar lounge area, with friends of both sexes, if that is what they prefer. Male members of the Press Club who were opposed to the admission of women now accept that it has caused no difficulty or unpleasantness. There are still all-male clubs which set their faces sternly against the admission of women, but where the women belong to the same profession, social stratum, or political persuasion, sex discrimination seems absurdly out of date.

When the Tavistock Study flew the kite of a single national woman's organization to act as a pressure group for their special concerns, the researchers probably were unaware of how many women have dreamed of an umbrella organization which would unite all the separate women's societies, large and small, and wield irresistible political force. The dream is so attractive that many women have tried to give it reality. First came the National Council of Women to which nearly a hundred societies are still affiliated, Catholics, Anglicans, Methodists, Jews; Conservatives, Liberals, and Labour women; the Abortion Law Reform Association and the Society for the Protection of Unborn Children and societies for the protection of animals as well as of children—but not the National Union of Townswomen's Guilds nor the National Federation of Women's Institutes, for historical reasons, in that the NCW was always a pressure group in the broadly political sense when the TGs and the WIs were exceedingly nervous of the 'political' label.

Next was the Women's Group on Public Welfare, started in 1939 under the chairmanship of the Rt. Hon. Margaret Bondfield to help cope with war-time civilian problems. It has been consulted over the years by Government departments and other bodies and has prepared many valuable reports and surveys. It also has the advantage of close links with a network of local 'Standing Conferences of Women's Organizations', with which it holds a national conference in alternate years. Now known as 'Women's Forum' it has fifty affiliates, including the NUTG and NFWI, and comes under the aegis of the National Council of Social Service. So it is prestigious and knowledgeable in very many fields and certainly in touch with women's thinking. So it is curious that in 1969 the Government turned a rather loosely organized 'women's consultative committee' into the Women's National Commission, which is Government funded and has a very small secretariat, with a senior civil servant, Dr Grace Thornton, as its secretary. The thirty-nine member organizations are limited to those of a certain size, with branches throughout the country, which excludes several radical, spearhead bodies like the Fawcett Society. The Government of the day always provides one of the co-chairmen and the voluntary organizations the other. The Commission provides an excellent platform for discussion, and one has the feeling that Governments (of whatever colour) like to think that through it they are fully informed of 'women's opinion' throughout the country. But if Ministers listened a little more carefully they would discover that it is absurd to expect a consensus of 'women's' opinion as it would be of 'men's', except on a very few issues which affect a majority of women in a way they do not affect men.

This impossibility—and surely undesirability—of getting women to speak always with one voice is the real reason why the dream of a single national organization of women has to be ruled out, but there is a pressing new reason for considering the possibility of running in closer harness . . . money. The NUTG is certainly not the only women's organization with money worries. The increase in postal and telephone charges is frightening. In its 1974 Budget the NUTG put them at £1,950. In the 1978 Budget it had to allocate £5,000. The printing and stationery budget, in these four years, increased from £3,000 to £6,000, headquarters' salaries from £35,000 to £53,000, and the cost of the statutory meetings of the executive, the Central Council and the National Council Meeting from £9,750 to £21,000—this huge jump reflecting, of course, the great rise in travel costs. On the other side of the balance sheet, between 1974 and 1978 the budgeted affiliation fees rose from £63,000 to £76,000 and the estimated Department of Education and Science grant from £5,600 to £8,100.

That the women's organizations like the Townswomen have to skimp on communication with their branches and local units is an alarming trend. National unity cannot be maintained without regular bulletins or communications, and regular visits by executive members and 'get-togethers'. The cost of running a London headquarters is also alarming. With rates, heating and lighting, and general maintenance soaring, the fine old houses maintained by the NUTG in Cromwell Place, South Kensington, the NFWI in Eccleston Street, S.W.1 and the NCW in Lower Sloane Street, S.W.3 are in danger of becoming a liability rather than an asset. If one large house could be used for all these, with, for instance, shared rooms for committee meetings etc, and perhaps some shared secretarial facilities, large savings would be possible... but problems of logistics and staffing would obviously be tricky, and problems of precedence and priority trickier still. It has been suggested several times that the time has now come when the Townswomen and the Women's Institutes might merge into a single organization—the geographical boundaries have not made much sense for years, with the villages receiving more 'incomers' from the towns and the reorganization of the local government system destroying the 'county federation' basis of the WIs. But the Townswomen would not like to be 'swallowed up' by the larger organization, and the WIs would not like their essentially rural interests to be dominated by the 'townies'.

Yet the future of the women's organizations, and indeed of many 'mixed' voluntary organizations, is really at risk and it is time the Government of the day had a look at the situation. It is surely not enough to fund the Women's National Commission or even the Women's Royal Voluntary Service, and hand out a few rather grudging thousands here and there to organizations whose 'charitable' aims are vetted and approved. The independent women's organization with its wide range of activities, some educational, some charitable, and some in the broadest sense 'political' has been such an important strand in the social fabric that it would be rather shocking if it were allowed to wither away just because inflation, VAT, income tax, etc, made it impossible to continue to fill its traditional function.

An urgent call for help came from the president of the National Council of Women, Mrs Helen Waldsax, at the annual conference of 1977: 'We would ask that the Government acknowledge in some constructive form the public service given by so many voluntary organizations to this country. Unless something is done the services provided by them may well have to be cut because of the steeply rising running costs. Should these organizations have to function at half strength, or even have to disappear, then the country possibly faces two serious risks. The source of supply of many specialist skills and of many voluntary workers may well be drastically cut, throwing a heavy burden on the already over-stretched statutory social services. In addition, the possible loss of any one of the organizations with their wealth of practical experience means that the Government is losing a most valuable means of finding out what problems ordinary men and women have to contend with and what the real impact is of legislation on those people in whose interest, presumably, laws are being passed. A very important democratic principle is at stake here and one that must not be ignored.'

Of course a Government injection of funds is not going to save the life of an organization which is no longer filling a useful function—as has been sadly seen too often in the industrial field. It is up to the organizations themselves to prove that they *are* still needed. The problem faced the NUTG acutely in the run-up to its golden jubilee celebrations for the year 1978–79. A jubilee steering committee, under the chairmanship of an executive member, Mrs Margaret Tierney, came up with a very different bunch of happenings from the silver jubilee celebrations, when the Duchess of Gloucester received purses to the value of £14,545 at the Royal Albert Hall, and Townswomen performed *The Gift*, a choral mime composed for the occasion by Dr Armstrong Gibbs. An 'Albert Hall spectacular' was again planned for 1979, a choir of 200, a specially written script on the theme 'Townswomen in the Spotlight' and the participation of many of the Townswomen who take part in Keep Fit and Medau classes, country dancing, Scottish dancing or any regular physical exercise. As part of the Townswomen's jubilation, they planned to gather for choir festivals in the four great cathedrals of Westminister Abbey, Liverpool, St Giles, Edinburgh, and Llandaff, on 9 December 1978.

But the programme of activities for the Golden Jubilee Year included some that would never have been dreamt of by the Founding Mothers—a competition to find the Car Driver of the Year, for instance. Quite a high proportion of the young mothers who are the potential new members of the NUTG are drivers and have at least the use of the family car. Practically all the National and Federation executives are car drivers nowadays and car ownership spans a wide social stratum. So the first two rounds of the TG car driver competition were devised to test the competitors' knowledge of the Highway Code, but at regional levels the competitors were required to take part in a driving test, and from each region two drivers were to go forward to a national driving contest of twenty-four competitors. Another new departure was the sporting events: bowls, golf, tennis and swimming. In early decades, Organization Women showed their skill as producers, chairmen, and conductors. Now, evidently, they were to go into training as umpires and referees.

'Will the jubilee produce a resurgence of enthusiasm?' was the crucial question during 1976 and 1977. And if so, in what way? The national chairman, Mrs Eileen Coram, would very much have liked to see Townswomen become more deeply involved in Europe, and one must hope that the younger generation of women, more fluent in foreign languages than their mothers, will see this as an imperative commitment in the future. There is, though, a rather surprising section of opinion which believes that the time has come for a return to fostering the home-making skills. Could it be true that the 'young marrieds' have rather missed out on enjoyment of these skills because the pattern of home-making has changed and because girls have been educated to expect to continue to work after marriage? There is, of course, still a strong wave of opinion that women should not be 'tied' to the home which expresses itself in resentment of housework. But if a woman is free to choose, and can have a job *and* a home and family, she may find that there is more to enjoy in home-making than she guessed. The impetus which leads women to take up pottery and painting could just as well find expression for many in various practical forms of needlework—and gardening.

The future cannot be known. What one feels absolutely sure of is that the spirit of voluntary service is not dead. The spate of voluntary organizations large and small which have sprung up or developed since World War II is proof of that. Thousands of women (and men too) give faithful service to Citizens' Advice Bureaux, to Marriage Guidance Councils, the Samaritans and all the 'self-help' organizations for the Single Women, for Pre-School Playgroups, Children in Hospital, for sufferers from chest and heart diseases, multiple sclerosis, mental disturbance, restricted growth, alcoholism, deafness, blindness—or just poverty and old age.

Organization Woman will never lack for stimulus to use her energy and brains, and it is unlikely that she will abandon the voluntary field entirely for a salaried career—a great many working women find a corner of their lives for at least one good cause. The other certainty is that in their new freedom women will not cease to seek out and enjoy the company of women, as Townswomen have now for fifty years.

The girls of the new age of the Women's Movement are apt to think that they were the first to discover the sisterhood of women. Of course they were not. Those benevolent conspirators of the 1850s experienced it; so did the first women doctors and lawyers; so did the suffrage workers, whether they were militant or constitutional; so did the early Townswomen who went knocking on doors in the thirties, and all who for half a century have flocked in their hundreds, even thousands, to conferences, rallies, and festivals. All these have known the precious sense of 'belonging' which is essential to real happiness and to stability in a complex industrial society.

Perhaps we of the women's organizations will need one another more, not less, as this century of staggering change moves to a close. The changes, scientific, technological, economic, and social are not likely to halt, or even slow down. The future sometimes looks a little frightening, especially for the home-oriented women who are not happy about what effect the new independence is going to have on family life. 'The common meeting ground' that is needed now is not of all women 'irrespective of race, creed or party', but of all women irrespective of whether they are young or old, married, single, divorced or deserted, whether they work in the home or outside it. In the United States, many young women wear a button badge with the words 'Sisterhood is Powerful'. The story of the National Union of Townswomen's Guilds is a proof that that is true.

Index